To Get Ahead in The Air Force

PRACTICE FOR AIR FORCE PLACEMENT TESTS

by DAVID R. TURNER, M.S. in Educ.

219 Park Avenue South, New York, N.Y. 10003

Third Edition B-2090
Second Printing, 1976

Copyright © 1975
by Arco Publishing Company, Inc.

All rights reserved. No part of this book may be
reproduced in any form, by any means, without
permission in writing from the publisher.

Published by Arco Publishing Company, Inc.
219 Park Avenue South, New York, N.Y. 10003

Library of Congress Catalog Card Number 74-80714
ISBN 0-668-01302-8 (Paper Edition)
     0-668-01505-5 (Cloth Edition)

Printed in the United States of America

CONTENTS

HOW TO USE THIS INDEX
Slightly bend the right-hand edge of the book. This will expose the corresponding Parts which match the index, below.

PART 1

PART 2

WHAT THIS BOOK WILL DO FOR YOU 5
How this book was prepared; what went into these pages to make them worth your while. How to use them profitably for yourself in preparing for your test. The essentials of successful study.

LET'S TALK ABOUT THE EXAM 7
Forewarned is forearmed with this comprehensive preview of the test you are about to take.

PART ONE
A MODEL EXAM FOR PRACTICE

A PREDICTIVE PRACTICE EXAMINATION 15
Similar to the one you must take, this exam is a practical yardstick for measuring your present knowledge and ability. It will help prepare you to get the grade you need for the school you want.

    General Technical Aptitude 21
        Word Knowledge. Analogies. Arithmetic.
    Clerical Ability and Aptitude 26
        Coding Speed. Accuracy. Sentence Completions.
    Electronics Aptitude 34
    Aptitude for General Mechanics 39
        Tool Knowledge. Space Perception.
        Tool Analogies. Shop Information.
    Aptitude for Motor Mechanics 48
        Mechanical Comprehension. Automotive Information.

PART TWO
PRACTICE FOR THE REAL THING.
SELECTED SUBJECTS

NUMERICAL RELATIONS 61
A chance to tackle those basic problems from which most examination questions are derived. Includes Profit and Loss, Addition of Fractions, Interest, Assessment, Cubic Volume, Literal Problems, Rate, Time and Distance, Time and Work, Proportions, and Mixture Problems. Simple, straightforward, step-by-step explanations. Sample questions with explanatory answers.

ARITHMETIC REVIEW TEST 71

GRAPH, CHART, AND TABLE INTERPRETATION 77
Designed not only to make you proficient in visual interpretation, but also to improve your reasoning and analytical ability.

...continued on next page

CONTENTS continued

PART

1

TOP SCORES ON VOCABULARY TESTS 93

Six valuable steps in building your word power. Also, two charts of prefixes and suffixes, with sample words, show how a knowledge of etymology can help increase your vocabulary.

2

CLERICAL SPEED AND APTITUDE 114

Massive, speeded practice in fundamental tests of perception and comparison. A chance to measure your ability, to understand these tasks, and to do them rapidly.

ADDRESS CHECKING 115

MATCHING LETTERS AND NUMBERS 119

CLASSIFICATION-CODING ABILITY 122

CODING PRACTICE 126

HIDDEN FIGURES 132

Mechanical aptitude and spatial relations test practice. 40 questions requiring you to find figures embedded in larger patterns. Answers.

PATTERN ANALYSIS AND COMPREHENSION 139

These questions test your understanding of spatial relations and present the type of problems found in making templates and patterns. They are a significant test theme in mechanical aptitude exams, and thus bear thorough practice. Familiarize yourself with basic instructions and understand the analytic method necessary to arrive at the correct answer. Visualizing figures . . . matching parts and figures . . . practice for view questions.

MECHANICAL INSIGHT TESTS 155

Selected from civil service and private industry tests, here are questions and answers (with clearly labeled diagrams) designed to gauge your mechanical aptitude, your inherent feeling for machinery, and your mechanical experience. Introduction . . . directions. Practice questions. Answers.

TOOL RECOGNITION TESTS 165

Exam-type questions to test your familiarity with the tools of your trade.

TEST-TAKING MADE SIMPLE 181

Test-taking strategy for successful exam performance. How to prepare yourself emotionally, factually, physically. During the exam . . . budgeting your time . . . following directions. "Musts" for the master test-taker.

ARCO BOOKS 189

You'll want to consult this list of Arco publications to order other invaluable career books related to your field. The list also suggests job opportunities and promotions that you might want to go after with an Arco self-tutor.

AIR FORCE PLACEMENT TESTS

WHAT THIS BOOK WILL DO FOR YOU

To get the greatest help from this book, please understand that it has been carefully organized. You must, therefore, plan to use it accordingly. Study this concise, readable book earnestly and your way will be clear. You will progress directly to your goal. You will not be led off into blind alleys and useless fields of study.

Arco Publishing Company has followed testing trends and methods ever since the firm was founded in 1937. We have specialized in books that prepare people for tests. Based on this experience it is our modest boast that you probably have in your hands the best book that could be prepared to help *you* score high. Now, if you'll take a little advice on using it properly, we can assure you that you will do well.

To write this book we carefully analyzed every detail surrounding the forthcoming examination . . .

* the job itself

* official and unofficial announcements concerning the examination

* all the available previous examinations

* many related examinations

* technical literature that explains and forecasts the examination.

As a result of all this (which you, happily, have not had to do) we've been able to create the "climate" of your test, and to give you a fairly accurate picture of what's involved. Some of this material, digested and simplified, actually appears in print here, if it was deemed useful and suitable in helping you score high.

But more important than any other benefit derived from this research is our certainty that the study material, the text and the practice questions are right for you.

The practice questions you will study have been judiciously selected from hundreds of thousands of previous test questions on file here at Arco. But they haven't just been thrown at you pell mell. They've been organized into the subjects that you can expect to find on your test. As you answer the questions, these subjects will take on greater meaning for you. At the same time you will be getting valuable practice in answering test questions. You will proceed with a sure step toward a worthwhile goal: high test marks.

Studying in this manner, you will get the feel of the entire examination. You will learn by "insight," by seeing through a problem as a result of experiencing *previous similar situations*. This is true learning according to many psychologists.

In short, what you get from this book will help you operate at top efficiency . . . make you give the best possible account of yourself on the actual examination.

CAN YOU PREPARE YOURSELF FOR YOUR TEST?

We believe, most certainly, that you *can* with the aid of this "self-tutor!"

It's not a "pony." It's not a complete college education. It's not a "crib sheet," and it's no HOW TO SUCCEED ON TESTS WITHOUT REALLY TRYING. There's nothing in it that will give you a higher score than you really deserve.

It's just a top quality course which you can readily review in less than twenty hours . . . a digest of material which you might easily have written yourself after about five thousand hours of laborious digging.

To really prepare for your test you must motivate yourself . . . get into the right frame of mind for learning from your "self-tutor." You'll have to urge *yourself* to learn and that's the only way people ever learn. Your efforts to score high on the test will be greatly aided by the fact that you will have to do this job on your own . . . perhaps without a teacher. Psychologists have demonstrated that studies undertaken for a clear goal . . . which you initiate yourself and actively pursue . . . are the most successful. You, yourself, want to pass this test. That's why you bought this book and embarked on this program. Nobody forced you to do it, and there may be nobody to lead you through the course. Your self-activity is going to be the key to your success in the forthcoming weeks.

Used correctly, your "self-tutor" will show you what to expect and will give you a speedy brush-up on the subjects peculiar to your exam. Some of these are subjects not taught in schools at all. Even if your study time is very limited, you should:

- Become familiar with the type of examination you will meet.

- Improve your general examination-taking skill.

- Improve your skill in analyzing and answering questions involving reasoning, judgment, comparison, and evaluation.

- Improve your speed and skill in reading and understanding what you read—an important part of your ability to learn and an important part of most tests.

- Prepare yourself in the particular fields which measure your learning—
  Vocabulary
  Problem solving
  Mathematics
  Arithmetic

This book will tell you exactly what to study by presenting in full every type of question you will get on the actual test. You'll do better merely by familiarizing yourself with them.

This book will help you find your weaknesses and find them fast. Once you know where you're weak you can get right to work (before the test) and concentrate your efforts on those soft spots. This is the kind of selective study which yields maximum test results for every hour spent.

This book will give you the *feel* of the exam. Almost all our sample and practice questions are taken from actual previous exams. Since previous exams are not always available for inspection by the public, these sample test questions are quite important for you. The day you take your exam you'll see how closely this book follows the format of the real test.

This book will give you confidence *now*, while you are preparing for the test. It will build your self-confidence as you proceed. It will beat those dreaded before-test jitters that have hurt so many other test-takers.

This book stresses the modern, multiple-choice type of question because that's the kind you'll undoubtedly get on your test. In answering these questions you will add to your knowledge by learning the correct answers, naturally. However, you will not be satisfied with merely the correct choice for each question. You will want to find out why the other choices are incorrect. This will jog your memory . . . help you remember much you thought you had forgotten. You'll be preparing and enriching yourself for the exam to come.

Of course, the great advantage in all this lies in narrowing your study to just those fields in which you're most likely to be quizzed. Answer enough questions in those fields and the chances are very good that you'll meet a few of them again on the actual test. After all, the number of questions an examiner can draw upon in these fields is rather limited. Examiners frequently employ the same questions on different tests for this very reason.

Probably the most important element of tests which you can learn is vocabulary. Most testers consider your vocabulary range an important indication of what you have learned in your life, and therefore, an important measuring rod of your learning ability. With some concentration and systematic study, you can increase your vocabulary substantially and thus increase your score on most tests.

After testing yourself, you may find that your reading ability is poor. It may be wise to take the proper remedial measures now.

If you find that your reasoning ability or your ability to handle mathematical problems is weak, there are ways of improving your skill in these fields.

There are other things which you should know and which various sections of this book will help you learn. Most important, not only for this examination but for all the examinations to come in your life, is learning how to take a test and how to prepare for it.

AIR FORCE PLACEMENT TESTS

LET'S TALK ABOUT THE EXAM

A great deal depends on your examination score, as you know. And this book will help you achieve your highest possible score. You'll get plenty of practice with relevant test subjects and questions. But first we want you to pick up a few facts about the test which may make things easier for you. Forgive us if some of these facts seem self-evident. Our experience has shown that this kind of information is sometimes overlooked . . . to the candidate's detriment.

The How and Why of A.S.V.A.B.

In 1966, the Assistant Secretary of Defense for Manpower and Reserve Affairs directed the services to explore the feasibility of a common aptitude test battery which could serve as an instrument for counseling high school students on vocational choices, provide appropriate military service qualification data, and be used in making job classification decisions about military enlistees.

A working group, consisting of personnel test experts from all of the military services, was set up to study the feasibility of such a test battery and to develop a prototype. The Armed Services Vocational Aptitude Battery (ASVAB) was developed from this effort. Test and measurement experts from the Army Research Institute, the Air Force Human Resources Laboratory, and the Naval Personnel Research and Development Center all contributed significantly to this developmental work. All of the services have engaged in this research over the past three decades through these research laboratories and the aptitude testing movement within the United States was pioneered by them.

Psychologists can predict with considerable accuracy the behavior of a group of people in a future situation from knowledge of their behavior in the present situation. Thus aptitude for learning a skill can be measured and applied in an operational selection situation such that people who are high on the measure are likely to be successful in jobs involving that skill while persons low on the measure are likely to perform inadequately. Such predictions are valuable in industry as well as in the military services in the dollar savings they represent in training and other personnel costs. One of the best ways to measure how people differ in aptitudes is by means of a test. Many such tests exist today. The ASVAB is one of those developed and validated by the military services for predicting success in military-oriented job areas. As military jobs are related to civilian jobs, the tests are useful in counseling a student concerning the area in which he is likely to succeed or in selection for the civilian counterparts to military occupations.

Questions Frequently Asked About A.S.V.A.B.

1. What is the Armed Services Vocational Aptitude Battery?

It is a battery of nine tests, derived from "common" content among the military service aptitude batteries. It is based on over three decades of military service research on the classification, placement and training of enlisted personnel.

2. How much time is required to administer the ASVAB?

Actual testing time is one hour and 52 minutes. With administration time, it requires approximately two and one-half hours.

3. Who administers the ASVAB?

A trained test administrator from one of the military services administers the battery and service personnel are used to help proctor the testing.

4. What ASVAB scores are reported?

Scores on all nine subtests, and five aptitude composite scores are reported. The test scores are Coding Speed, Word Knowledge, Arithmetic Reasoning, Tool Knowledge, Space Perception, Mechanical Comprehension, Shop Information, Automotive Information and Electronics Information. The aptitude composites are General-Technical, Clerical, Electronics, General Mechanics and Motor Mechanics. All scores and composites are reported in percentile form, and are calibrated against a national sample of youth.

The aptitude composites are formed from combinations of the nine test scores and are designed as composite measures relevant to training success for clusters of occupations. The five aptitude areas are:

General-Technical—describes the student's ability for occupations requiring academic ability. The composite is composed of verbal and mathematical components of the battery.

Clerical—describes the student's ability relevant to clerical and administrative occupations. The composite is composed of the battery components concerned with verbal ability and clerical speed and accuracy.

Electronics—describes student's ability relevant to electrical and electronic occupations. The composite consists of tests dealing with electrical information and with understanding of mechanical principles.

General Mechanics—describes student's ability in terms of those capabilities relevant to a variety of mechanical and trade jobs. The composite consists of tests assessing shop information and spatial ability.

Motor Mechanics—describes the student's ability relevant to engine repair and other related jobs. It is composed of measures of automotive information and understanding of mechanical principles.

Official Sample Questions That Forecast the Test

Content selected for inclusion in the ASVAB consisted of the following nine group-administered tests:

1. Coding Speed Test. This is a test of clerical speed and accuracy. At the top of each test page is a group of words with a code number beside each word. Each test item consists of one of the key words from the top of the page, followed by code number choices.

The task is to identify the correct code number for that word in accordance with the code at the top of the page. This test emphasizes speed; the examinee is given 100 such items and is required to accurately complete as many as possible in seven minutes. A sample set of this type item is shown next. (Answers to these and subsequent sample items are presented at the end of this section.)

Questions that Forecast the Test / 9

KEY			
auto 2715		house 3451	
bread 1413		train 2864	
QUESTIONS		**ANSWER Choices**	
	A	B	C	D
1. train	1413	2715	2864	3451
2. bread	1413	2715	2864	3451
3. auto	1413	2715	2864	3451
4. train	1413	2715	2864	3451
5. house	1413	2715	2864	3451

2. Word Knowledge Test. This test presents 25 vocabulary words. Each of the vocabulary words is contained in a sentence and is followed by four alternative answers. From among the four alternatives, the examinee must select the word which means most nearly the same thing as the underlined word in the item stem. In this and all subsequent tests in the battery, speed is not emphasized; while there is a time limit on the tests, it is ample for most examinees. Two sample Word Knowledge items are given below:

(6) It was a *small* table.
6-A sturdy
6-B round
6-C cheap
6-D little

(7) There will be *variable* winds.
7-A shifting
7-B chilling
7-C steady
7-D mild

3. Arithmetic Reasoning Test. This test presents 25 reasoning problems involving arithmetic processes. For each problem, the examinee must solve the problem and select the correct answer from among four alternatives. Two sample problems are:

(8) A boy buys a can of beans for 20 cents, potato chips for 10 cents, and cookies for 15 cents. How much does he pay for all?
8-A 30 cents
8-B 35 cents
8-C 45 cents
8-D 50 cents

(9) If John can stack 2/3 of a cord of wood in one hour, how long will it take him to stack four cords of wood?
9-A 6 hours
9-B 5 hours
9-C 4 hours 20 minutes
9-D 2 hours 40 minutes

4. Tool Knowledge Test. This test has 25 pictorial questions about tools and equipment. Each item presents a picture of a tool or piece of equipment, followed by four more drawings of various tools or pieces of equipment. The examinee must select the one of the four alternatives that "goes best" with the stem. Two sample items are shown below:

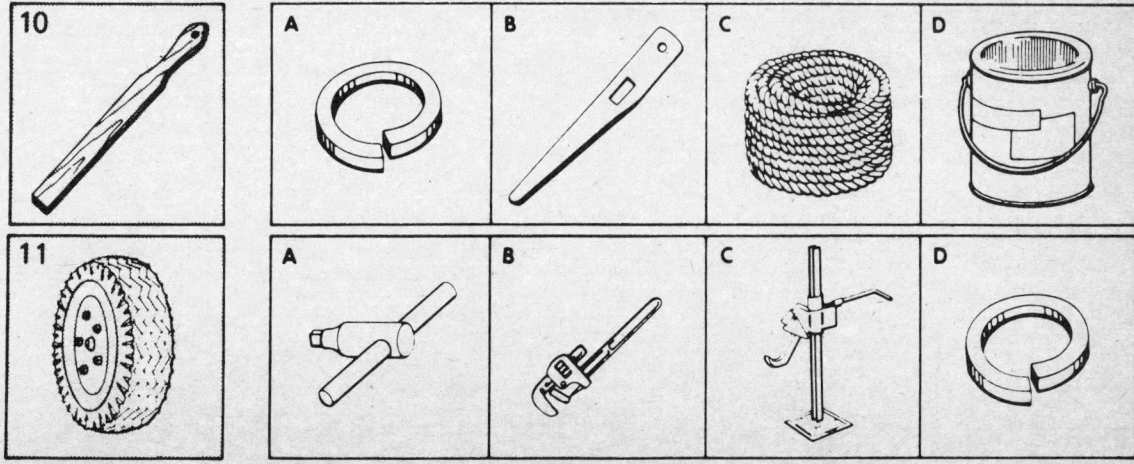

5. **Space Perception Test.** This is also a pictorial test. It consists of 25 items, each of which shows a flat pattern followed by four drawings of three-dimensional figures. Broken lines on the pattern show where it is to be folded. The subject's task is to select the one of the three-dimensional figures which could be made from the pattern by folding it on the dotted lines. Two samples are shown below:

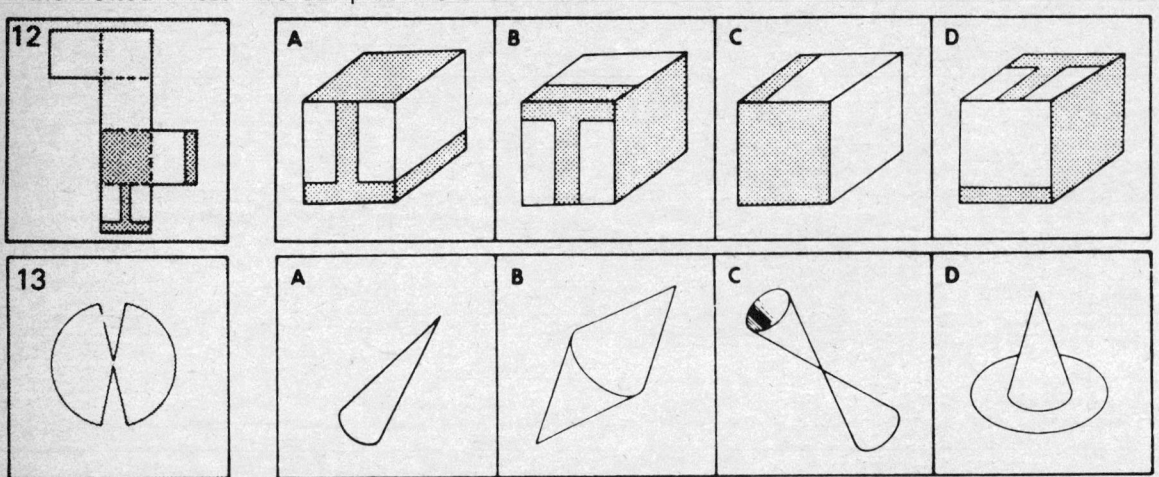

6. **Mechanical Comprehension Test.** This is a 25 item test in which a drawing illustrates a mechanical principle and a question is asked about it. The correct answer must be selected from four alternatives. Two sample items are shown below:

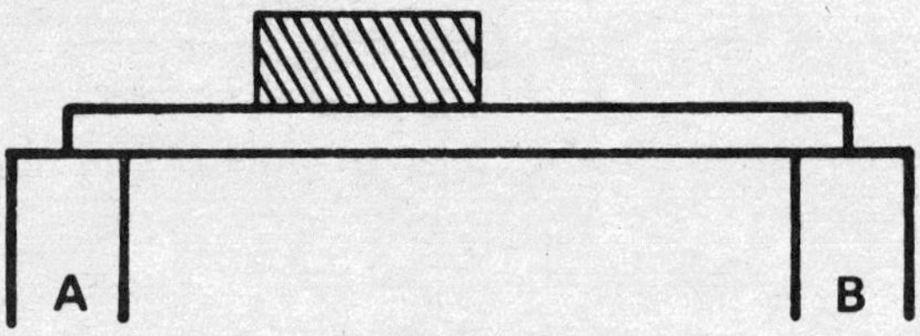

(14) Which upright supports the greater part of the load?
14-A Upright A
14-B Upright B
14-C They support it equally
14-D Cannot be determined

(15) Which of the following is correct if gear Z drives to the right (R)?
15-A Gear Y turns L, and gear X turns R
15-B Gear Y turns R, and gear X turns R
15-C Gear Y turns L, and gear X turns L
15-D Gear Y turns R, and gear X turns L

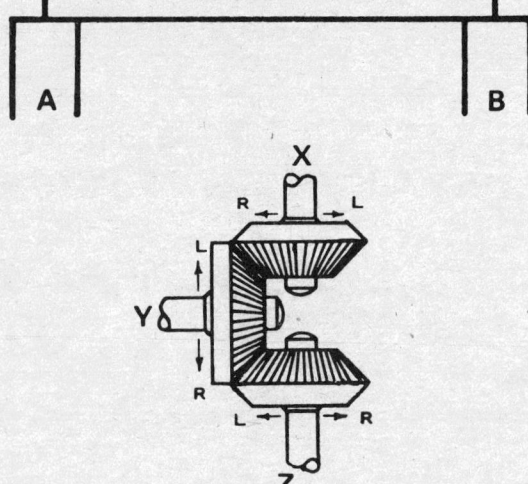

7. **Shop Information Test.** In this test, about half the items contain drawings. The test consists of 25 questions about shop practices and the use of tools. The examinee is to select the correct answer from among four alternatives. Two sample questions are shown:

(16) Which of these is used when sawing an exact angle through a board?

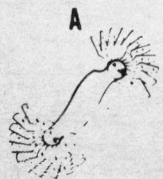 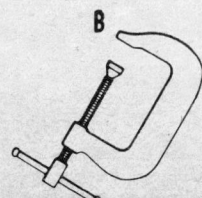 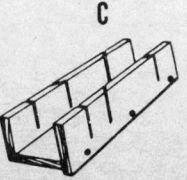 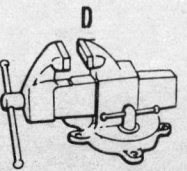

(17) The expression "18 gauge", when used in reference to sheet metal, indicates the
17-A plating
17-B quality of the metal
17-C thickness of the metal
17-D weight per square foot

8. Automotive Information Test. This test has 25 questions about automobile parts or their operation. The correct answer must be selected from four alternatives. Two sample questions are shown below:

(18) Jerky application of power to the crankshaft is eliminated by the
18-A crankcase
18-B main springs
18-C shock absorbers
18-D flywheel

(19) The function of the rotor is to
19-A open and close the distributor points
19-B rotate the distributor cam
19-C distribute electricity to the spark plugs
19-D rotate the distributor shaft

9. Electronics Information Test. This test consists of 25 questions involving elementary principles of electricity and electronics. The examinee must select the correct answer to each question from among four alternatives. Two sample items are shown below:

(20) In the circuit shown, what is at X?
20-A switch
20-B battery
20-C resistor
20-D light bulb

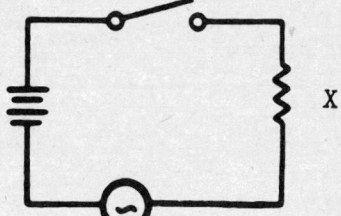

(21) Mechanical energy is converted into electrical energy by a
21-A generator
21-B turbine
21-C converter
21-D motor

KEY TO SAMPLE ITEMS

Item Number	Correct Answer	Item Number	Correct Answer
1	C	11	C
2	A	12	A
3	B	13	C
4	C	14	A
5	D	15	A
6	D	16	C
7	A	17	C
8	C	18	D
9	A	19	C
10	D	20	C
		21	A

HOW TESTS ARE USED

An effective fighting force needs the right kind of man as well as the right kind of equipment. The right kind of man is the man who is suited to his job; he meets the requirements and he is not wasted. If it is known what the requirements are and what the characteristics of the men are, the jobs and men can be matched.

Effective Utilization of Manpower Means Matching Jobs and Men. It does not mean that only the best possible men will be accepted. The manpower barrel has a bottom and the "cream of the crop" is at best only a thin layer. How far down the barrel it is necessary to go is a matter of high-level policy and depends on how great the need is. It also depends on how successfully the men who are taken are used. The Armed Services need to know how the manpower barrel is made up. It is the overall objective of personnel measurement to provide the essential information on the abilities which make up the nation's manpower.

Personnel Research Is Concerned With Discovering Techniques That Will Help Match People With Jobs. On the one hand, each job must be analyzed into the tasks which make it up and the skills needed to do the job. On the other, the abilities and skills that men and women bring with them from civilian life, or that they acquire in the services must be identified and described.

DIFFERENCES AMONG PEOPLE

The men and women who must be selected and assigned to training courses and jobs vary in many ways. The fact that each individual possesses more of some abilities than of others is important to the Armed Services. Effective utilization of manpower is not possible without knowledge of the strengths and weaknesses of the individuals that make up the manpower pool. It is a severe loss to fail to use to advantage a man capable of developing into a good leader, just as it is a severe loss to place a man in a position of leadership and find out too late that he is incapable of carrying out his responsibilities.

Differences in Physical Characteristics. Even after screening by the physical examination at the induction station and subsequent physical conditioning, soldiers differ widely in health, strength, size, and endurance. Some men can march 30 miles a day with full field equipment; others can cover only a few miles under the same conditions. Some can resist extremes of temperature, others cannot; some can maintain their efficiency at high altitudes, others lose it; some can see well at night, others are practically night blind. No matter how effective the screening or conditioning, soldiers will not show any great uniformity in physical characteristics.

Differences in Psychological Characteristics—Ability and Personality. The differences among soldiers in abilities and personality characteristics are just as large and as important as are the differences in physique, stamina, and the keenness of their senses. However, these abilities and personality characteristics cannot be observed as directly as can physical traits. It is not possible to tell by looking at a man whether he can add or spell, repair a carbine, lead a squad, or be aggressive under fire. Nor is it possible to tell by such direct observation whether the man can learn to do these things in the relatively short time available for training. To obtain useful estimates of psychological characteristics, it is necessary to use other methods

Differences in Effects of Training. Among men in the same training situation or in the same job the range in ability, and in capacity to absorb training, may be tremendous. Men differ also in the level of skill they can reach with training. For instance, it is exceedingly doubtful if the poorest performers could be brought up to the level of the best even if limitless time were available. Differences among men are not always ironed out by training. Differences in level of performance may even increase under a program of instruction. Those who are more skillful to start with may improve faster than the less skillful, with the result that the range of abilities after training may be even greater than before.

As you can see from this and what will follow, the United States Armed Forces use psychological tests to make the most effective possible use of the individual. To the extent that you understand this, your doubts, your fears, and your hesitations should be removed.

AIR FORCE PLACEMENT TESTS

PART ONE

A Model Exam for Practice

DIRECTIONS FOR ANSWERING QUESTIONS

DIRECTIONS: For each question read all the choices carefully. Then select that answer which you consider correct or most nearly correct. Write the letter preceding your best choice next to the question. Should you want to answer on the kind of answer sheet used on machine-scored examinations, we have provided several such facsimiles. On some machine-scored exams you are instructed to "place no marks whatever on the test booklet." In other examinations you may be instructed to mark your answers in the test booklet. In such cases you should be careful that no other marks interfere with the legibility of your answers. It is always best NOT to mark your booklet unless you are sure that it is permitted. It is most important that you learn to mark your answers clearly and in the right place.

FOR THE SAMPLE QUESTION that follows, select the appropriate letter preceding the word which is most nearly the same in meaning as the capitalized word:

1. DISSENT: (A) approve   (B) depart
                      (C) disagree   (D) enjoy

DISSENT is most nearly the same as (C), disagree, so that the acceptable answer is shown thus on your answer sheet:

Practice Using Answer Sheets

Alter numbers to match the practice and drill questions in each part of the book.
Make only ONE mark for each answer. Additional and stray marks may be counted as mistakes.
In making corrections, erase errors COMPLETELY. Make glossy black marks.

AIR FORCE PLACEMENT TESTS

PREDICTIVE PRACTICE EXAMINATION

This Predictive Practice Examination is patterned on the actual exam. We emphasize that it is not a copy of the actual exam, which is guarded closely and may not be duplicated. The exam you'll take may have more difficult questions in some areas than you will encounter on this Predictive Practice Exam. On the other hand, some questions may be easier, but don't bank on it. This book is meant to give you confidence . . . not over-confidence.

The time allowed for the entire examination is 2 hours. In order to create the climate of the test to come, that's precisely what you should allow yourself . . . no more, no less. Use a watch and keep a record of your time, especially since you may find it convenient to take the test in several sittings.

In constructing this Examination we tried to visualize the questions you are *likely* to face on your actual exam. We included those subjects on which they are *probably* going to test you.

Although copies of past exams are not released, we were able to piece together a fairly complete picture of the forthcoming exam.

A principal source of information was our analysis of official announcements going back several years.

Critical comparison of these announcements, particularly the sample questions, revealed the testing trend; foretold the important subjects, and those that are likely to recur.

In making up the Tests we predict for your exam, great care was exercised to prepare questions having just the difficulty level you'll encounter on your exam. Not easier; not harder, but just what you may expect.

The various subjects expected on your exam are represented by separate Tests. Each Test has just about the number of questions you may find on the actual exam. And each Test is timed accordingly.

The questions on each Test are represented exactly on the special Answer Sheet provided. Mark your answers on this sheet. It's just about the way you'll have to do it on the real exam.

As a result you have an Examination which simulates the real one closely enough to provide you with important training.

Proceed through the entire exam without pausing after each Test. Remember that you are taking this Exam under actual battle conditions, and therefore you do not stop until told to do so by the proctor.

Certainly you should not lose time by trying to mark each Test as you complete it. You'll be able to score yourself fairly when time is up for the entire Exam.

Correct answers for all the questions in all the Tests of the Exam appear at the end of the Exam.

ANALYSIS AND TIMETABLE: PREDICTIVE PRACTICE EXAMINATION

This table is both an analysis of the exam that follows and a priceless preview of the actual test. Look it over carefully and use it well. Since it lists both subjects and times, it points up not only what to study, but also how much time to spend on each topic. Making the most of your study time adds valuable points to your examination score.

SUBJECT TESTED	Time Allowed	SUBJECT TESTED	Time Allowed
GENERAL TECHNICAL APTITUDE	25"	APTITUDE FOR GENERAL MECHANICS	30"
Word Knowledge	10"	Tool Knowledge	10"
Verbal Analogies	5"	Tool Analogies	5"
Arithmetic Reasoning	10"	Space Perception	5"
		Shop Information	10"
CLERICAL ABILITY AND APTITUDE	25"	APTITUDE FOR MOTOR MECHANICS	20"
Coding Speed	7"	Mechanical Comprehension	10"
Clerical Accuracy	8"	Automotive Information	10"
Sentence Completion	10"		
ELECTRONICS APTITUDE	20"		
Electronics	10"	For the Entire Composite Examination: All Tests...	2 hours [120"]
Electricity	10"		

ANSWER SHEET FOR PREDICTIVE EXAMINATION

TEST I. WORD KNOWLEDGE

TEST II. VERBAL ANALOGIES

TEST III. ARITHMETIC REASONING

TEST IV. CLERICAL ACCURACY

TEST V. CLERICAL ACCURACY

18 / Practice For Air Force Placement Tests

TEST VI. CODING SPEED

TEST VII. SENTENCE COMPLETION

TEST VIII. ELECTRONICS

TEST IX. ELECTRICITY

1. ____ 2. ____ 3. ____ 4. ____ 5. ____ 6. A B C D E 7. A B C D E 8. A B C D E
9. A B C D E 10. A B C D E 11. A B C D E 12. A B C D E 13. A B C D E 14. A B C D E 15. A B C D E 16. A B C D E
17. A B C D E 18. A B C D E 19. A B C D E 20. A B C D E 21. A B C D E 22. A B C D E 23. A B C D E 24. A B C D E

TEST X. TOOL KNOWLEDGE

1. ____ 2. ____ 3. ____ 4. ____ 5. ____ 6. ____ 7. ____ 8. ____
9. ____ 10. ____ 11. ____ 12. ____ 13. ____ 14. ____ 15. ____ 16. ____
17. ____ 18. ____ 19. ____ 20. ____ 21. ____ 22. ____ 23. ____ 24. ____
25. ____ 26. ____ 27. ____ 28. ____ 29. ____ 30. ____ 31. ____ 32. ____

TEST XI. TOOL ANALOGIES

1. A B C D E 2. A B C D E 3. A B C D E 4. A B C D E 5. A B C D E 6. A B C D E 7. A B C D E 8. A B C D E

TEST XII. SPACE PERCEPTION

1. A B C D E 2. A B C D E 3. A B C D E 4. A B C D E 5. A B C D E 6. A B C D E 7. A B C D E 8. A B C D E
9. A B C D E 10. A B C D E 11. A B C D E 12. A B C D E 13. A B C D E 14. A B C D E 15. A B C D E 16. A B C D E

TEST XIII. SHOP INFORMATION

1. A B C D E 2. A B C D E 3. A B C D E 4. A B C D E 5. A B C D E 6. A B C D E 7. A B C D E 8. A B C D E
9. A B C D E 10. A B C D E 11. A B C D E 12. A B C D E 13. A B C D E 14. A B C D E 15. A B C D E 16. A B C D E
17. A B C D E 18. A B C D E 19. A B C D E 20. A B C D E 21. A B C D E 22. A B C D E 23. A B C D E 24. A B C D E
25. A B C D E 26. A B C D E 27. A B C D E 28. A B C D E 29. A B C D E 30. A B C D E 31. A B C D E 32. A B C D E

TEST XIV. MECHANICAL COMPREHENSION

1. A B C D E 2. A B C D E 3. A B C D E 4. A B C D E 5. A B C D E 6. A B C D E 7. A B C D E 8. A B C D E
9. A B C D E 10. A B C D E 11. A B C D E 12. A B C D E 13. A B C D E 14. A B C D E 15. A B C D E 16. A B C D E
17. A B C D E 18. A B C D E 19. A B C D E 20. A B C D E 21. A B C D E 22. A B C D E 23. A B C D E 24. A B C D E

TEST XV. AUTOMOTIVE INFORMATION

A NOTE ABOUT TEST TIMES.

The time allotted for each Test in each Examination in this book is based on a careful analysis of all the information now available. The time we allot for each test, therefore, merely suggests in a general way approximately how much time you should expend on each subject when you take the actual Exam. We have not, in every case, provided precisely the number of questions you will actually get on the examination. It's just not possible to know what the examiners will finally decide to do for every Test in the Examination. It might be a good idea to jot down your "running" time for each Test, and make comparisons later on. If you find that you're working faster, you may assume you're making progress. Remember, we have timed each Test uniformly. If you follow all our directions, your scores will all be comparable.

General Technical Aptitude.
Allow 25 minutes for these Tests.

TEST I. WORD KNOWLEDGE
TIME: 10 Minutes

DIRECTIONS: For each question in this test, select the appropriate letter preceding the word which is most nearly the same in meaning as the italicized word in each sentence.

1. Franklin was a man of *exceptional* ability.
   (A) well-trained (B) active
   (C) mechanical (D) self-educated
   (E) unusual

2. Their aim seems to be to *thwart* our plans.
   (A) simplify (B) direct
   (C) rely on (D) block
   (E) keep up with

3. He heard the warning cry of another *pedestrian*.
   (A) agent (B) walker
   (C) passenger (D) workingman
   (E) traffic officer

4. They boasted about the *superiority* of their product.
   (A) beauty (B) abundance
   (C) excellence (D) popularity
   (E) permanence

5. We considered their point of view *absurd*.
   (A) disgusting (B) old-fashioned
   (C) insincere (D) reasonable
   (E) foolish

6. Before long this machine will be *obsolete*.
   (A) out-of-date (B) broken down
   (C) as good as new (D) replaced
   (E) remodeled

7. In her lifetime she *surmounted* many difficulties.
   (A) overlooked (B) escaped
   (C) stirred up (D) overcame
   (E) complained about

8. The police were *lax* in enforcing parking regulations.
   (A) cross (B) faithful
   (C) not fair (D) too late
   (E) not strict

9. The door was *cunningly* concealed.
   (A) partly (B) cleverly
   (C) amusingly (D) completely
   (E) easily

10. The letter *emphasized* two important ideas.
    (A) introduced (B) overlooked
    (C) contrasted (D) questioned
    (E) stressed

11. Our neighbor *purchased* his home last year.
    (A) bought (B) rented
    (C) painted (D) remodeled
    (E) built

12. The only sound was the *steady* ticking of the clock.
    (A) noisy (B) rapid
    (C) regular (D) cheerful
    (E) tiresome

13. The desks in our room are *stationary*.
    (A) heavy (B) not movable
    (C) metal (D) easily adjustable
    (E) standard

14. Before signing the papers, Mr. Edmond consulted his *attorney*.
    (A) banker (B) clerk
    (C) lawyer (D) secretary
    (E) employer

15. We imitate those whom we admire.
    (A) protect (B) attract
    (C) study (D) copy
    (E) appreciate

16. They reached the *summit* of the mountain by noon.
    (A) base (B) wooded area
    (C) side (D) face
    (E) top

17. The motorist *heeded* the signals.
    (A) worried about (B) passed by
    (C) took notice of (D) laughed at
    (E) disagreed with

18. The *severity* of their criticism upset us.
    (A) purpose (B) harshness
    (C) method (D) suddenness
    (E) unfairness

19. We made a very *leisurely* trip to California.
    (A) roundabout (B) unhurried
    (C) unforgetable (D) tiresome
    (E) speedy

20. The little girl shook her head *vigorously*.
    (A) sadly (B) hopefully
    (C) sleepily (D) thoughtfully
    (E) energetically

END OF TEST

Go on to the next Test in the Examination, just as you would do on the actual exam. Check your answers when you have completed the entire Examination. The correct answers for this Test, and all the other Tests, are assembled at the conclusion of this Examination.

TEST II. VERBAL ANALOGIES

TIME: 5 Minutes

DIRECTIONS: In each of the following questions the FIRST TWO words in capital letters go together in some way. Find how they are related. Then write the correct letter to show which one of the last five words goes with the THIRD word in capital letters in the same way that the second word in capital letters goes with the first.

1. PERSPIRATION is to PORES as HAIR is to
   (A) endoderm
   (B) head
   (C) diathermy
   (D) electrolysis
   (E) filament

2. LIQUID is to SYPHON as SMOKE is to
   (A) chimney
   (B) fire
   (C) flame
   (D) flue

3. EXTORT is to WREST as CONSPIRE is to
   (A) entice
   (B) plot
   (C) deduce
   (D) respire
   (E) convey

4. WIDOW is to DOWAGER as CONSORT is to
   (A) enemy
   (B) constable
   (C) companion
   (D) distaff
   (E) curette

5. EMINENT is to LOWLY as FREQUENT is to
   (A) often
   (B) frivolous
   (C) enhance
   (D) soon
   (E) rare

6. GAUDY is to OSTENTATIOUS as DEJECTED is to
   (A) oppressed
   (B) inform
   (C) rejected
   (D) depressed

7. SALT is to MINE as MARBLE is to
   (A) palace
   (B) engraving
   (C) stone
   (D) quarry
   (E) sapphire

8. BRICK is to BUILDING as LEATHER is to
   (A) steer
   (B) hide
   (C) belt
   (D) horse
   (E) calf

9. BASS is to LOW as SOPRANO is to
   (A) intermediate
   (B) feminine
   (C) alto
   (D) eerie
   (E) high

10. SHOE is to FOOT as HELMET is to
    (A) steel
    (B) head
    (C) combat
    (D) duel
    (E) football

11. FINGER is to TACTILE as NOSE is to
    (A) proboscis
    (B) smell
    (C) olfactory
    (D) redolent
    (E) perfume

12. WATER is to FLUID as IRON is to
    (A) metal
    (B) rusty
    (C) solid
    (D) rails
    (E) mines

TEST III. ARITHMETIC REASONING

TIME: 10 Minutes

DIRECTIONS: Each problem in this test involves a certain amount of logical reasoning and thinking on your part, besides the usual simple computations, to help you in finding the solution. Read each problem carefully and choose the correct answer from the five choices that follow. Mark E on your answer sheet, if none of the suggested answers agree with your answer.

1. Find the interest on $25,800 for 144 days at 6% per annum. Base your calculations on a 360-day year.

   (A) $619.20   (B) $619.02
   (C) $691.02   (D) $691.20
   (E) None of these

2. A court clerk estimates that the untried cases on the docket will occupy the court for 150 trial days. If new cases are accumulating at the rate of 1.6 trial days per day (Saturday and Sunday excluded) and the court sits 5 days a week, how many days' business will remain to be heard at the end of 60 trial days?

   (A) 168 trial days   (B) 185 trial days
   (C) 188 trial days   (D) 186 trial days
   (E) None of these

3. The visitors section of a courtroom seats 105 people. The court is in session 6 hours of the day. On one particular day 486 people visited the court and were given seats. What is the average length of time spent by each visitor in the court? Assume that as soon as a person leaves his seat it is immediately filled and that at no time during the day is one of the 105 seats vacant. Express your answer in hours and minutes.

   (A) 1 hr. 20 min.   (B) 1 hr. 18 min.
   (C) 1 hr. 30 min.   (D) 2 hr.
   (E) None of these

4. If paper costs $1.46 per ream and 5% discount is allowed for cash, how many reams can be purchased for $69.35 cash? Do not discard fractional part of a cent in your calculations.

   (A) 49 reams   (B) 60 reams
   (C) 50 reams   (D) 53 reams
   (E) None of these

5. How much time is there between 8:30 a.m. today and 3:15 a.m. tomorrow.

   (A) 17¾ hrs.   (B) 18 hrs.
   (C) 18⅔ hrs.   (D) 18½ hrs.
   (E) None of these

6. How many days are there between September 19th and December 25th, both inclusive?

   (A) 98 days   (B) 96 days
   (C) 89 days   (D) 90 days
   (E) None of these

7. A clerk is requested to file 800 cards. If he can file cards at the rate of 80 cards an hour, the number of cards remaining to be filed after 7 hours of work is

   (A) 40   (B) 250
   (C) 140   (D) 260
   (E) None of these

8. An officer's weekly salary is increased from $80.00 to $90.00. The per cent of increase is, most nearly,

   (A) 10 per cent   (B) 11 1/9 per cent
   (C) 12½ per cent   (D) 14 1/7 per cent
   (E) None of these

9. If there are 245 sections in the city, the average number of sections for each of the 5 boroughs is

(A) 50 sections   (B) 49 sections
(C) 47 sections   (D) 59 sections
    (E) None of these

10. If a section had 45 miles of street to plow after a snow storm and 9 plows are used, each plow would cover an average of how many miles?

    (A) 7 miles   (B) 6 miles
    (C) 8 miles   (D) 5 miles
        (E) None of these

11. If a crosswalk plow engine is run 5 minutes a day for ten days in a given month, it would run how long in the course of this month?

    (A) 50 min.   (B) 1½ hrs.
    (C) 1 hr.   (D) 30 min.
        (E) None of these

12. If the department uses 1500 men in manual street cleaning and half as many more to load and drive trucks, the total number used is

    (A) 2200 men   (B) 2520 men
    (C) 2050 men   (D) 2250 men
        (E) None of these

13. If an inspector issued 186 summonses in the course of 7 hours, his hourly average of summonses issued was

    (A) 23 summonses   (B) 26 summonses
    (C) 25 summonses   (D) 28 summonses
        (E) None of these

14. If, of 186 summonses issued, one hundred were issued to first offenders, then there were how many summonses issued to other than first offenders?

    (A) 68   (B) 90
    (C) 86   (D) 108
        (E) None of these

15. A truck going at a rate of 20 miles an hour will reach a town 40 miles away in how many hours?

    (A) 3 hrs.   (B) 1 hr.
    (C) 4 hrs.   (D) 5 hrs.
        (E) None of these

16. If a barrel has a capacity of 100 gallons, it will contain how many gallons when it is two-fifths full?

    (A) 20 gal.   (B) 60 gal.
    (C) 40 gal.   (D) 80 gal.
        (E) None of these

17. If a salary of $3000 is subject to a 20 percent deduction, the net salary is

    (A) $2,000   (B) $2,400
    (C) $2,500   (D) $2,600
        (E) None of these

18. If $1000 is the cost of repairing 100 square yards of pavement, the cost of repairing one square yard is

    (A) $10   (B) $150
    (C) $100   (D) $300
        (E) None of these

19. If a man's base pay is $3000 and it is increased by a bonus of $350 and a seniority increment of $250, his total salary is

    (A) $3,600   (B) $3,500
    (C) $3,000   (D) $3,700
        (E) None of these

20. If an annual salary of $2160 is increased by a bonus of $720 and by a service increment of $120, the total pay rate is

    (A) $2,960   (B) $3,960
    (C) $2,690   (D) $3,000
        (E) None of these

END OF PART
If you finish before the allotted time is up, work on this part only.
When time is up, proceed directly to the next part and do not return to this part.

Clerical Aptitude and Ability.

TEST IV. CLERICAL ACCURACY

TIME: 4 Minutes

DIRECTIONS: This is a test of your speed and accuracy in comparing addresses. For Part I of the test, blacken the proper space under A in the Answer Sheet if the two addresses are exactly alike in every way. Blacken B if they are not alike in every way. For Part II of the test, go back to number 1 on the Answer Sheet. But this time blacken the space under D if the two addresses are exactly alike in every way. Blacken the space under E if they are not exactly alike in every way.

PART I

1. 240 Winthrop Ave.   240 Winthrop Ave.
2. 332 Macon St.   332 Malcolm St.
3. 3517 Beverly Rd.   3517 Beverley Rd.
4. 182 Wilson Ave.   182 Willson Ave.
5. 50 Leffert Ave.   50 Leffert Ave.
6. 494 Seward Pk.   494 Seward Lane
7. 292 Montauk Ave.   292 Montalk Ave.
8. 3053 Bedford Ave.   2053 Bedford Ave.
9. 280 Parkside Ave.   280 Parkside Ave.
10. 419 Van Siclen Ave.   419 Van Sicklen Ave.
11. 766 Howard Ave.   766 Howard Ave.
12. 471 Ralph Ave.   417 Ralph Ave.
13. 8421 Glenwood Rd.   8421 Glenword Rd.
14. Bayside, L.I.   Bayside, N.Y.
15. 718 Dun Ct.   718 Dun Ct.
16. 453 Sheffield St.   453 Shefield St.
17. 1440 50 St.   1440 55 St.

PART II

1. 160 Quincy St.   160 Quincy St.
2. 1001 Rutland Rd.   1001 Rutland Pl.
3. 5714 Farragut Pl.   5714 Farragut Pl.
4. 206 Albemarle Rd.   206 Albemarl Rd.
5. 1332 Throop Ave.   1332 Troop Ave.
6. 222 Franklin Rd.   222 Franklen Rd.
7. April, Ga.   April, Va.
8. 84 S. Weirfield   84 S. Wierfield
9. 49 Bokee Ct.   49 Bokee Ct.
10. 4739 N. Marion St.   4739 N. Marion St.
11. 167 22nd Ave. E   167 27th Ave. E
12. 205 W. 77th Rd.   250 W. 77th Rd.
13. 1108 E. Chauncey Blvd.   1108 E. Chauncey Blvd.
14. 7 Union Plaza   7 Union Place
15. 3721 Filmore Ave.   3721 Filmoor Ave.
16. 919 Garfield Te.   919 Garfield Te.
17. 4316 Marino St.   4361 Marino St.

TEST V. CLERICAL ACCURACY

TIME: 4 Minutes

DIRECTIONS: This is a test of your speed and accuracy in comparing addresses. For Part I of the test, blacken the proper space under A in the Answer Sheet if the two addresses are exactly alike in every way. Blacken B if they are not alike in every way. For Part II of the test, go back to number 1 on the Answer Sheet. But this time blacken the space under D if the two addresses are exactly alike in every way. Blacken the space under E if they are not exactly alike in every way.

PART I

1. 356 Clifton Pl. N   356 Clifton Pl. N.
2. 9401 W. McDonald Ave.   9401 W. MacDonald Ave.
3. 2834 W. 15th St.   2843 W. 15th St.
4. 406 7th Ave. S.   406 7th Ave.
5. 4114 Purdue, La.   4114 Purdue, Ia
6. 723 S. Macon St.   723 S. Mason St.
7. 320 S. Webster St.   302 S. Webster St.
8. 577 Wnona Blvd.   577 Winona Blvd.
9. 8022 Washington St.   822 Washington St.
10. 5432 Ave. H N.W.   5432 Ave. H N.W.
11. 3374 Fifth Ave.   3374 Fitch Ave.
12. 62 W. Mataqua Pl.   62 W. Matakwa Pl.
13. 291 S.W. Adams St.   219 S.W. Adams St.
14. 585 N. Park Pl.   585 N. Park Pl.
15. 8604 23rd Ave.   8604 23rd Ave.
16. 244 W. Covert Sq.   244 W. Covert Sq.
17. 498 McLaren Pl.   498 Maclaren Pl.

PART II

1. 48 S. Rinaldi Rd.   48 S. Rinaldo Rd.
2. 82 Severn Dr. S.   82 Severn Dr. S.
3. 435 W. Hendricks   435 W. Hendrix
4. 20 Hubard Pl.   20 Hubbard Pl.
5. 51 Chamber St.   51 Chamber St.
6. 2015 Dorchester Rd.   2015 Dorchestor Rd.
7. 356 Miller Ave.   356 Mills Ave.
8. 45 Fleet Walk   45 Fleet Rd.
9. 1528 E. 9 St.   1528 E. 9 St.
10. 56 Monument Walk   56 Monument Rd.
11. 186 Hudson Blvd.   186 Hudson Bldg.
12. 53 Woodbine St.   53 Woodbine St.
13. 130 Martens Ave.   130 Martins Ave.
14. 3720 Nautilus Ave.   3270 Nautilus Ave.
15. 53 C Wyona Dr.   53 C Wyona Dr.
16. 511 Jaffry Ct.   511 Jaffrie Ct.
17. 76 Herzl St.   76 Herzel St.

TEST VI. CODING SPEED

TIME: 7 Minutes

DIRECTIONS: The Code Identification Key contains a group of words with a Code Number beside each word. Each test question consists of one of the words from the Key followed by five possible Code Numbers arranged in columns labelled A, B, C, D and E. Choose the one Code Number for each word that corresponds to the number given in the Code Identification Key. On your answer sheet, blacken the letter of the column in which the correct Code Number appears.

```
                    CODE IDENTIFICATION KEY
     pear..........9572     table.........4163     silver........8569
     beach.........8451     tree..........3490     door..........6301
     house.........2015     boat..........7751     garden........4972
                            tiger.........2508
```

QUESTIONS	A	B	C	D	E
1. boat	8569	6301	2508	7751	9572
2. table	8569	7751	4163	2015	3490
3. door	8569	6301	4163	7751	3490
4. pear	8569	8451	4163	7751	9572
5. tree	4972	6301	2508	2015	3490
6. garden	4972	9572	2015	4163	6301
7. beach	4972	8451	4163	2508	6301
8. silver	8569	8451	4163	7751	9572
9. house	8569	8451	2508	2015	3490
10. tiger	8569	9572	2508	2015	6301
11. silver	4163	7751	4972	8569	6301
12. table	4163	8451	9572	2015	3490
13. boat	4163	8451	4972	7751	6301
14. beach	4163	8451	2508	7751	9572
15. tree	4972	3490	2508	8569	6301
16. tiger	4972	8451	2508	7751	3490
17. house	8451	8569	2508	4163	2015
18. pear	8569	7751	9572	2015	6301
19. garden	4972	7751	4163	2015	3490
20. door	4972	6301	4163	2508	3490

CODE IDENTIFICATION KEY

pear..........9572	table.........4163	silver........8569
beach.........8451	tree..........3490	door..........6301
house.........2015	boat..........7751	garden........4972
	tiger.........2508	

QUESTION	A	B	C	D	E
21. beach	8569	8451	9572	7751	2015
22. silver	4972	8569	9572	3490	2015
23. boat	4972	6301	9572	7751	3490
24. table	4163	6301	2508	7751	2015
25. garden	4972	8451	2508	4163	6301
26. tiger	4972	8569	2508	2015	3490
27. pear	8569	8451	4163	2015	9572
28. door	8569	6301	9572	2015	3490
29. house	4163	9572	2508	2015	3490
30. tree	8451	9572	4163	7751	3490
31. garden	4972	8451	9572	7751	6301
32. pear	4972	8451	4163	2015	9572
33. table	8569	6301	4163	2508	3490
34. boat	8451	9572	2508	7751	2015
35. beach	8451	8569	4163	3490	2508
36. tiger	4972	6301	2508	7751	2015
37. door	8569	6301	2015	7751	9572
38. silver	8569	6301	4972	2508	3490
39. house	8451	9572	2015	7751	2508
40. tree	4163	6031	4972	2508	3490
41. table	4972	9572	4163	7751	3490
42. beach	8451	8569	9572	2015	6301
43. pear	4972	9572	2508	7751	3490
44. tiger	8569	8451	4972	2508	9572
45. garden	4972	9572	4163	7751	3490
46. silver	8569	8451	2508	7751	6301
47. door	8569	8451	4972	3490	6301
48. tree	4163	8451	2015	2508	3490
49. house	8569	6301	9572	2015	3490
50. boat	8569	6301	4163	7751	3490

CODE IDENTIFICATION KEY

army.........4873	ocean.........7293	salad.........6591
chair.........8741	party.........5894	film.........8436
dress.........6720	window.........3914	cash.........6209
	carpet.........2395	

QUESTIONS	A	B	C	D	E
51. ocean	6209	8741	7293	5894	4873
52. dress	6720	6209	7293	6591	3914
53. salad	6720	8436	7293	6591	5894
54. army	3914	8741	7293	2395	4873
55. film	6209	8436	6591	3914	4873
56. cash	6209	8741	6591	3914	5894
57. window	6720	8436	3914	2395	5894
58. chair	6720	6209	6591	8741	4873
59. carpet	8436	2395	7293	3914	5894
60. party	6720	8741	7293	2395	5894
61. salad	6209	4873	6591	2395	5894
62. film	6209	8436	7293	6591	3914
63. chair	6720	8741	7293	2395	4873
64. window	3914	4873	6591	8741	5894
65. ocean	3914	2395	7293	6591	4873
66. army	6209	8741	8436	5894	4873
67. cash	6720	8436	7293	6209	3914
68. dress	6720	8741	6591	2395	4873
69. carpet	6209	2395	7293	5894	4873
70. party	3914	8741	7293	5894	4873
71. window	8436	6209	7293	2395	3914
72. ocean	6720	8741	7293	5894	4873
73. party	6209	8741	7293	2395	5894
74. chair	6209	8741	6591	2395	3914
75. salad	6720	8741	6591	7293	5894
76. carpet	6720	2395	8436	8741	5894
77. cash	6209	2395	6591	7293	4873
78. film	6209	8436	7293	2395	4873
79. army	6720	8741	8436	5894	4873
80. dress	6720	8741	6591	5894	3914

CODE IDENTIFICATION KEY

army.........4873	ocean.........7293	salad.........6591
chair.........8741	party.........5894	film..........8436
dress.........6720	window........3914	cash..........6209
	carpet........2395	

QUESTIONS	A	B	C	D	E
81. chair	8436	8741	6591	7293	3914
82. salad	6209	4873	6591	2395	3914
83. army	6209	8436	6591	5894	4873
84. window	6720	4873	8436	7293	3914
85. dress	6720	6209	7293	5894	3914
86. party	6209	8436	6591	5894	4873
87. cash	6720	8436	7293	6209	3914
88. carpet	6720	2395	6591	7293	3914
89. ocean	6209	8741	7293	8436	3914
90. film	8436	6209	6591	2395	4873
91. dress	6720	8741	7293	6591	5894
92. army	6720	2395	8436	7293	4873
93. cash	6720	4873	8436	6209	5894
94. salad	6209	4873	6591	8741	3914
95. chair	6720	8741	8436	6591	3914
96. ocean	6720	2395	7293	8741	3914
97. carpet	8436	2395	6591	8741	5894
98. film	8436	2395	5894	6209	3914
99. party	6720	6209	6591	8741	5894
100. window	6720	2395	8436	3914	4873

TEST VII. SENTENCE COMPLETION

TIME: 10 Minutes

DIRECTIONS: Each of the completion questions in this test consists of an incomplete sentence. Each sentence is followed by a series of lettered words, one of which best completes the sentence. Select the word or words that best completes the meaning of each sentence.

1. The admiration the Senator earns is _____ by his _____ instinct for getting onto the front pages.
   (A) concocted . . . proverbial
   (B) evolved . . . haughty
   (C) belied . . . aggressive
   (D) engendered . . . unerring
   (E) transcended . . . dogged

2. The accelerated growth of public employment _____ the dramatic expansion of budgets and programs.
   (A) parallels
   (B) contains
   (C) revolves
   (D) escapes
   (E) populates

3. So great is the intensity of Shakespeare's dramatic language that the audience becomes _____ and sees messages and equivocations everywhere, until the play becomes an apocalypse of _____ and fall.
   (A) stunned . . . rise
   (B) hallucinated . . . temptation
   (C) aroused . . . doubt
   (D) dulled . . . zeal
   (E) weary . . . disgust

4. Not every _____ mansion, church, battle site, theater, or other public hall can be preserved.
   (A) novel
   (B) structured
   (C) comparative
   (D) unknown
   (E) venerable

5. Man is still a _____ in the labor market.
   (A) glut
   (B) possibility
   (C) commodity
   (D) resumption
   (E) provision

6. As we moved on to Melford shortly after noon on Saturday, the clear air and the rolling _____ made one wonder whether this festival would lead all others, at least in altitude.
   (A) stones
   (B) hovels
   (C) skyline
   (D) oaks
   (E) terrain

7. Witness the long waiting list for the overworked psychiatrists and psychologists and the twentieth-century _____ for lying on the couch talking about oneself and the neuroses that have resulted from a too intense _____ with oneself.
   (A) wish . . . inspection
   (B) process . . . tirade
   (C) plan . . . understanding
   (D) fad . . . preoccupation
   (E) garb . . . implication

8. The book will be _____ by every Western student of the USSR, and it will be a thrilling adventure for any reader.
   (A) skimmed
   (B) perused
   (C) rejected
   (D) blasphemed
   (E) borrowed

9. With this realization, the people suddenly found themselves left with _____ moral values and little ethical _____.
   (A) obsolete . . . perspective
   (B) established . . . grasp
   (C) portentous . . . insinuation
   (D) extreme . . . judgment
   (E) continued . . . pronouncement

10. There is a notion abroad that history has gotten away from us; that our lives are beyond control; that there are no points of _____ which mean anything any more.
    (A) conference   (B) inference
    (C) prudence   (D) incidence
    (E) reference

11. I cannot honestly number myself among the pious and I have frequently had the experience of being _____ among the unholy.
    (A) regenerated   (B) deteriorated
    (C) compiled   (D) consigned
    (E) inflamed

12. These avant-garde thinkers believe that the major peace movements are ineffective because the thinking that underlies these movements is old-fashioned, confused, _____ and out-of-step with the findings of _____ science.
    (A) stimulating . . . natural
    (B) delusionary . . . behavioral
    (C) loaded . . . true
    (D) uncertain . . . physical
    (E) blatant . . . scholastic

13. Today, we who read Latin return far more often to the exuberance of Apuleius than to the carefully molded _____ of Cicero.
    (A) literature   (B) redundancies
    (C) objects   (D) piracies
    (E) platitudes

14. If the process of decision-making was _____ a half-century or more ago, consider how it has become _____ since.
    (A) dedicated . . . simplified
    (B) complicated . . . compounded
    (C) revived . . . encouraged
    (D) imbedded . . . obvious
    (E) enhanced . . . improved

15. Scientists should have choice as to what areas they explore, and certainly have the _____ right and obligations as _____ to influence what use is made of their discoveries.
    (A) impeccable . . . teachers
    (B) inescapable . . . philosophers
    (C) definitive . . . recorders
    (D) divine . . . lecturers
    (E) ethical . . . humanists

16. Under the contest rules, the award goes to an undergraduate college student who has collected a _____ personal library.
    (A) distinguished   (B) well-managed
    (C) modified   (D) precise
    (E) stocked

17. The consequences of the establishment of the colonies were a rapid and careless _____ of natural resources, and _____ human suffering.
    (A) depletion . . . appalling
    (B) cancellation . . . remarkable
    (C) disappearance . . . planned
    (D) development . . . unfailing
    (E) disintegration . . . compelled

18. The Crusades can be seen as the first great collective military _____ in which all Europe participated.
    (A) embarrassment   (B) compilation
    (C) review   (D) drawing board
    (E) enterprise

19. The first essential in building a missile submarine is the _____ of literally millions of parts.
    (A) application
    (B) reassembling
    (C) integration
    (D) infiltration
    (E) assignment

20. The _____ researchers had heard that kind of talk often before, but what came next _____ them.
    (A) avid . . . encouraged
    (B) asinine . . . revived
    (C) studious . . . involved
    (D) assembled . . . jolted
    (E) fatigued . . . enervated

END OF PART
If you finish before the allotted time is up, work on this part only.

Electronics Aptitude.
Allow 20 minutes for these Tests.

TEST VIII. ELECTRONICS

TIME: 10 Minutes

DIRECTIONS: For each question in this test, read carefully the stem and the four lettered choices that follow. Choose the answer which you consider correct or most nearly correct. Mark the answer sheet for the letter you have chosen: A, B, C, or D.

1. A D.C. wattmeter is essentially a combination of
   (A) a voltmeter and an ammeter
   (B) two ammeters
   (C) two voltmeters
   (D) a current and potential transformer.

2. Of the following meters, the one that does *not* have the zero at the center of the scale is the
   (A) control battery ammeter
   (B) main tie-line ammeter
   (C) main tie-line reactive volt-ammeter
   (D) main tie-line wattmeter.

3. A shunt in conjunction with a shunt-type ammeter is used in measuring D.C. current where
   (A) it is desired to isolate the instrument from the main circuit
   (B) the current fluctuates greatly in value
   (C) it is not practical to carry the full load current through the instrument
   (D) the accompanying D.C. voltage is high.

4. High A.C. voltages are usually measured with a
   (A) voltmeter and current transformer
   (B) millivoltmeter and shunt
   (C) voltmeter and multiplier
   (D) potential transformer and voltmeter.

5. In the course of normal operation the instrument which will be *least* effective in indicating that a generator may overheat because it is overloaded is
   (A) an ammeter
   (B) a voltmeter
   (C) a wattmeter
   (D) a stator thermocouple.

6. Large currents in D.C. circuits are practically always measured with a
   (A) ammeter and multiplier
   (B) millivoltmeter and multiplier
   (C) ammeter and current transformer
   (D) millivoltmeter and shunt.

7. A millivoltmeter having a full scale deflection of 50 mv. is used with a 100-ampere, 50-millivolt shunt in a d.c. circuit. This combination is normally used to measure
   (A) voltage   (B) current
   (C) power   (D) resistance.

8. In the telemetering equipment the purpose of the glow tube is to provide
   (A) adequate illumination to read the meter
   (B) protection against high line voltage
   (C) rectification of the line current
   (D) a means of discharging the equipment.

9. A cycle counter is used in testing
   (A) relays   (B) ammeters
   (C) wattmeters   (D) voltmeters.

10. The insulation resistance of a transformer winding is readily measured with
    (A) a wattmeter   (B) an ammeter
    (C) a megger   (D) a Kelvin bridge.

11. To measure the voltage across a load you would
    (A) connect a voltmeter across the load
    (B) connect an ammeter across the load
    (C) connect a voltmeter in series with the load
    (D) connect an ammeter in series with the load.

12. Your foreman told you to measure the insulation resistance of some feeders. To do this you would use
    (A) a megger
    (B) a bell test
    (C) a magneto test
    (D) a service man from the Utility Company.

13. You are to check the Power Factor of a certain electrical load. You cannot get a Power Factor Meter. You would use
    (A) an ammeter, a wattmeter and a voltmeter
    (B) a voltmeter and an ammeter
    (C) a wattmeter
    (D) a Kilo-watt Hour Meter.

14. The power factor of a single phase alternating current motor may be found by using one of the following sets of AC instruments:
    (A) one voltmeter and one phase-rotation meter
    (B) one voltmeter and one ammeter
    (C) one voltmeter, one ammeter, and one wattmeter
    (D) one voltmeter, one ammeter, and one watt-hour meter.

15. The correct value of the resistance of a field coil can be measured by using
    (A) a Schering bridge
    (B) an ammeter and a voltmeter
    (C) a Kelvin double bridge
    (D) a Maxwell bridge.

16. The hot wire voltmeter
    (A) is a high precision instrument
    (B) is used only for D.C. circuits
    (C) reads equally well on D.C. and/or A.C. circuits
    (D) is used only for A.C. circuits.

17. An A.C. ammeter is calibrated to read R.M.S. values. This also means that this meter is calibrated to read the
    (A) average value   (B) peak value
    (C) effective value   (D) square value.

18. To increase the range of D.C. ammeters you would use
    (A) a current transformer
    (B) an inductance
    (C) a condenser
    (D) a shunt.

19. The electric meter *NOT* in itself capable of measuring both D.C. and A.C. voltages is the
    (A) Darsonval voltmeter
    (B) electrodynamometer voltmeter
    (C) iron vane voltmeter
    (D) inclined-coil voltmeter.

20. To increase the range of an A.C. ammeter the one of the following which is most commonly used is
    (A) a current transformer
    (B) an inductance
    (C) a condenser
    (D) a straight shunt (not U-shaped).

END OF TEST

Go on to the next Test in the Examination, just as you would do on the actual exam. Check your answers when you have completed the entire Examination. The correct answers for this Test, and all the other Tests, are assembled at the conclusion of this Examination.

TEST IX. ELECTRICITY

TIME: 10 Minutes

DIRECTIONS: Below we present a number of representative jobs. Although the correct steps for each job are given, they are not placed in the proper order. Examine each job and decide which step should come first. On your answer sheet, place the number of this step. Then insert the numbers of the remaining steps, so that when you have finished the numbers can be read in proper job order.

1. In soldering an electric cable, you are assigned to tin the soldering copper.
   (1) The copper should be properly heated.
   (2) Ammonium chloride should be applied to soldering copper together with the solder until copper is tinned.
   (3) Copper should be wired until shiny on an emery cloth.
   (4) The copper should be cleaned and polished with ammonium chloride solution and filed.

2. In the rewinding of an electric motor, you are assigned to wind an electromagnet. What procedure would you employ?
   (1) Polarity of magnet should be determined.
   (2) Core should be wound with No. 20 d.c.c. wire.
   (3) Wire should be attached to the plus and minus terminals.
   (4) A soft iron core that has no magnetism should be selected.
   (5) Core should be tested to find whether it is non-magnetic.

3. You are assigned to a job which requires splicing the ends of connecting wires in an outlet box. What would be the correct method for you to follow?
   (1) Joint should be properly protected by friction tape.
   (2) Wires should be securely entwined.
   (3) Solder joint so that flux and solder run smoothly on heated wires.
   (4) Scrape insulation from cable.
   (5) Joint should be properly protected by rubber plate.
   (6) Remove oxides from surface of wire.

4. You are working on a job when a fuse in a lighting circuit blows out. You have to discover and put in another fuse in its place. What method would you employ in carrying out this task?
   (1) The fuse which has blown out should be removed from the fuse block.
   (2) The line should be traced and the fuse block discovered.
   (3) The bulb which no longer gives light should be investigated for a defective filament.
   (4) The fuses should be carefully examined for defects.
   (5) A new fuse which has the same amperage should be screwed in.
   (6) The circuit should be closed in order to determine whether the new fuse operates properly.

5. An important assignment has been given to you to carry out. You are told that two door bells are to be put in, using a parallel circuit. Further instructions state that both bells are to be operated from one push button and two dry cells. After careful consideration, in what manner would you proceed to carry out this assignment?

   (1) The binding post nuts should be carefully examined in order to see that they are properly tightened.

   (2) Since an electric doorbell requires a current, the button should be pushed and the circuit tested.

(3) The binding posts should be connected with the wires which have been provided.

(4) The length of No. 18. d.c.c., which is the bell wire best suited for his purpose, is to be decided upon.

(5) The staples which have been insulated should be driven in place to carry out the job properly.

(6) The door bells should be mounted, then the button pushed to see if they work properly and the cells sufficiently dried.

DIRECTIONS: For each question in this test, read carefully the stem and the four lettered choices that follow. Choose the answer which you consider correct or most nearly correct. Mark the answer sheet for the letter you have chosen: A, B, C, or D.

6. Alternating currents may be increased or decreased by means of
   (A) a generating machine
   (B) a dynamo
   (C) a transformer
   (D) a motor.

7. The best of the following conductors of electricity is
   (A) silver wire
   (B) mica
   (C) nickel and chromium wire
   (D) gold.

8. Different amounts of resistance in a circuit may be introduced by means of
   (A) a voltmeter
   (B) an electromagnet
   (C) an ammeter
   (D) a good connection.

9. In sockets, extension cord is protected by means of the .... knot
   (A) sheepshank
   (B) clove hitch
   (C) fire
   (D) underwriters'.

10. The fuse plug contains a safety element composed of
    (A) a piece of metal that has a high resistance and a low melting point
    (B) a piece of metal that has a low resistance and a high melting point
    (C) a piece of metal that has a low resistance
    (D) a piece of metal that has a high melting point.

11. Storage battery electrolite is formed by the dissolving of .... acid in water
    (A) hydrochloric
    (B) sulphuric
    (C) acetic
    (D) atric.

12. The electric pressure or electromotive force is measured by
    (A) the volt
    (B) the electric meter
    (C) the watt
    (D) kilowatt.

13. The unit of measurement for electrical resistance to currents is
    (A) the ohm
    (B) the ampere
    (C) the volt
    (D) the watt.

14. Electricity is sold by the kilowatt which equals .... watts.
    (A) 1,000
    (B) 2,000
    (C) 10,000
    (D) 100.

15. The unit for measuring electrical capacity is
    (A) farad
    (B) volt
    (C) ohm
    (D) watt.

16. The central terminal of a dry cell is said to be
    (A) positive
    (B) negative
    (C) neutral
    (D) charged.

17. The spark-plug used in automobiles produces electrical energy at .... voltage
    (A) high
    (B) low
    (C) medium
    (D) no.

18. A D.C. series motor that has the current reversed, turns in the .... direction
    (A) opposite
    (B) same
    (C) reverse
    (D) wrong.

19. The current used for charging storage batteries is
    (A) direct
    (B) alternating
    (C) negative
    (D) positive.

20. The starting motor of an automobile requires a high
    (A) amperage
    (B) voltage
    (C) capacity
    (D) degree of insulation.

21. Receptacles in a house-lighting system are regularly connected in
    (A) parallel
    (B) series
    (C) diagonal
    (D) perpendicular.

22. Wire connections should encircle binding posts in the .... manner the nut turns to lighten.
    (A) opposite
    (B) same
    (C) reverse
    (D) different.

23. The headlights to automobiles are found to be connected ordinarily in
    (A) parallel
    (B) series
    (C) diagonal
    (D) perpendicular.

END OF PART
If you finish before the allotted time is up, work on this part only.
When time is up, proceed directly to the next part and do not return to this part.

Aptitude for General Mechanics.
Allow 30 minutes for these Tests.

TEST X. TOOL KNOWLEDGE

TIME: 10 Minutes

DIRECTIONS: The items listed below refer to the use of tools shown on the following pages. Read each item, and for the operation given, select the proper tool to be used.

Read and answer each question carefully. Select the best answer and mark the proper space on the answer sheet.

1. Laying out the angle of cut on the side supports for stair treads.
2. Cutting a brick accurately.
3. Marking lines parallel to the edge of a board.
4. Coupling nickel plated pipes.
5. Finishing the flat surface of a cement floor.

6. Checking that the side of a concrete form is vertical.
7. Drilling a 3/4" hole in a 6" channel iron on the job.
8. Locating the center of a circular plate having a diameter of 12".
9. Forging an iron ring.
10. Bending a 1/2" rod for a U-support for a 6" pipe.

11. Coupling iron pipe for a handrail.
12. Chamfering the edge of a cement curb.
13. Filling joins in old brickwork.
14. Setting glazed tile on a wall.
15. Driving a drill for a hole through concrete for a 1" pipe.

16. Grooving a cement floor to form blocks.
17. Laying out an accurate line for a saw cut as 90° to the edge of a board.
18. Holding sheet metal together for welding.
19. Locating a point for a hole in the floor directly under a point in the ceiling.
20. Cutting a channel in concrete for a pipe with the aid of tool "U."

21. Marking off a number of equal small distances.
22. Laying out a horizontal line in the center of a wall.
23. Driving a carpenter's chisel.
24. Driving a drill for a 1/4" hole in a column.
25. Drilling holes in wood with auger bits.

26. Driving a screwdriver bit.
27. Making a chalk line.
28. Forcing a dove-tail joint together.
29. Bending thin sheet copper into the shape of a cylinder.
30. Marking a corner to be rounded on a board.
31. Flattening the end of a 1" iron pipe on a steel plate.

TEST X.

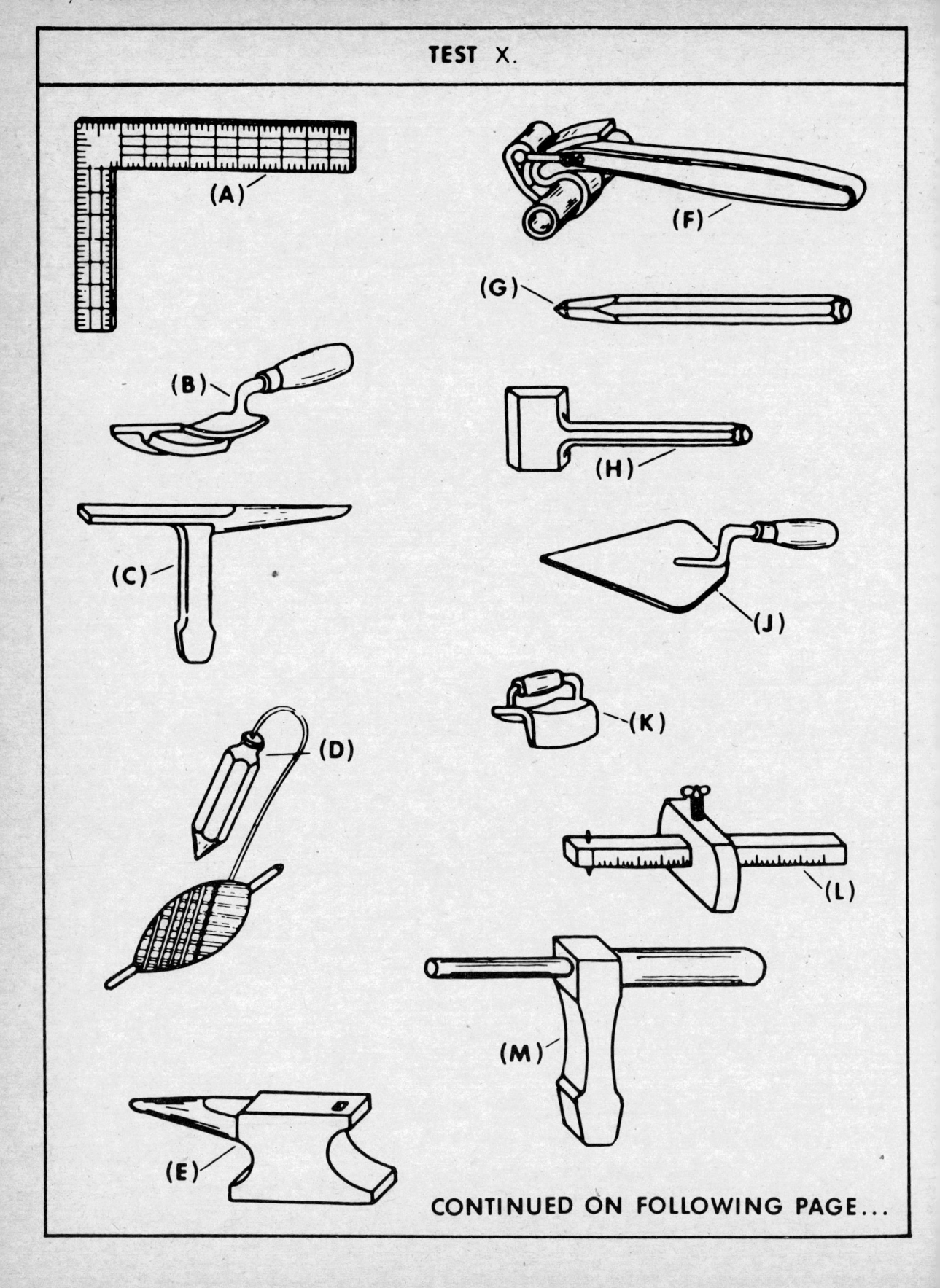

CONTINUED ON FOLLOWING PAGE...

TEST X.

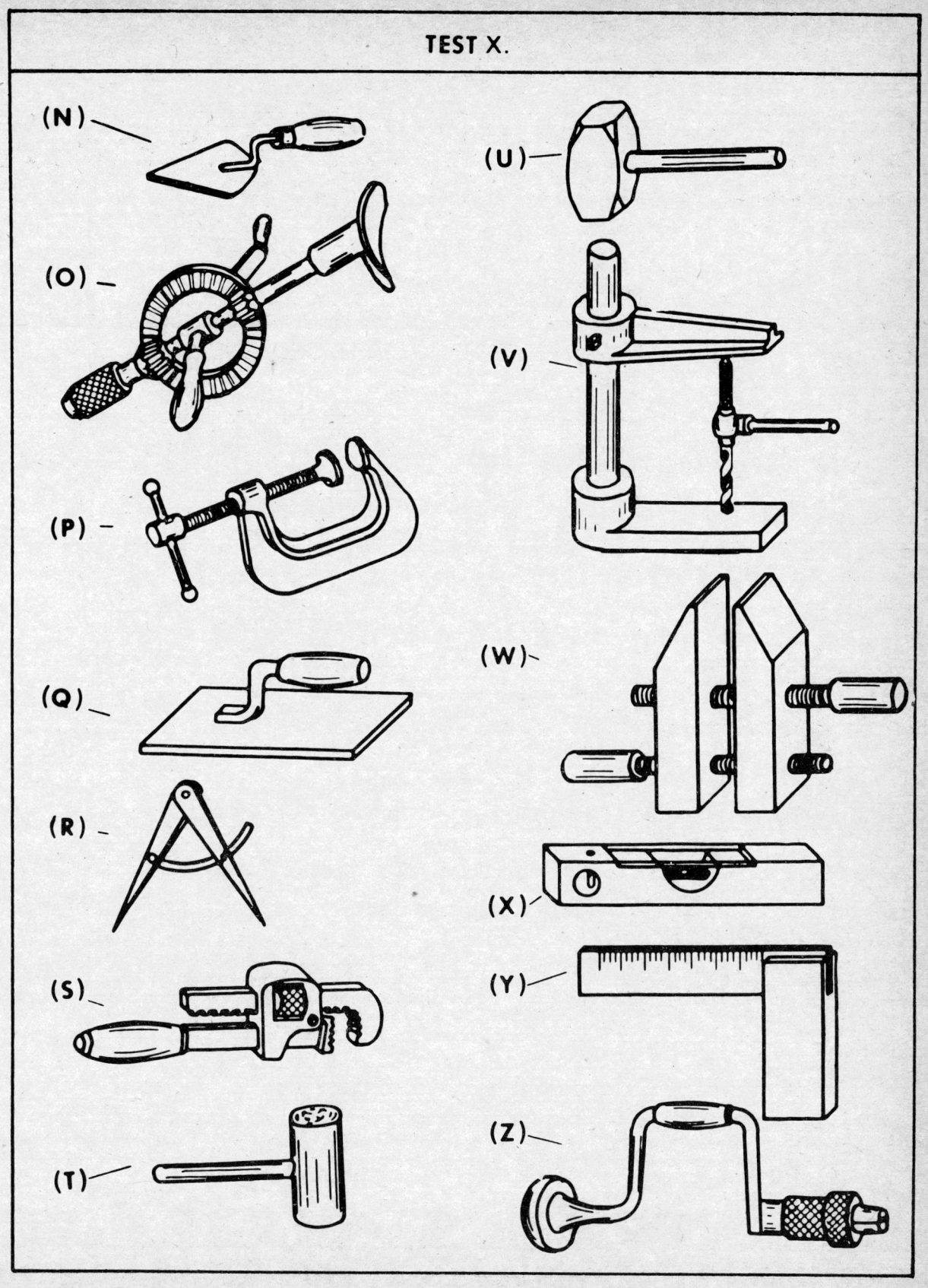

(N)

(O)

(P)

(Q)

(R)

(S)

(T)

(U)

(V)

(W)

(X)

(Y)

(Z)

END OF TEST
Go on to the next Test in the Examination.

42 / *Practice For Air Force Placement Tests*

TEST XI. TOOL ANALOGIES

TIME: 5 Minutes

DIRECTIONS: Each question in this test consists of a numbered picture followed by four lettered illustrations marked A, B, C, & D. The problem is to determine which of the four lettered pictures goes best with the numbered tool or machine part. For each question blacken the space on your answer sheet corresponding to the letter of the best answer.

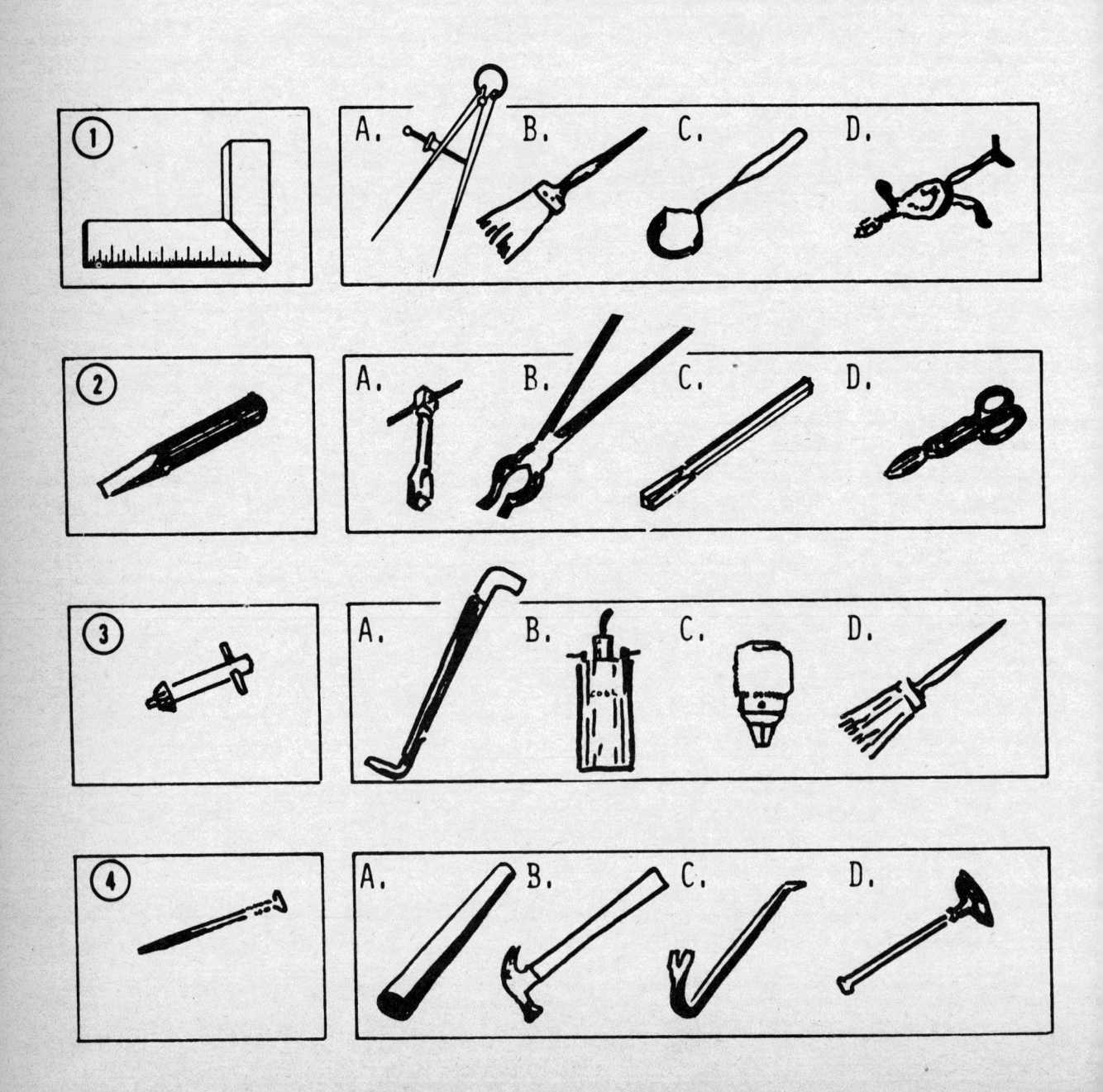

Predictive Practice Examination / 43

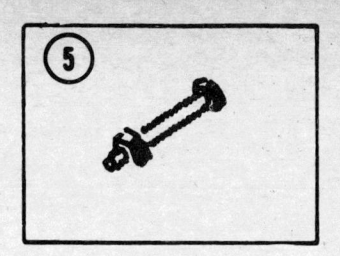

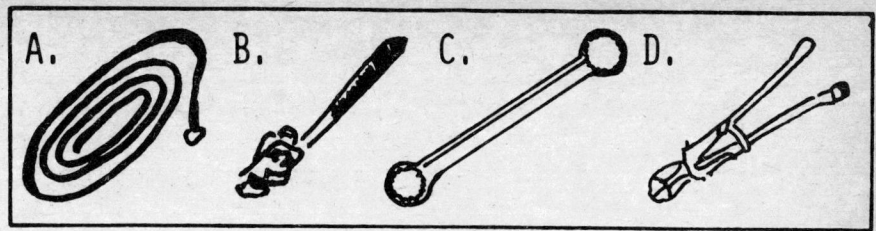

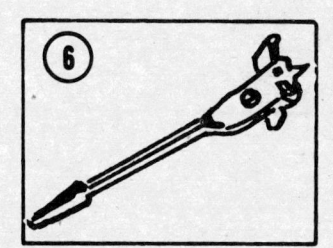

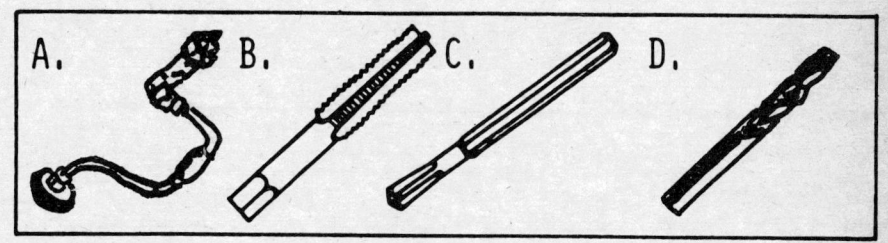

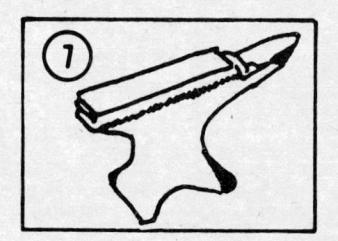

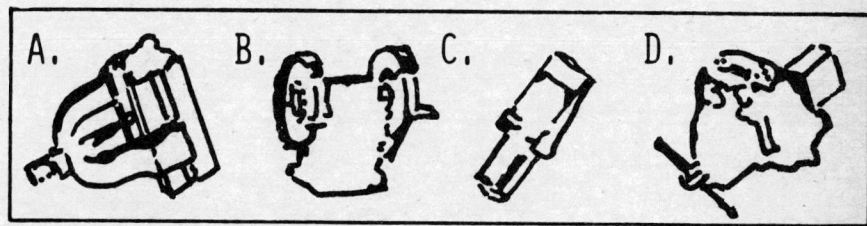

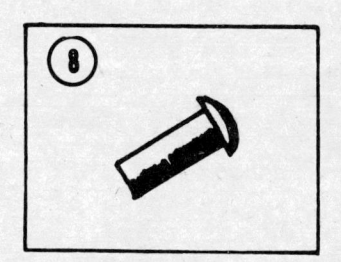

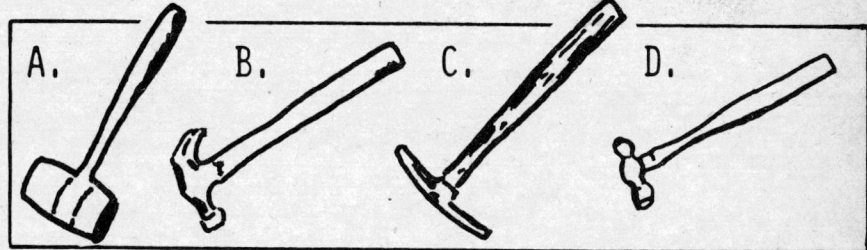

END OF TEST

Go on to the next Test in the Examination, just as you would do on the actual exam. Check your answers when you have completed the entire Examination. The correct answers for this Test, and all the other Tests, are assembled at the conclusion of this Examination.

TEST XII. SPACE PERCEPTION

TIME: 5 Minutes

DIRECTIONS: Each question in this test consists of a numbered picture showing a piece of cardboard that is to be folded. The dotted lines show where folds are to be made. The problem is to choose the lettered picture, A, B, C, or D which would be made by folding the cardboard in the numbered picture. For each question blacken the space on your answer sheet corresponding to the letter of the best answer.

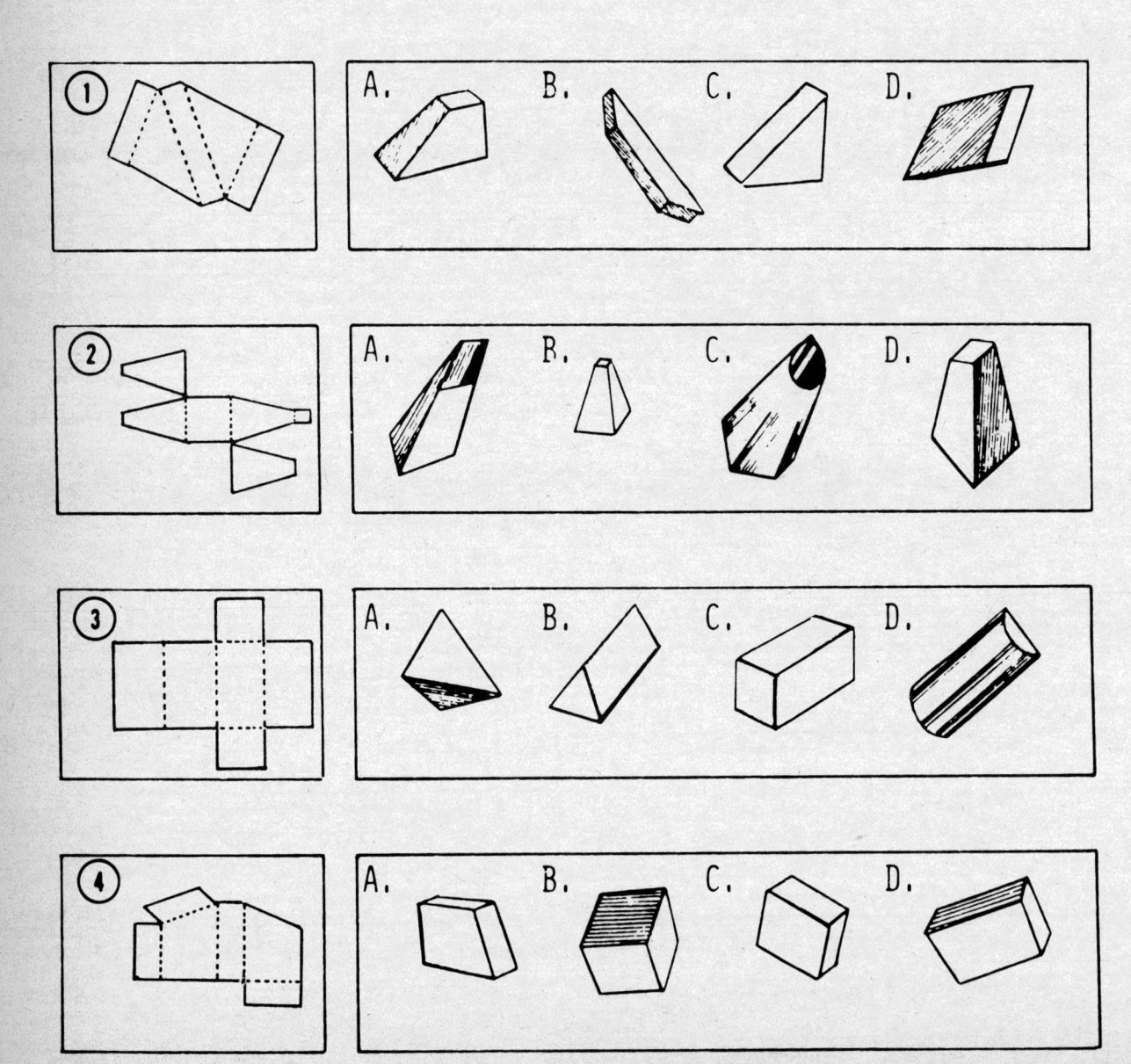

Predictive Practice Examination / 45

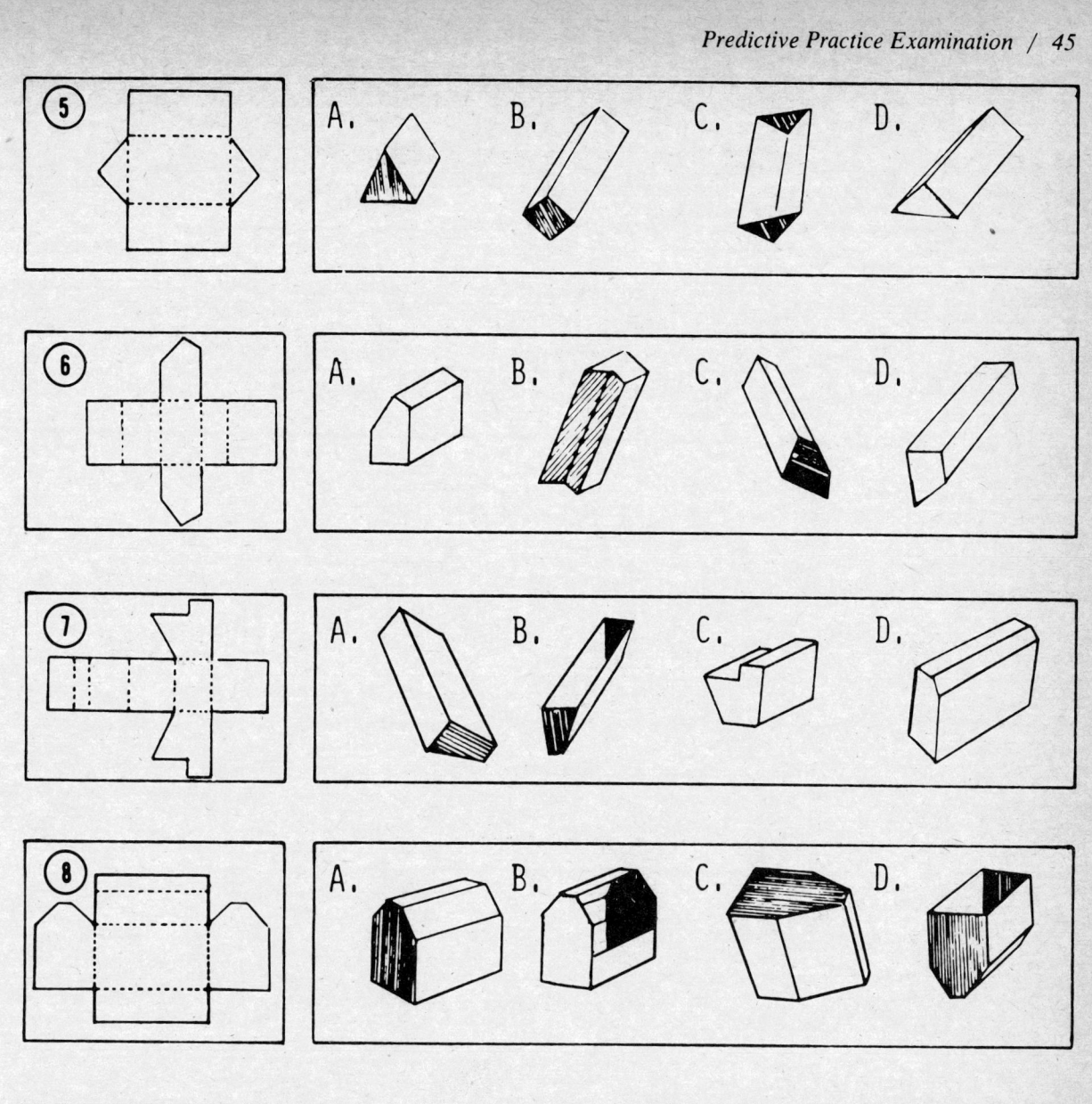

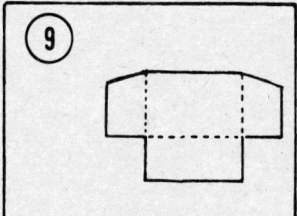

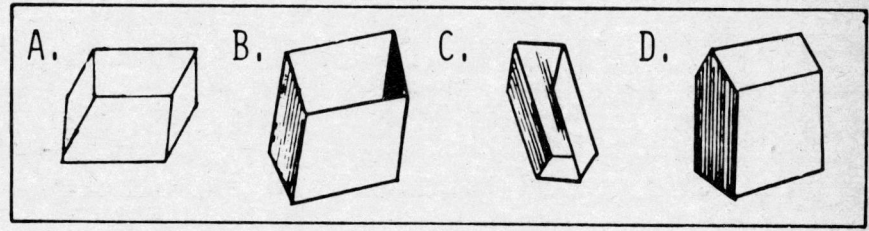

END OF TEST

Go on to the next Test in the Examination, just as you would do on the actual exam. Check your answers when you have completed the entire Examination. The correct answers for this Test, and all the other Tests, are assembled at the conclusion of this Examination.

TEST XIII. SHOP INFORMATION

TIME: 10 Minutes

DIRECTIONS: For each question read all the choices carefully. Then select that answer which you consider correct or most nearly correct. Blacken the answer space corresponding to your best choice, just as you would do on the actual examination.

1. A certain type of paint is capable of covering about 400 square feet of wall surface per gallon. How many gallons of this type of paint will be required to cover a wall that measures 73 1/2 feet by 15 feet?
   (A) 1 1/2 gallons (B) 2 3/4 gallons
   (C) 5 gallons (D) 6 1/2 gallons

2. A train leaves Terminal "a" for Terminal "b;" at the same time, another train leaves Terminal "b" for Terminal "a." Train leaving "a" travels at the rate of 45 miles per hour. Train leaving "b" travels at the rate of 25 miles per hour. The distance between "a" and "b" is 1540 miles. How long after leaving Terminals will the two trains pass?
   (A) 20 hours (B) 21 hours
   (C) 21 1/2 hours (D) 22 hours

3. A steam shovel excavates 2 cubic yards every 40 seconds. At this rate, the amount excavated in 45 minutes is:

   (A) 90 cubic yards
   (B) 135 cubic yards
   (C) 900 cubic yards
   (D) 3,600 cubic yards.

The four departments of a railroad shop occupy floor space as follows:

Inspector shop, 3300 square feet; machine shop, 1700 square feet; paint shop, 1500 square feet; truck shop, 2000 square feet. The yearly heating cost for the entire shop is $1870. This expense is distributed on the basis of the floor space occupied by each department.

4. What amount should be charged to the inspection shop?
   (A) $726   (C) $440
   (B) $374   (D) $330

5. What amount should be charged to the machine shop?
   (A) $726   (C) $440
   (B) $374   (D) $330

6. What amount should be charged to the paint shop?
   (A) $726   (C) $440
   (B) $374   (D) $330

7. What amount should be charged to the truck shop?
   (A) $726
   (B) $374
   (C) $440
   (D) $330

8. If measured accurately, 36 square yards of floor surface will be found to contain:
   (A) 324 square feet   (C) 200 sq. feet
   (B) 800 square feet   (D) 144 sq. feet.

9. The hypotenuse of a right triangle whose sides are 3 feet and 4 feet is:
   (A) 7 feet   (B) 9 feet
   (C) 5 feet   (D) 8 feet.

10. One brass rod measures 3 5/16 inches long and another brass rod measures 2 3/4 inches long. Together their length is:
    (A) 6 9/16   (B) 5 1/8
    (C) 6 1/16   (D) 5 1/16.

11. 4000 sheets of 8" x 11" paper are purchased at $12.00 a ream for 32" x 44" stock. If there are 500 sheets in a ream the cost is:
    (A) $12.00   (B) $24.00
    (C) $ 6.00   (D) $ 5.00.

12. 20 board feet of lumber are purchased at $120 per M. The cost is:
    (A) $12.00   (B) 60¢
    (C) $2.40   (D) $24.00.

13. The sum of 5 feet 2 3/4 inches; 8 feet 1/2 inch; and 12 1/2 inches is:
    (A) 14 feet 3 3/4 inches
    (B) 14 feet 5 3/4 inches
    (C) 14 feet 9 1/4 inches
    (D) 15 feet 1/2 inch.

14. A train traveling at 30 miles per hour will go one mile in:
    (A) 1/2 minute   (B) 2 minutes
    (C) 4 minutes   (D) 5 minutes.

15. The number of sacks necessary for a 4 inch sidewalk 6 ft. wide and 27 ft. long at 6 sacks of cement per cubic yard of concrete is:
    (A) 12   (B) 6
    (C) 36   (D) 9.

16. A barrel, containing an equal number of bolts and nuts, weighs 60 lbs. If each bolt weighs 1/6 of a lb. and is 5 times as heavy as the nut, the number of nuts in the barrel is:
    (A) 300   (B) 360
    (C) 50   (D) 72.

17. If iron weighs 0.25 lb. per cubic inch, an iron bar 8'-6" by 4" by 1/2" weighs:
    (A) 4.25 lbs.   (B) 51 lbs.
    (C) 68 lbs.   (D) 204 lbs.

18. A mechanic who receives $0.75 per hour, and works 9 hours a day for 5 days, will earn a total of:
    (A) $28.00   (B) $30.00
    (C) $31.20   (D) $33.75.

19. The circumference of a circle is given by the formula C = 2πR, where C is the circumference, R is the radius, and π is approximately 3 1/7. The circumference of an oil drum having a diameter of one foot and nine inches is therefore about:
    (A) 132 inches   (B) 66 inches
    (C) 33 inches   (D) 17 inches.

20. The area of a circle having a diameter of one inch is closest to:
    (A) 3/4 square inch
    (B) 1 square inch
    (C) 1 1/3 square inches
    (D) 1 1/2 square inches.

21. The total surface area of a 5-inch solid cube is:
    (A) 100 square inches
    (B) 125 square inches
    (C) 150 square inches
    (D) 200 square inches.

22. To change cubic feet into cubic yards:
    (A) multiply by 27
    (B) multiply by 3
    (C) divide by 3
    (D) divide by 27.

23. Using measuring cans without any intermediate marks, two gallons of oil can be accurately measured from a barrel and put in a bearing using:
    (A) an 8 gallon and a 4 gallon can
    (B) two 4 gallon cans
    (C) a 6 gallon and a 4 gallon can
    (D) a 1 1/2 gallon and a 6 gallon can.

24. Six men can wire 3 rooms in 4 hours. At this rate, 4 men can wire 2 rooms in:
    (A) 2 hours   (B) 4 hours
    (C) 4 1/2 hours   (D) 6 hours.

25. The number of 125-pound weights that can be lifted safely with a chain hoist of half-ton capacity is:
    (A) 4   (B) 8   (C) 10   (D) 14.

END OF SECTION

If you finish before the allotted time is up, check your work on this section only. When time is up, proceed directly to the next section and do not return to this section.

Aptitude for Motor Mechanics.
Allow 20 minutes for these Tests.

TEST XIV. MECHANICAL COMPREHENSION

TIME: 10 Minutes

DIRECTIONS: For each question read all the choices carefully. Then select that answer which you consider correct or most nearly correct. Blacken the answer space corresponding to your best choice, just as you would do on the actual examination.

1. Examine Figure 1 on the next page, and determine which of the following statements is true.
   (A) If the nut is held stationary and the head turned clockwise, the bolt will move up.
   (B) If the head of the bolt is held stationary and the nut is turned clockwise, the nut will move down.
   (C) If the head of the bolt is held stationary and the nut is turned clockwise, the nut will move up.
   (D) If the nut is held stationary and the bolt is turned counter-clockwise, the nut will move down.

2. Referring to Figure 2, which one of the following statements is true?
   (A) If the nut is held stationary and the head turned clockwise, the bolt will move down.
   (B) If the head of the bolt is held stationary and the nut is turned clockwise, the nut will move down.
   (C) If the head of the bolt is held stationary and the nut is turned clockwise, the nut will move up.
   (D) If the nut is held stationary and the head turned counter-clockwise, the bolt will move up.

3. Figure 3 shows a bolt and nut and five numbered pieces. If all of the pieces are long enough to go through the bolt, and if the circular hole extends through the bolt and through the other side of the nut, which piece must you use to fix the nut in a stationary position?
   (A) 1   (B) 2
   (C) 3   (D) 4
           (E) 5.

4. Examine the tenon and the numbered mortises in Figure 4. The tenon best fits into the mortise numbered
   (A) 1   (B) 2
   (C) 3   (D) 4
           (E) 5.

5. In making the tenon in figure 4, the best of the following tools to use is
   (A) hammer   (B) knife
   (C) saw   (D) drill
           (E) bit.

6. Study the gear wheels in Figure 5, then determine which of the following statements is true.
   (A) If you turn wheel M clockwise by means of the handle, wheel P will also turn clockwise.
   (B) It will take the same time for a tooth of wheel P to make a full turn as it will for a tooth of wheel M.
   (C) It will take less time for a tooth of wheel P to make a full turn than it will take a tooth of wheel M.
   (D) It will take more time for a tooth of wheel P to make a full turn than it will for a tooth of wheel M.
   (E) The faster wheel P is turned, the slower wheel M will turn.

7. If wheel M in Figure 5 makes 16 full turns, the number of full turns made by wheel P will be
   (A) 20   (B) 12
   (C) 10   (D) 18

Predictive Practice Examination / 49

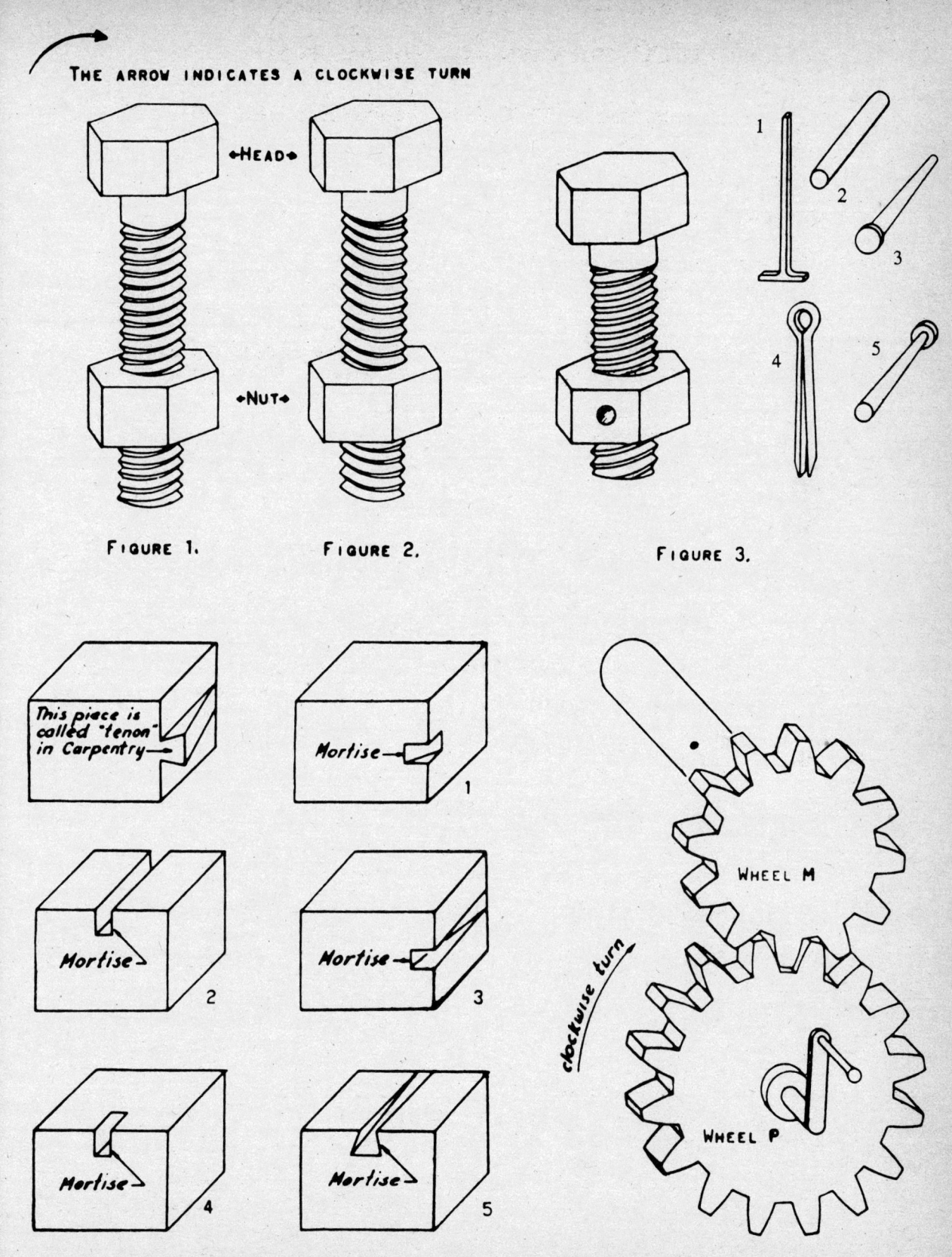

THE ARROW INDICATES A CLOCKWISE TURN

FIGURE 1. ←Head→ ←Nut→

FIGURE 2.

FIGURE 3.

FIGURE 4.
- This piece is called "tenon" in Carpentry
- Mortise 1
- Mortise 2
- Mortise 3
- Mortise 4
- Mortise 5

FIGURE 5.
Wheel M
Wheel P
clockwise turn

50 / Practice For Air Force Placement Tests

8) Referring to Figure 5, the number of teeth shown on wheel M is
(A) 12   (B) 14
(C) 16   (D) 10
(E) 15.

9) Referring to Figure 5, the number of teeth shown on wheel P is
(A) 10   (B) 18
(C) 16   (D) 17
(E) 19.

10) A bar measuring exactly three inches in length is pivoted at one end and a movement of 0.120 inches is noted at the opposite end. The movement of a point on the bar exactly 7/8" from the pivot end will be
(A) .015 inches   (B) .105 inches
(C) .035 inches   (D) .35 inches.

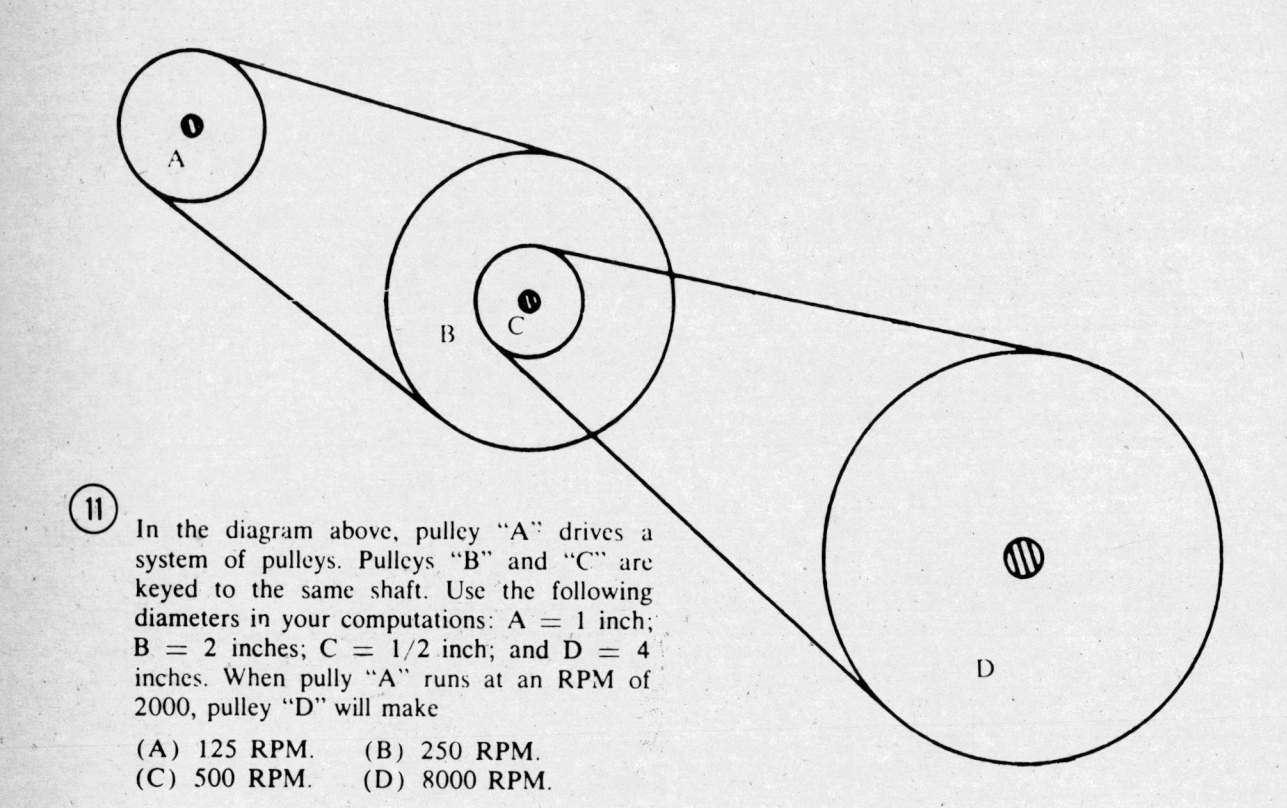

11) In the diagram above, pulley "A" drives a system of pulleys. Pulleys "B" and "C" are keyed to the same shaft. Use the following diameters in your computations: A = 1 inch; B = 2 inches; C = 1/2 inch; and D = 4 inches. When pully "A" runs at an RPM of 2000, pulley "D" will make

(A) 125 RPM.   (B) 250 RPM.
(C) 500 RPM.   (D) 8000 RPM.

⑫

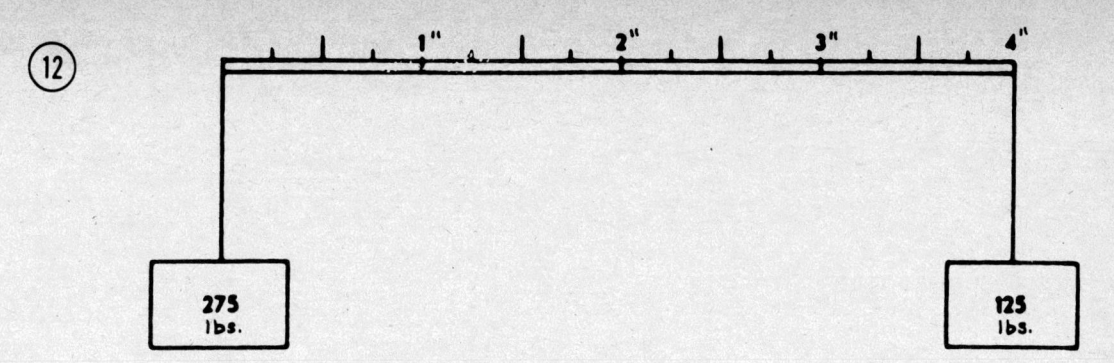

The bar above, which is exactly four inches in length, has a two hundred seventy-five pound weight hung on one end and a one hundred twenty-five pound weight on the opposite end. In order that the bar will just balance, the distance from the two hundred seventy-five pound weight to the fulcrum point should be (In your computation neglect the weight of the bar.)
(A) 1/2 inch   (B) 3/4 inch
(C) 1 inch   (D) 1 - 1/4 inches
    (E) 1 - 1/2 inches.

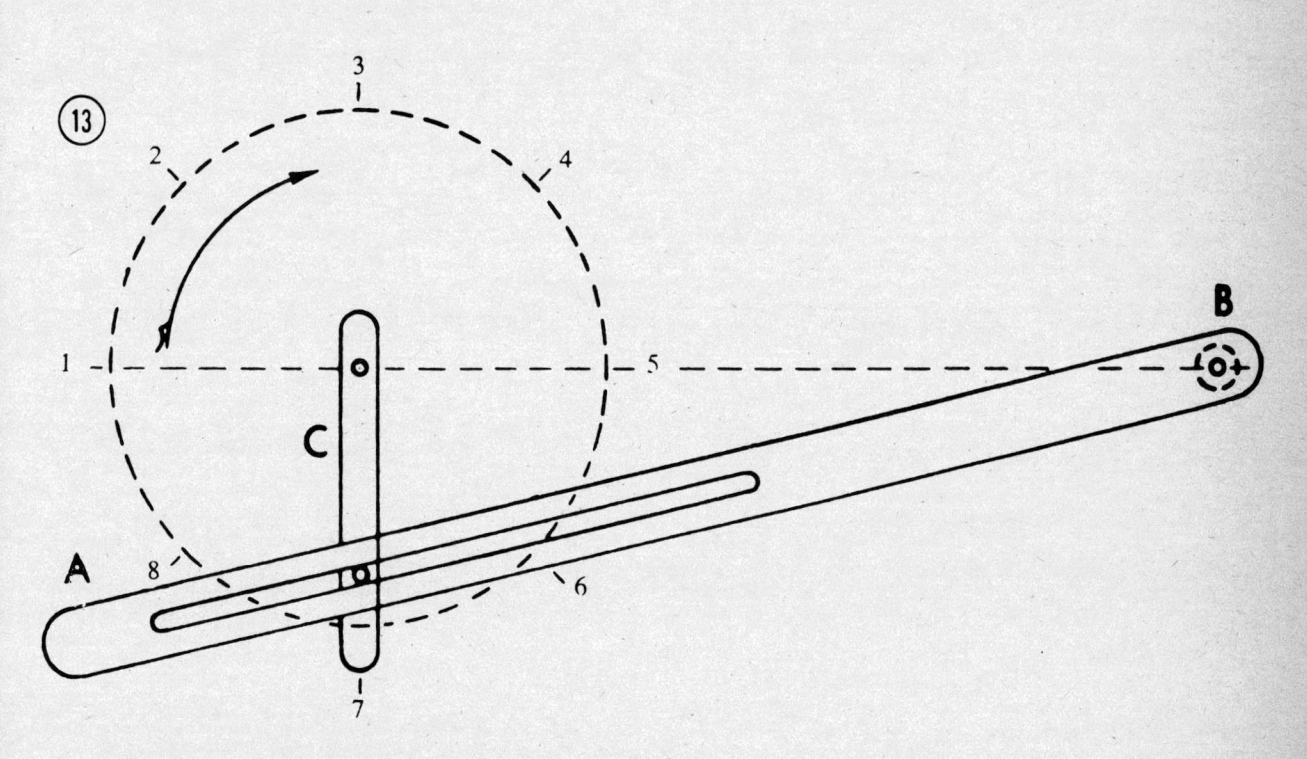

⑬

In the diagram above, crank arm "C" revolves at a constant speed of 400 RPM and drives the lever "AB". When lever "AB" is moving the fastest arm "C" will be in position
(A) 1   (B) 5
(C) 6   (D) 7.

14. In the diagram shown, the axle eight inches in diameter has attached a handle 28 inches in diameter. If a force of 50 lb. is applied to the handle, the axle will lift a weight of
(A) 224 lb.   (B) 200 lb.
(C) 175 lb.   (D) 88 lb.
(E) 75 lb.

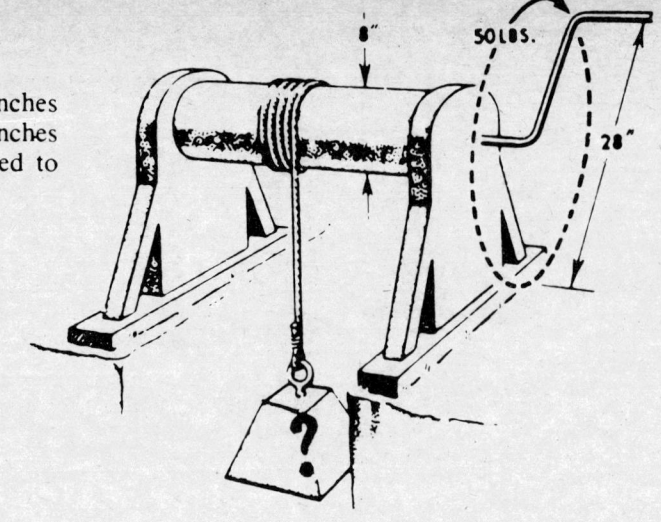

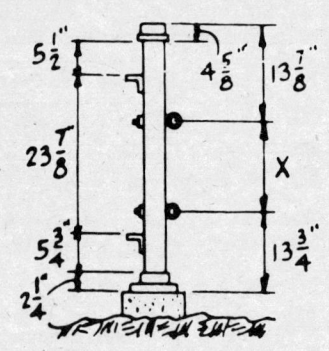

15. On the post, the dimension marked "X" is
(A) 9 3/4"   (B) 10 3/4"
(C) 13 3/8" (D) 14 3/8"

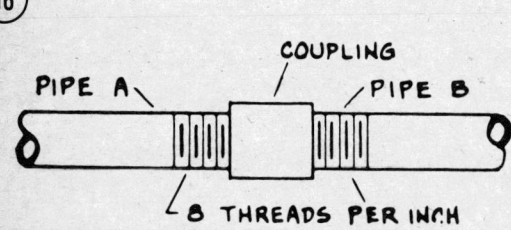

16. If pipe A is held in a vise and pipe B is turned ten revolutions with a wrench, the overall length of the pipes and coupling will decrease
(A) 5/8 inch   (B) 1 1/4 inches
(C) 2 1/2 inches (D) 3 3/4 inches.

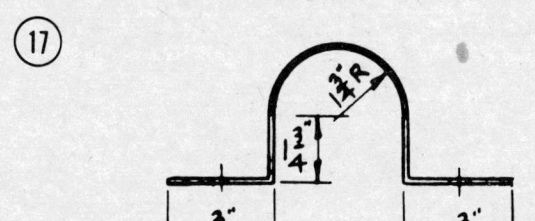

17. The strap-iron bracket shown will support a pipe. The required straight length of strap-iron to make the bracket is
(A) 20 1/2 inches   (B) 17 inches
(C) 15 inches   (D) 13 1/4 inches.

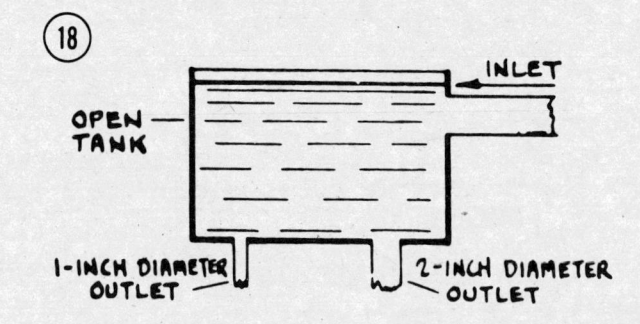

18. Eight gallons per minute of water flow at a given time from the one-inch outlet in the tank shown. What is the amount of water flowing at that time from the two-inch outlet?
(A) 64 gallons per minute
(B) 32 gallons per minute
(C) 16 gallons per minute
(D) 2 gallons per minute.

TEST XV. AUTOMOTIVE INFORMATION

TIME: 10 Minutes

DIRECTIONS: Read and answer each question carefully. Select the best answer and blacken the proper space on the answer sheet.

1. Most automobile engines run according to the
   (A) rotary cycle
   (B) intake-exhaust cycle
   (C) four-stroke cycle
   (D) two-stroke cycle

2. In calculating the "Indicated" horsepower of a gasoline engine by means of a formula, the item that is *NOT* considered in the calculations is usually the
   (A) number of power strokes per cycle
   (B) pressure exerted on the piston during the power stroke
   (C) diameter of the piston
   (D) length of the piston

3. In reference to the internal combustion engine, the term "Mechanical Efficiency" is frequently used. The meaning of this term is best defined as the
   (A) thermal efficiency divided by the volumetric efficiency
   (B) thermal efficiency multiplied by the volumetric efficiency
   (C) indicated horsepower divided by the brake horsepower
   (D) brake horsepower divided by the indicated horsepower

4. It is common practice today for some manufacturers to make the outside surface of aluminum alloy pistons highly resistant to wear by
   (A) spheroidizing   (C) anodizing
   (B) case hardening (D) annealing

5. Many gasoline engines today are being built with cylinder heads of cast aluminum alloy. The reason for using aluminum is mainly because it
   (A) is a better conductor of heat
   (B) will not rust
   (C) has less expansion per degree F. than cast iron
   (D) is lighter in weight

6. When reference is made to the "Compression Ratio" of an automotive gasoline engine, this is best described to be the
   (A) volume above the piston at top dead center
   (B) displacement volume as the piston moves down to bottom dead center
   (C) total volume of a cylinder divided by its clearance volume
   (D) displacement volume of a cylinder divided by its clearance volume

7. When the piston of a gasoline engine is said to be in "Rock" position, it is meant that the
   (A) piston has reached rock bottom of its stroke
   (B) crankshaft cannot move without causing the piston to move
   (C) crankshaft can move about 20° without causing the valves to open or close
   (D) crankshaft can move about 15° without causing the piston to move up or down

8. Manifolds are used to conduct
   (A) gases out of an engine only
   (B) gases into an engine only
   (C) gases into or out of an engine
   (D) heat into the piston

9. A modern six-cylinder passenger car will run most economically and efficiently at an approximate speed of
   (A) 20 mph   (C) 40 miles per hour
   (B) 30 mph   (D) 50 miles per hour

10. An engine, such as is used in automobiles, is called
    (A) diesel engine
    (B) external-combustion engine
    (C) internal-combustion engine
    (D) three cycle engine

11. Cam ground pistons are used primarily because
    (A) they can be used in badly worn engines without reboring the cylinders
    (B) their use increases the compression ratio
    (C) their use aids in the lubrication of the cylinder walls
    (D) they eliminate piston slap in engine warm-up and permit expansion

12. The total piston displacement, in cubic inches, of a 6-cylinder engine having a 4" bore and a 3½" stroke is most nearly
    (A) 84
    (B) 168
    (C) 216
    (D) 264

13. In the four stroke cycle gasoline engine, the sequence of the steps in each cylinder to complete a cycle is which one of the following?
    (A) Intake stroke, power stroke, compression stroke, exhaust stroke
    (B) Intake stroke, compression stroke, exhaust stroke, power stroke
    (C) Intake stroke, exhaust stroke, compression stroke, power stroke
    (D) Intake stroke, compression stroke, power stroke, exhaust stroke

14. Assume that an intake manifold gauge reads 10 inches of vacuum. This means that the pressure is most nearly
    (A) 10 inches of mercury above a perfect vacuum
    (B) 10 inches of water below atmospheric pressure
    (C) 5 pounds per square inch more than engine exhaust pressure
    (D) 5 pounds per square inch less than the outside pressure

15. If non-hydraulic valve lifters are used, for an L-head type gasoline engine, the total number of removable valve guides normally required for a six-cylinder engine are most nearly
    (A) 6
    (B) 12
    (C) 18
    (D) 24

16. The one of the following that is not a common type of poppet valve for four stroke cycle gasoline engines is the
    (A) shroud valve
    (B) plain valve
    (C) tulip valve
    (D) mushroom valve

17. If a semi-floating type piston pin arrangement is used in a gasoline engine it is usually found that
    (A) snap rings are commonly used
    (B) the piston should be cam ground
    (C) a split bearing is required
    (D) a connecting rod bushing is not needed

18. If a 3½ x 3¾ inch cylinder is used in a 6 cylinder engine, the engine displacement in cu. in. will be most nearly
    (A) 36.09
    (B) 72.18
    (C) 108.27
    (D) 216.54

19. Gasoline engine cylinders must be round and true and have highly finished surfaces. The surfaces are usually produced by the following operations in the order shown
    (A) grinding, boring, plating
    (B) plating, grinding, honing
    (C) boring, grinding, honing
    (D) boring, honing, grinding

20. Removable valve guides are usually made of
    (A) hardened steel
    (B) forged steel
    (C) cast bronze
    (D) cast iron

CORRECT ANSWERS FOR PREDICTIVE EXAMINATION

(Please try to answer the questions on your own before looking at our answers. You'll do much better on your test if you follow this rule.)

TEST I. WORD KNOWLEDGE

1. E	5. E	9. B	13. B	17. C
2. D	6. A	10. E	14. C	18. B
3. B	7. D	11. A	15. D	19. B
4. C	8. E	12. C	16. E	20. E

TEST II. VERBAL ANALOGIES

1. A	3. B	5. E	7. D	9. E	11. C
2. D	4. C	6. D	8. C	10. B	12. C

TEST III. ARITHMETIC REASONING

1. A	5. E	9. B	13. B	17. B
2. D	6. A	10. D	14. C	18. A
3. B	7. E	11. A	15. E	19. A
4. C	8. C	12. D	16. C	20. D

TEST IV. CLERICAL ACCURACY

1. AD	4. BE	7. BE	10. BD	13. BD	16. BD
2. BE	5. AE	8. BE	11. AE	14. BE	17. BE
3. BD	6. BE	9. AD	12. BE	15. AE	

TEST V. CLERICAL ACCURACY

1. AE	4. BE	7. BE	10. AE	13. BE	16. AE
2. BD	5. BD	8. BE	11. BE	14. AE	17. BE
3. BE	6. BE	9. BD	12. BD	15. AD	

TEST VI. CODING SPEED

1. D	14. B	27. E	40. E	53. D	65. C	77. A	89. C
2. C	15. B	28. B	41. C	54. E	66. E	78. B	90. A
3. B	16. C	29. D	42. A	55. B	67. D	79. E	91. A
4. E	17. E	30. E	43. B	56. A	68. A	80. A	92. E
5. E	18. C	31. A	44. D	57. C	69. B	81. B	93. D
6. A	19. A	32. E	45. A	58. D	70. D	82. C	94. C
7. B	20. B	33. C	46. A	59. B	71. E	83. E	95. B
8. A	21. B	34. D	47. E	60. E	72. C	84. E	96. C
9. D	22. B	35. A	48. E	61. C	73. E	85. A	97. B
10. C	23. D	36. C	49. D	62. B	74. B	86. D	98. A
11. D	24. A	37. B	50. D	63. B	75. C	87. D	99. E
12. A	25. A	38. A	51. C	64. A	76. B	88. B	100. D
13. D	26. C	39. C	52. A				

TEST VII. SENTENCE COMPLETION

1. D	5. C	9. A	13. E	17. A
2. A	6. E	10. E	14. B	18. E
3. B	7. D	11. D	15. E	19. C
4. E	8. B	12. B	16. A	20. D

TEST VIII. ELECTRONICS

1. A	6. D	11. A	16. C
2. B	7. B	12. A	17. C
3. C	8. B	13. A	18. D
4. D	9. A	14. C	19. A
5. B	10. C	15. B	20. A

TEST IX. ELECTRICITY

1. 1423	6. C	11. B	16. A	21. A
2. 42351	7. D	12. A	17. D	22. B
3. 462351	8. B	13. A	18. B	23. A
4. 324156	9. D	14. A	19. A	
5. 435126	10. A	15. A	20. A	

TEST X. TOOL KNOWLEDGE

1. A	6. X	11. S	16. B	21. R	25. Z	30. R
2. H	7. V	12. K	17. Y	22. X	26. Z	31. U
3. L	8. A	13. N	18. P	23. T	27. D	
4. F	9. E	14. J	19. D	24. O or U	28. T	
5. Q	10. E	15. U	20. G		29. M	

TEST XI. TOOL ANALOGIES

1. A   2. D   3. C   4. B   5. D   6. A   7. C   8. D

TEST XII. SPACE PERCEPTION

1. C   3. C   5. D   7. C   9. A
2. B   4. A   6. A   8. B

TEST XIII. SHOP INFORMATION

1. B   6. D   11. C   16. A   21. C
2. D   7. C   12. C   17. B   22. D
3. B   8. A   13. A   18. D   23. C
4. A   9. C   14. B   19. B   24. B
5. B   10. C   15. A   20. A   25. B

TEST XIV. MECHANICAL COMPREHENSION

1. C   4. E   7. B   10. C   13. B   16. B
2. B   5. C   8. A   11. A   14. C   17. C
3. D   6. D   9. C   12. D   15. D   18. B

TEST XV. AUTOMOTIVE INFORMATION

1. C   5. A   9. B   13. D   16. A   19. C
2. D   6. C   10. C   14. D   17. D   20. D
3. D   7. D   11. D   15. B   18. D
4. C   8. C   12. D

Use the results of the Examination you have just taken to diagnose yourself. Pinpoint the areas in which you show the greatest weakness. Fill in the Diagnostic Table to spotlight the subjects in which you need the most practice.

DIAGNOSTIC TABLE

SUBJECT TESTED	QUESTIONS ANSWERED CORRECTLY ON EXAM		
	Strong	Average	Weak
WORD KNOWLEDGE	17 - 20	10 - 16	1 - 9
VERBAL ANALOGIES	10 - 12	6 - 9	1 - 5
ARITHMETIC REASONING	17 - 20	10 - 16	1 - 9
CLERICAL ACCURACY	60 - 68	46 - 59	1 - 45
CODING SPEED	85 - 100	64 - 84	1 - 63
SENTENCE COMPLETIONS	17 - 20	10 - 16	1 - 9
ELECTRONICS	17 - 20	10 - 16	1 - 9
ELECTRICITY	20 - 23	13 - 19	1 - 12
TOOL KNOWLEDGE	28 - 31	21 - 27	1 - 20
TOOL ANALOGIES	7 - 8	4 - 6	1 - 4
SPACE PERCEPTION	7 - 9	4 - 6	1 - 3
SHOP INFORMATION	22 - 25	15 - 21	1 - 14
MECHANICAL COMPREHENSION	15 - 18	9 - 14	1 - 8
AUTOMOTIVE INFORMATION	17 - 20	10 - 16	1 - 9

AIR FORCE PLACEMENT TESTS

PART TWO

Practice For The Real Thing. Selected Subjects

Arco Practice Answer Sheet

Alter numbers to match the practice and drill questions in each part of the book.

MAKE GLOSSY BLACK MARKS.

Make only ONE mark for each answer. Additional and stray marks may be counted as mistakes. In making corrections, erase errors COMPLETELY.

AIR FORCE PLACEMENT TESTS

NUMERICAL RELATIONS

"Hark how the numbers softly clear, gently steal upon the ear . . . adding to golden numbers, golden numbers."

Solutions To Basic Problems

Ten "basic" types of problems are explained and solved in this section. They are followed by previous exam questions which you should be able to solve if you are adequately prepared for the mathematical part of your exam. Each of the ten "basic" problem types are solved in step-by-step fashion. Most of the problems you will face on an actual exam are either like one of these ten types, or a variation of one, since the principles they apply encompass a vast number and variety of problems. Study these example problems which have been solved for you.

Profit and Loss

1. Hammers are bought for $18.00 a dozen. In order to gain 40%, what must the selling price per hammer be?
    (A) $2.10   (B) $2.00
    (C) $2.50   (D) $3.00

SOLUTION: To find the selling price we must multiply the cost by the rate of profit or loss.

In this case the cost is $18.00 divided by 12; $18.00 being the cost of an entire dozen. Since there is a profit of 40% we must multiply the cost by 1.40 or 140%. (If we sold something at 100% of its cost, we should be getting what we paid for it.)

$$\frac{18}{12} \times 1.40 = \begin{array}{r} 18 \\ \times\ 1.40 \\ \hline 720 \\ 18 \\ \hline 25.20 \end{array} \quad \text{Answer} \quad \begin{array}{r} 2.10 \\ 12\overline{)25.20} \end{array}$$

To find the rate of profit or loss, we first find the actual profit or loss and then find what percent of the COST this is.

2. Hammers are bought for $30.00 a dozen and sold at $3.50 each. The rate of profit on the transaction is:
    (A) 30%   (B) 40%
    (C) 50%   (D) 45%

SOLUTION: Multiplying $3.50 by 12 to find the cost of a dozen hammers:

$$\$3.50 \times 12 = \$42.00$$

Subtracting the cost from the selling price to find the actual profit:

$$\begin{array}{r} \$42.00 \\ -\ 30.00 \\ \hline \$12.00 \end{array}$$

Finding what percent of the cost the profit is involves converting a fraction into a percent.

S1334

We multiply the fraction by 100 and perform the indicated divisions:

$$\frac{\$12}{\$30} \times 100 =$$

Answer $\quad 30\overline{)1200}40\%$

Addition of Fractions

3. If we add 8-1/5, 45-5/8, 2-17/20, 14-1/2, and 1-21/40 the answer will be
   (A) 70-8/10   (B) 72-7/10
   (C) 72-1/5   (D) 70-7/10.

SOLUTION: In adding mixed numbers like these, we perform three additions: The addition of the whole numbers, the addition of the fractions, and combination of the added whole numbers and fractions. Adding the whole numbers presents no difficulty. Our sum is 70.

To add the fractions we must first find the least common denominator. In this case it is 40.

Then for each separate fraction we divide the denominator into the common denominator and multiply the resulting quotient by the numerator.

We add all these products and divide by the common denominator. Here are the actual calculations:

$$\begin{array}{r} 40 \\ 8\text{-}1/5 \quad 8 \\ 45\text{-}5/8 \quad 25 \\ 2\text{-}17/20 \quad 34 \\ 14\text{-}1/2 \quad 20 \\ 1\text{-}21/40 \quad 21 \end{array}$$

$$\frac{108}{40} = 2\frac{28}{40} = 2\frac{7}{10}$$

$$\begin{array}{r} 70 \\ +\ 2\ \frac{7}{10} \\ \hline 72\ \frac{7}{10} \end{array}$$ **Answer**

Interest

4. $1,850 is invested for 50 days at a rate of 5%. The interest return is
   (A) $12.00   (B) $10.00
   (C) $12.67   (D) $13.00.

SOLUTION: While there are many short cuts used by banks and commercial houses in computing interest, the best plan for the candidate is to understand thoroughly all the steps involved in this computation and to use them all intelligently.

If we multiply the principal by the rate of interest, and the length of time the money draws interest, we have the amount of interest due.

If the money were to bear interest for a year we would only have to multiply $1,850 by 5% (5/100) in this example. However, the money only bears interest for 50 days or 50/365 of a year. The rest is done by simple cancellation.

$$\frac{\$1850 \times 5 \times 50}{100 \times 365} = \frac{925}{73} = \$12.67 \text{ \textbf{Answer}}$$

Expressed as a formula, interest may be computed thus: $P \times R \times T = I$. If we are given interest, principal and time, and asked to find the Rate, the operation may be expressed thus:

$$R = \frac{I}{P \times T}$$

And if we are given R, T, and I, and asked to find the Principal, this is the formula:

$$P = \frac{I}{R \times T}$$

5. What amount of money yields $40.00 per month if invested at an annual rate of 5%
(A) $9,000   (B) $9,500
(C) $9,600   (D) $9,400.

SOLUTION: To find the principal we must divide interest by rate by time.

If we multiply $40.00 per month by twelve we find the interest yield for a year. $40 × 12 = $480.00. The Time factor in this problem is now one year.

For the rest we have only to follow out our formula:

$$P = \frac{I}{R \times T} = P = \frac{\$480}{\frac{5}{100} \times 1}$$

DIVISION OF FRACTIONS: At this point an interesting difficulty presents itself: The division of fractions. To divide $80 by 5/100 we have simply to invert the fraction and multiply thus:

$$\$480 \div \frac{5}{100} = \$480 \times \frac{100}{5} = \$9,600 \quad \textbf{Answer}$$

6. A woman invested $4,000 in a speculative venture for 9 months. A second woman invested $6,000 in the same business for 6 months. The net gain was $720.00. What was the second woman's return on her investment if all the profits were divided between the two women?
(A) $360   (B) $700
(C) $400   (D) $350.

SOLUTION: So far as regards dividends, the investment of $6,000 for 6 months is the same as the investment of $36,000 for 1 month. The same statement can be made regarding $4,000 for 9 months.

First Woman — $4,000 for 9 months = $36,000 for 1 month.

Second Woman — $6,000 for 6 months = $36,000 for 1 month.

Both $72,000 for 1 month.

It is a coincidence that the shares of the two women in this example are the same. However, the procedure here is exactly the same as though they had different shares.

We find what part the second woman's share bears to the total. We then take this proportion of the total income and our result is the second woman's share.

$$\frac{36,000}{72,000} \times \frac{720}{1} = \$360 \quad \textbf{Answer}$$

7. The rate of interest on a principal of $10,000 that will yield $80.00 in 65 days is
(A) 4%   (B) 5.5%
(C) 4.49%   (D) 6%.

SOLUTION: The formula here is

$$R = \frac{I}{P \times T}$$

Substituting, we have:

$$R = \frac{\$80}{10,000 \times \frac{65}{365}} = \frac{\$80}{\frac{650,000}{365}} =$$

$$\$80 \times \frac{365}{650,000} = \frac{29,200}{650,000}$$

CONVERTING A FRACTION INTO A PERCENT: This is a simple operation if the proper steps be known and taken. We must convert the fraction $\frac{29,200}{650,000}$ into a percent so that we may properly express the rate of interest.

To change a fraction into a percent we must multiply the fraction by 100 and then carry through the indicated division.

$$\frac{29,200}{650,000} \times 100 = \frac{2,920,000}{650,000} =$$

$$650,000 \overline{)2,920,000} \quad 4.49\% \quad \textbf{Answer}$$

Assessment

8. If a piece of property is assessed at $45,700 and the tax rate on real property is $2.40 per $1,000, the amount of tax that must be paid on this property is
   (A) $110   (B) $112
   (C) $109.68   (D) $109.

SOLUTION: Since the tax rate is $2.40 per $1,000, we must determine how many thousands of dollars are involved. To do this, we divide $45,700 by $1,000. And the result is 45.7.

When we multiply 45.7 by $2.40, we learn the amount of the tax—
$109.68 **Answer**

9. $60,000 worth of land is assessed at 120% of its value. If the tax rate is $2.56 per 1,000 the amount of tax to be paid is
   (A) $190   (B) $195
   (C) $184.32   (D) $180.

SOLUTION: To find how much the land has been assessed:

$$60{,}000 \times \frac{120}{100} = \frac{720{,}000}{10} = \$72{,}000$$

If tax is $2.56 per $1,000, multiply:

```
    2.56
   × 72
    512
   1792
 $184.32  Answer
```

Cubic Volume

10. A bin measures 14 feet by 9 feet by 7½ feet. Allowing 4/5 bushel of grain per cubic foot, how many bushels will the bin hold?

SOLUTION: Length × Width × Height = Cubic Area.

$$14 \times 9 \times 7\tfrac{1}{2} = \overset{7}{\cancel{14}} \times 9 \times \frac{15}{\cancel{2}} = 945 \text{ cubic ft.}$$

Since each cubic foot of space holds 4/5 bushel of grain:

$$\overset{189}{\cancel{945}} \times \frac{4}{\cancel{5}} = 756 \text{ Bushels.} \textbf{ Answer}$$

Literal Problems

11. If L explosions occur during a given month and result in Q dollars of loss, the average loss per explosion in dollars is:
   (A) L × Q   (B) Q/L
   (C) L/A   (D) 12K/2P
   (E) none.

SOLUTION: This is a simple problem in determining an average. The presence of letters rather than numbers makes it slightly more difficult by imposing upon us the burden of using fundamental principles rather than habitual modes of action.

The average loss per explosion is the total loss divided by the number of explosions, or the average loss per explosion equals

$$\frac{\text{Total amount of loss}}{\text{Number of explosions}}$$

Since the total loss in a given month is Q and the number of explosions is L we may say that the average loss per explosion is $\frac{Q}{L}$ **Answer**

12. If there is a total of J garbage trucks in operation in New York City, covering a total street mileage of N miles at an average speed of E miles per hour, we can find the average street mileage per truck from the above data, without considering
   (A) the number of cars
   (B) the total street mileage
   (C) the average speed
   (D) any of these values
   (E) any further data besides the above.

SOLUTION: The average street mileage per truck is the total street mileage divided by the total number of trucks, that is, the average street mileage per truck = $\frac{\text{Total street mileage}}{\text{Total No. of trucks}}$ (if we had 20 trucks covering a total street mileage of 300 miles then the average mileage covered by each truck is 15 miles or $\frac{300}{20} = 15$ miles.)

From this it is clear that the average speed of the trucks does not come into the consideration of the average mileage per truck and therefor answer (C) is correct.

13. During 1964, T families took out insurance policies, representing an increase of M families over the number taking them in 1962. In 1963, however, the number taking out insurance was P less than in 1962. If there were R insurance agents in each of these 3 years, the average number of policies written per insurance agent in 1963 was:
   (A) $\frac{T - M}{P \quad R}$
   (B) $\frac{T - M - P}{R}$
   (C) $\frac{M + T - R}{R}$
   (D) $\frac{T + M + P}{R}$

SOLUTION: We must first determine how many people took out insurance in 1963 and get this quantity in terms of T, M, and P.

in 1964—T families took out insurance.

in 1962—T − M families took out insurance (since 1964 is an increase of M over 1962.)

in 1963—(no. in 1962) − P (since it was P less than 1962) = T − M − P = Total number of Policies in 1937.

Now the average number of policies per insurance agent:

$\frac{\text{Total number of policies in 1963}}{\text{Total number of insurance agents in 1963}}$ =

Answer $\frac{T - M - P}{R}$

14. Clerk A sorts B letters per hour, clerk C sorts D letters per hour. The D letters which clerk C sorts exceed those which clerk A sorts by 10 letters per hour. Measured in number sorted per 8-hour day, clerk C exceeds A by:
   (A) D − B × 10
   (B) (D − B) × 8
   (C) D + C − A + B
   (D) C + D − A + B

SOLUTION: The D letters sorted per hour by clerk C exceeds (is greater than) the B letters sorted per hour by clerk A, by an amount of 10 letters per hour, or D is 10 more than B. In symbols: D = B + 10.

In 8 hours, clerk C will have sorted 8 D letters while clerk A will have sorted 8 B letters and since the difference in one hour is 10 letters, in 8 hours, the difference will be 8 × 10. 8D = 8B + 80 or bringing 8 B to the other side: 8D − 8B = 80 or factoring out the 8 on the left.

We have 8 (D − B) = 80 which is the amount of letters by which clerk C's output exceeds clerk A's output and hence answer (B) above is correct.

15. The annual salary of a machinist is R dollars more than that of his assistant. His assistant earns V dollars annually. The amount in monthly salary, by which the machinist exceeds his assistant is given by:
   (A) $\frac{V - R}{13}$
   (B) $\frac{RV}{12}$
   (C) R − V
   (D) 12V − R
   (E) $\frac{R}{12}$

SOLUTION: The annual salary of the machinist is V + R dollars. The annual salary of his assistant is V dollars. The monthly salary of the machinist is $\frac{V}{12} + \frac{R}{12}$ dollars. (Since in a year the machinist receives 12 times as much as he receives in a month, we divide the yearly salary by 12 to find the amount earned in one month.) Similarly, the monthly salary of his assistants is $\frac{V}{12}$ dollars. Therefore the machinist's monthly salary exceeds his assistant's salary, monthly, by $\frac{R}{12}$ dollars. **Answer (E) is correct.**

16. A family of 5 has two employed members earning L dollars a month. The family receives a total semi-monthly relief allowance of M dollars. If the rent allowance is N dollars, and the amount spent for food is twice that for rent, the amount spent monthly for all items other than food and rent is:

(A) $L + 2M - 3N$ (B) $\underline{N + L + M}$

(C) $L + M - 2N$

SOLUTION: The amount spent monthly for all items other than food and rent is the total income for one month minus the total expenditure for food and rent.

Total income = $L + 2M$ (since M is a semi-monthly allowance, the monthly allowance is 2M or M multiplied by 2.)

Total exp. for food and rent = N (for rent) + $2N$ (food)—since the amount spent for other items = $L + 2M - N - 2N = L + 2M - 3N$. **Answer**

17. If psychological studies of college students show K per cent to be emotionally unstable, the number of college students not emotionally unstable per one hundred college students is:
(A) 100 minus K   (B) 100 times (K minus)
(C) K minus 1

SOLUTION: Since K percent = $\frac{K}{100}$ in 100 students, K% of 100 are emotionally unstable then $\frac{K}{100} \times 100 = K$ students are unstable. Therefore the remaining students are emotionally stable and they number $100 - K$.

Rate, Time, and Distance Problems

In all these problems the formula to be followed is very simple:
Rate (speed) × Time = Distance.

If you are given the RATE and DISTANCE and are asked to find time then you simply make the obvious modification in the formula:

$$\text{Time} = \frac{\text{Distance}}{\text{Rate}}$$

To find rate given distance and time:
$$\frac{\text{Distance}}{\text{Time}} = \text{Rate}$$

There are many complications that can be introduced but if these fundamental ideas can be kept clearly in view few difficulties will be encountered.

18. Two hikers start walking from the city line at different times. The second hiker whose speed is 4 miles per hour starts 2 hours after the first hiker whose speed is 3 miles per hour. Determine the amount of time and distance that will be consumed before the second hiker catches up with the first.

SOLUTION: Since the first man has a 2 hour headstart and is walking at the rate of 3 miles per hour he is 6 miles from the city line when the second hiker starts.

Rate × Time = Distance.

Subtracting 3 miles per hour from 4 miles per hour gives us 1 mile per hour or the difference in the rates of speed of the two men. In other words, the second hiker gains one mile on the first hiker in every hour.

Since there is a 6 mile difference to cut down and it is cut down one mile every hour, it is clear that the second hiker will need 6 hours to overtake his companion.

In this time he will have traveled $4 \times 6 = 24$ or 24 miles. The first hiker will have been walking 8 hours since he had a 2 hour headstart $8 \times 3 = 24$.

19. The same two hikers start walking toward each other along a road connecting two cities which are 60 miles apart. Their speeds are the same as in the preceding problem, 3 and 4 miles per hour. How much time will elapse before they meet?

SOLUTION: In each hour of travel toward each other the men will cut down a distance equal to the sum of their speeds. $3 + 4 = 7$ miles per hour. To meet they must cut down 60 miles, and at 7 miles per hour this would be

$$\frac{D}{R} = T \quad \frac{60}{7} = 8\frac{4}{7} \text{ hours.}$$

20. The problem might also have asked: "How much distance must the slower man cover before the two hikers meet?" In such case we should have gone through the same steps plus one additional step:

The time consumed before meeting was $8\frac{4}{7}$ hours. To find the distance covered by the slower hiker we merely multiply his rate by the time elapsed.

$$R \times T = D \quad 3 \times 8\frac{4}{7} = 25\frac{5}{7} \text{ Answer}$$

Time and Work Problems

21. If A does a job in 6 days, and B does the same job in 3 days, how long will it take the two of them, working together, to do the job?

SOLUTION: Almost any problem of this type can be solved quite simply by fractions, without resorting to higher mathematics.

A. If A does the whole job in 6 days, he will do 1/6 of the job in one day.
   If B does the whole job in 3 days, he will do 1/3 of the job in one day.

B. $1/3 + 1/6 = 1/2$

C. 1/2 of the job will be finished in one day if the two men work together.

D. The whole job will be finished in two days.

EXPLANATION OF SOLUTION:

A. If you are given the time that a job takes you have merely to find the reciprocal of that time in order to find how much of the work would be done in one day. Finding the reciprocal simply means inverting the figure.

If you do a job in 2 1/2 days, you would do 2/5 of the job in one day.

$$2\ 1/2 = 5/2$$

Finding the reciprocal or inverting:

$$5/2 = 2/5$$

Another way of looking at the same operation:

All of the work is done in 5/2 days. In other words it takes 5 half days to finish the job. In one half day 1/5 of the job would be completed, and consequently in one day (2/2) 2/5 of the job would be completed.

CAUTION: If the total time for the job is given in HOURS you will, by getting the reciprocal, find what fraction of the work is done in one HOUR. The procedure for the rest of the problem, of course, is the same as above, except that the answer is in hours.

B. The total time must be reduced to a fraction of the total job because it would not do to simply add the time consumed by each man. 3 days and 6 days added together yield nine days, which is merely

TIME and tells us nothing of the AMOUNT OF WORK. But 1/3 and 1/6 do represent amounts of work.

C. Adding these two fractions together we discover the part of the job that would be completed in one day.

D. If we are told that a certain fraction represents the amount of work done in one day and if we wish to find how long the entire job would take, we find the reciprocal of the fraction.

$$\frac{1}{2} \text{ in 1 day} \quad \frac{2}{2} \text{ (or all) in } \frac{2}{1} \text{ days.}$$

Two principles should be kept in mind.

1. To find the part, invert the time.
2. To find the time, invert the part.

22. A and B working together do a job in 4½ days. B, working alone, is able to do the job in 10 days. How long would it take A, working alone, to do the job?

SOLUTION: All of the job in 9/2 days. $\frac{2}{9}$ of the job in 1 day.
If B takes 10 days to do the job alone he will do 1/10 of the job in one day.

To find the work done by A in one day we subtract B's work from the amount of work done by the two men together in one day.

$$2/9 - 1/10 = \frac{20 - 9}{90} = \frac{11}{90}$$

11/90 represents the portion of the total job done by A in one day.

Inverting, we found how long it would take him to do the entire job.

$$\frac{90}{11} = 8\frac{2}{11} \text{ Days.}$$

23. If A can do a job in 6 days which B can do in 5-1/2 days, and C can do in 2-1/5 days, how long would the job take if A, B, and C were working together?

SOLUTION:

A Does the job in 6 days: 1/6 of the job in 1 day.
B Does the job in 5-1/2 days: 2/11 of the job in 1 day.
C Does the job in 2-1/5 days: 5/11 of the job in 1 day.

Adding the work done by A, B, and C in one day to find the work done by all three in one day.

$$\frac{1}{6} + \frac{2}{11} + \frac{5}{11} = \frac{11 + 12 + 30}{66} = \frac{53}{66}$$

Finding the reciprocal of $\frac{53}{66}$ in order to find how long the total job would take:

$$\frac{66}{53} = 1\frac{13}{53} \text{ Days.} \quad \textbf{Answer}$$

24. One pipe fills a pool in 20 minutes, a second can fill the pool in 30 minutes, and a third can fill it in 10 minutes. How long would it take the three together to fill the pool?

SOLUTION: First pipe—fills in 20 minutes—fills 1/20 of pool in 1 minute.
Second pipe—fills in 30 minutes—fills 1/30 of pool in 1 minute.
Third pipe—fills in 10 minutes—fills 1/10 of pool in 1 minute.

Adding three fractions together to determine what part of the pool will be filled in one minute when the three pipes are working together.

$$1/20 + 1/30 + 1/10 = \frac{3 + 2 + 6}{60} = \frac{11}{60}$$

If 11/60 of the pool is filled in one minute the reciprocal of the fraction will tell us how many minutes will be required to fill the whole pool.

$$\frac{60}{11} = 5\frac{5}{11} \text{ Minutes.} \quad \textbf{Answer.}$$

Problems in Proportions

25. If 5 men can build 6 miles of railroad track in 40 days, how many miles of track can be built by 3 men in 15 days?

SOLUTION: One of the best methods of solving such problems is by directly making the necessary cancellations, divisions, and multiplications.

In this example, we wish to find how many miles of track will be built if both the number of workers and the working time are reduced. It is easily seen that the amount of track constructed will be less than under the old conditions. But how much less?

Since we now have 3 men where before there were 5, we may assume that so far as man-power is concerned, production will be 3/5 as high as when 5 men were working. Consequently:

$$6 \times \frac{3}{5} = \frac{18}{5} = 3\frac{3}{5} \text{ Miles of track.}$$

Thus we know that if 3 men worked 40 days they would build 3-3/5 miles of track.

But another factor serves to lessen production. And that is the decrease in time. Only 15 days are expended, or 15/40 of the time that was expended before. Consequently:

$$3\frac{3}{5} + \frac{15}{40} = \frac{18}{5} \times \frac{15}{40}$$
$$= \frac{270}{200} = 1\frac{7}{20} \text{ Miles of track.}$$

The two arithmetical operations just shown can, of course, be combined into one. Thus:

$$6 \times \frac{3}{5} \times \frac{15}{40} = 1\frac{7}{20} \text{ Miles of track.}$$

26. If 5 men build 6 miles of railroad track in 40 days, how many miles of track can be built by 8 men working 90 days?

SOLUTION: Here we have a problem which is similar to the previous one, with this exception: more men are working a longer period of time and consequently the answer will yield not a reduced but an increased number of miles of track.

If we multiply a number by a fraction whose value is less than one, we are reducing the value of that number. If, however, we multiply the number by a fraction whose value is more than one, we are increasing the value of that number. In solving this problem, then, we would not multiply $6 \times \frac{40}{90} \times \frac{5}{8}$. That would produce a number less than 6 and we know that our answer should be more than 6 since we have more men working a longer time than were required to produce 6 miles of track. The proper way of expressing the facts given in the example is:

$$6 \times \frac{90}{40} \times \frac{8}{5} = \frac{4320}{200} = 21\frac{12}{20} \text{ Miles of track.}$$
Answer

Some examples indicate an increase in one factor and a decrease in another.

27. If 10 men earn $500 in 12 days, how much will 6 men earn in 15 days?

SOLUTION: The number of men involved decreases and consequently the fraction will be less than one. The smaller number will therefore be the numerator.

$$\$500 \times \frac{6}{10}$$

The number of days worked increases and so the fraction will be more than one. The larger number will therefore be the numerator.

$$\$500 \times \frac{6}{10} \times \frac{15}{12} = \frac{45,000}{120} = \$375$$
Answer

Mixture Problems

28. A wine merchant has 32 gallons of wine worth $1.50 a gallon. If he wishes to reduce the price to $1.20 a gallon, how many gallons of water must he add?
    (A) 10   (B) 9
    (C) 8   (D) 7.

SOLUTION: First let us find the cost of the 32 gallons of undiluted wine at the old price.
$$32 \times \$1.50 = \$48.00.$$

$48, then, is the value of the wine that is ultimately to be mixed with water. By the conditions of the problem, $48 will be the price realized from the sale of the wine at the new price of $1.20.

To find how many gallons of wine we shall have at the new price let us divide $48 by $1.20, the new price. The answer, of course, is 40. We see then that we must have 40 gallons of the $1.20 wine.

This is 8 gallons more than the undiluted wine. And that difference of 8 gallons is made up by water.

29. A bakery shop sold 3 kinds of cake. The prices of these three kinds were 25¢, 30¢, and 35¢ per pound. The income from these sales was $36. If the number of pounds of each kind of cake sold was the same, how many pounds were sold?

SOLUTION: To buy all three kinds of cake would cost 25¢ + 30¢ + 35¢ = 90¢.

If we divide $36, the total income, by 90¢, the total price of the three kinds of cake, we will know how many times each kind of cake was sold in order to realize the $36. $\frac{\$36.00}{\$.90} = 40.$
Since there were just as many of each kind of cake sold, the total number of pounds sold = 40 × 3 = 120. **Answer**

30. The number of dimes in a cash register was equal to the number of quarters. There were five times as many nickels as quarters. All these coins together totalled $120. How many of each were there?

SOLUTION: Let us again make groups, this time of coins. A group will consist of five nickels + 1 quarter + 1 dime which equals 60¢. If we divide $120 by 60¢ we find that there are 200 such 60¢ groups contained in $120. Since there are 5 nickels in every one of the 200 groups we multiply 200 by 5 to find the number of nickels—1,000. There are 200 dimes and 200 quarters.

AIR FORCE PLACEMENT TESTS

ARITHMETIC REVIEW EXAMINATION

The questions in this chapter are provided as practice for the kind of questions you will be asked to answer on your test. Do them all carefully yourself and then compare your answers with those given at the end of the chapter. These questions have been scientifically designed to bring out all the tricks and difficulties you may expect to encounter on your test. When you have practiced with them you will be better able to cope with the actual test questions. Try to work quickly and accurately. If your score on the first trial is less than 70% right you should plan to do the chapter over at some later date. And when you do it over you should expect to note an improvement in your score. Let at least two weeks elapse before trying it for the second time.

PREVIOUS TEST QUESTIONS FOR PRACTICE

DIRECTIONS: For each question in this test, read carefully the stem and the four lettered choices that follow. Choose the answer which you consider correct or most nearly correct. Mark the answer sheet for the letter you have chosen: A, B, C, or D.

1. A real estate dealer buys a house and lot for $4,400. He pays $125 for painting, $175 for plumbing, and $100 for grading and walks. At what price must he sell the property to make a profit of $12\frac{1}{2}\%$?

   (A) $6,000   (B) $5,400
   (C) $5,600   (D) $5,800

2. An automobile cost $1,200. It depreciated in value 45% the first year, 20% of the reduced value the second year, and 20% of the second reduced value the third year. What was it worth at the end of the third year?

   (A) $425   (B) $432.80
   (C) $180   (D) $422.40

3. If the income of a certain city is $6,950,000, and 1.81¢ of each dollar is expended for Parks, Libraries and Museums, the total amount spent for Parks, Libraries and Museums will be

   (A) $25,795   (B) $135,795
   (C) $125,795   (D) $12,579.

4. A desk has a marked price of $100. Discounts of 20% and 25% are allowed. The dealer's profit is 30% of the selling price, and his cost of doing business is 10% of the selling price. What is the cost of the desk to the dealer?

   (A) $40   (B) $50
   (C) $24   (D) $36

5. What is the sum of 8-1/3, 4/5, 5-1/4, and 4-3/8?

   (A) 18-91/120   (B) 17-91/120
   (C) 18-17/24   (D) 17-5/24

6. If 1/3 gallon of milk is added to 4/5 gallon, how many quarts of milk will there be?

   (A) 4-2/15 qts.   (B) 4-1/30 qts.
   (C) 4-8/15 qts.   (D) 4-3/5 qts.

7. A man invests $500 at the rate of 6%. How much interest is due him at the end of 3 years and 60 days? (Consider a year as 360 days.)
   (A) $125   (B) $105
   (C) $85   (D) $95

8. A mortgage on a house in the amount of $4,000 provides for quarterly payments of $200 plus interest on the unpaid balance at $4\frac{1}{2}\%$. The total second payment to be made is
   (A) $371   (B) $285.50
   (C) $242.75   (D) $240.00

9. A man borrowed $1,200 at 6% on June 1, 1953; on Sept. 25, 1954, he paid the note in full with interest. What was the amount of payment made? (Consider a year as 360 days.)
   (A) $1,295.40   (B) $1,289.55
   (C) $1,298.35   (D) $1,295.08

10. A certain property is assessed at $55,000, and the tax rate is $4.85 per $1,000. What is the amount of the tax to be paid on this property?
   (A) $256.75   (B) $276.75
   (C) $286.75   (D) $266.75

11. $120,000 worth of land is assessed at 115% of its value. If the tax rate is $2.80 per $1,000, the amount of tax to be paid is
   (A) $384.60   (B) $386.40
   (C) $368.80   (D) $384.25

12. Blocks of real estate in a certain area are assessed at $20,000 each. The tax rate is 90¢ per $500. What amount of tax is due on each block?
   (A) $54.00   (B) $48.00
   (C) $36.00   (D) $28.00

13. The number of cubic feet of soil it takes to fill a flower box 3 ft. long, 8 in, wide, and 1 ft. deep is
   (A) 2   (B) 4-2/3
   (C) 12   (D) 24

14. If a man can get 1/3 bushel of berries per cubic foot, how many bushels can be get into a box measuring 5 ft. square by 1 ft. deep?
   (A) 5   (B) 9-1/2
   (C) 9-1/3   (D) 8-1/3

15. A carton is 10 ft. long, 4 ft. wide, and 6 in. deep. When packed with machine parts, the carton weighs 60 lbs. How many pounds of machine parts can be packed into a cubic foot of the carton?
   (A) 10   (B) 3
   (C) 6   (D) 8

16. A certain highway intersection has had A accidents over a ten-year period, resulting in B deaths. What is the yearly average death rate for the intersection?
   (A) $A + B - 10$ (B) $B/10$
   (C) $10 - A/B$ (D) $A/10$

17. A typist can address approximately R envelopes in a 7-hour day. A list containing S addresses is submitted with a request that all all envelopes by typed within T hours. The number of typists needed to complete this task would be
   (A) $\dfrac{7RS}{T}$ (B) $\dfrac{S}{7RT}$
   (C) $\dfrac{R}{7ST}$ (D) $\dfrac{S}{\dfrac{R \times T}{7}}$

18.   Clerk X earns $L per year. Clerk Y earns $R less per month. Both earn yearly increments of $T up to S years. At the end of P years, which is less than S years, the excess of Clerk X's earnings over Clerk Y's will be
   (A) 12PR
   (B) 12P(L minus R)
   (C) 12PT(L plus R)
   (D) P(T plus L minus R)

19. A car traveling a distance of 900 miles averages 50 m.p.h. the first 3 hours of travel, 45 m.p.h. for the 4th and 5th hours, and 40 m.p.h. for the remainder of the trip. How long did it take the car to go 900 miles?
   (A) 16-1/2 hours   (B) 18-1/2 hours
   (C) 21-1/2 hours   (D) 23 hours

20. An airplane on a trans-Atlantic flight took 18 hours to get from New York to its destination, a distance of 3,000 miles. To avoid a storm, however, the pilot went off his course, adding a distance of 200 miles to the flight. How fast did the plane travel?
   (A) 179.6 m.p.h.   (B) 163.4 m.p.h.
   (C) 166.6 m.p.h.   (D) 177.7 m.p.h.

21. Two cars start toward each other along a road between two cities which are 450 miles apart. The speed of the first car is 35 m.p.h. and that of the second 48 m.p.h. How much time will elapse before they meet?
(A) 5.42 hours   (B) 6.01 hours
(C) 4.98 hours   (D) 5.25 hours

22. A city pumping station can pump 3,600,000 gallons of water in 24 hours. The pump is operated on an average of 14 hours a day. The population of the city is 15,000. What is the average number of gallons of water pumped every day for each resident of the city?
(A) 145 gals.   (B) 140 gals.
(C) 132 gals.   (D) 1,200 gals.

23. Two men working together can build a cabinet in 2½ days. The first man, working alone, can build the cabinet in 6 days. How long would it take the second man to build the cabinet working alone?
(A) 5-1/7 days   (B) 3-7/8 days
(C) 4-2/7 days   (D) 4-3/10 days

24. One man can load a truck in 25 minutes; a second can load it in 50 minutes, and a third can load it in 10 minutes. How long would it take the three together to load the truck?
(A) 5-3/11 min. (B) 8-1/3 min.
(C) 6-1/4 min.   (D) 10 min.

25. If 4 typists can type 600 letters in 3 days, how many letters can 2 typists complete in one day?   (A) 100 letters   (B) 120 letters
(C) 90 letters   (D) 150 letters

26. If 12 factory workers produce 120 units in 20 days, how many units can 18 workers produce in 50 days?
(A) 375   (B) 350
(C) 325   (D) 450

27. If 15 construction workers earn $2,800 in 18 days, how much will 8 workers earn in 25 days?
(A) $2,900   (B) $2,074
(C) $1,843   (D) $2,650

28. Population figures for a certain area show there are 1½ times as many single men as single women in the area. Total population is 18,000. There are 1,122 married couples, with 756 children. How many single men are there in the area?
(A) 5,893   (B) 9,874
(C) 3,498   (D) 9,000

29. A dairyman has 4 gallons of milk worth 25¢ a quart. How much water must he add to make it worth 18¢ a quart?
(A) 1.2 gallons (B) 3.7 quarts
(C) 6.2 quarts   (D) 3 gallons

30. A car dealer sold 3 different makes of cars. The price of the first make was $1,800, of the second $2,200, and the third $2,600. The income from these sales was $26,400. If the number of each make sold was the same, how many cars were sold?
(A) 12   (B) 10
(C) 8   (D) 6

31. If it takes 3 men 56 minutes to fill a trench 4′ × 6′ × 5′, and two of the men work twice as rapidly as the third, the number of minutes that it will take the two faster men alone to fill this trench is
(A) 70 minutes
(B) 60 minutes
(C) 50 minutes
(D) impossible to determine from the above data.

32. Your office wishes to purchase an adding machine. Company X offers you a standard model, less discounts of 10% and 5%. Company Y offers you the same model at the same list price, less discounts of 5% and 10%. Of the two plans, the total discount given by Company X, compared to that given by Company Y, is
(A) much larger (B) slightly larger
(C) equal   (D) slightly less.

33. The dimensions of an office are 25 feet by 15 feet. It is to be fitted with desks 4 feet by 3 feet. The distance between the front of one desk and the rear of another should be 3 feet while the distance between the sides of 2 desks should be 4 feet. Assuming that no desk is placed closer than 1 ft. from any wall, the optimum number that can be placed in the office is
(A) 6   (B) 8
(C) 10   (D) 12

74 / Practice For Air Force Placement Tests

34. Two pieces of meat which together weighed 40 lbs. were sold for the same sum. What did the 12¢ piece weigh if they were worth 18¢ and 12¢ a pound?
(A) 24
(B) 20
(C) 30
(D) 40.

35. How many houses worth $12,000 each can a real estate agent buy for 1,000 bungalows worth $900 each?
(A) 75
(B) 74
(C) 73
(D) 72.

36. Suppose that the loss of water pressure in a hose due to friction is uniformly L pounds per square inch for every foot of hose. Of the following, the best estimate of the total loss in terms of pressure per square inch in a hose H feet long is
(A) H plus L pounds
(B) H times L pounds
(C) H divided by L pounds
(D) L divided by H pounds
(E) none of the foregoing.

37. Suppose that the amount of money that the Fire Department has saved the citizens of the City of New York in 1940 is estimated at P dollars. If this sum is to be increased at least 100 per cent in 1941, then the saving in 1941 must be at least
(A) equivalent to the ratio between P and 100
(B) commensurate with a sum derived by arithmetic manipulation involving P, 100, and a third value not given in the problem
(C) 100 times P dollars
(D) twice P dollars
(E) a sum of money not accurately described in any of the foregoing options.

38. The velocity of a fire engine which is traveling to a fire is computed by
(A) multiplying distance by time
(B) dividing distance by time
(C) squaring the force with which the earth attracts the engine
(D) means of the moment of inertia
(E) use of the Pythagorean Theorem.

39. Suppose that R persons were rescued from burning buildings by firemen in 1940. Suppose also that P persons perished in burning buildings in 1940. If R is less than S but greater than T and P is less than both M and N, it may safely be concluded that
(A) the sum of R and T is greater than S
(B) the sum of M and N is greater than P
(C) R is between M and N times as great as P
(D) R exceeds P to an indeterminate degree lying somewhere between S and N
(E) none of the foregoing options is correct.

40. In an experiment, a sprinkler system discharging W gallons of water per hour extinguished a fire covering a floor of A square yards in T minutes. The amount of water actually used to put out the fire was
(A) W times T divided by 60
(B) 60 times W divided by T
(C) 60 times W times T
(D) T divided by the fraction whose numerator is W and denominator 60
(E) none of the foregoing.

41. Suppose that a ladder consists of four sections, each R feet in length. When the ladder is extended, adjacent sections overlap for a distance of S feet to strengthen the interlocking. The total overall length of the ladder, when fully opened, is
(A) 4 R feet
(B) 4 R minus 3 S feet
(C) 4 R minus 4 S feet
(D) 4 R minus 6 S feet
(E) none of the foregoing.

42. In the New York City Fire Department there are A firemen, D lieutenants, E captains, and G chiefs of various ranks. Suppose that, for comparative purposes, promotional opportunities are evaluated as the ratio of the number of promotional positions to the number of positions at the entrance level. In accordance with this method, promotional opportunities in the uniformed force of the Fire Department in New York City are evaluated as
(A) G divided by the sum of A plus D plus E
(B) the sum of D plus E plus G divided by the number of firemen
(C) A divided by the sum of D plus E plus G
(D) the sum of A plus D divided by the sum of E plus G
(E) a fraction about which it is known only that the numerator is greater than the denominator.

43. Suppose that the number of fires occurring in a particular type of dwelling decreased C per cent in 1939, as compared with 1938, but then increased C per cent in 1940, as compared with 1939. Then the number of fires occurring in that type of dwelling during 1940, as compared with 1938, is
(A) decreased by the per cent equal to C squared divided by 100
(B) unchanged
(C) increased by the per cent equal to the fraction whose numerator is 100 minus C and denominator is 100
(D) decreased by the per cent equal to the square of the fraction C over 100
(E) dependent on the temporal distance between 1938 and 1939 as contrasted with that between 1939 and 1940.

44. In the year 1940, fires occurred in K "Type Z" multiple dwellings. It is known that L per cent of the M multiple dwellings in New York City are of "Type Z". The fraction of "Type Z" multiple dwellings in which fires occurred during 1940 is
(A) K divided by L times M
(B) L times M divided by 100 K
(C) K divided by the quantity 100 times L times M
(D) 100 K divided by the quantity L times M
(E) none of the foregoing.

45. Suppose that the amount of money spent for supplies in 1946 for a division in a City department was $15,650. This represented an increase of 12% over the amount spent for supplies for this division in 1945. The amount of money spent for supplies for this division in 1945 was most nearly
(A) $13,973 (B) $13,772
(C) $14,346 (D) $13,872.

46. Suppose that a group of five clerks have been assigned to insert 24,000 letters into envelopes. The clerks perform this work at the following rates of speed: Clerk A, 1100 letters an hour; Clerk B, 1450 letters an hour; Clerk C, 1200 letters an hour; Clerk D, 1300 letters an hour; Clerk E, 1250 letters an hour. At the end of two hours of work, Clerks C and D are assigned to another task. From the time that Clerks C and D were taken off the assignment, the number of hours required for the remaining clerks to complete this assignment is
(A) less than 3 hours
(B) 3 hours
(C) more than 3 hours, but less than 4 hours
(D) more than 4 hours.

47. Six gross of special drawing pencils were purchased for use in a City department. If the pencils were used at the rate of 24 a week, the maximum number of weeks that the six gross of pencils would last is
(A) 6 weeks (B) 12 weeks
(C) 24 weeks (D) 36 weeks.

48. A stock clerk had 600 pads on hand. He then issued 3/8 of his supply of pads to Division X, 1/4 to Division Y, and 1/6 to Division Z. The number of pads remaining in stock is
(A) 48 (B) 125
(C) 240 (D) 475.

49. If a certain job can be performed by 18 clerks in 26 days, the number of clerks needed to perform the job in 12 days is
(A) 24 clerks (B) 30 clerks
(C) 39 clerks (D) 52 clerks.

50. A department vehicle has completed the first 5 miles of a 10 mile trip in 10 minutes. To complete the entire trip at an average rate of 45 miles per hour, the vehicle must travel the remaining 5 miles in
(A) 3 minutes (B) 5 minutes
(C) 10 minutes (D) 15 minutes
(E) 20 minutes.

51. Assume that the average time required for a department vehicle to reach the scene of an emergency is M minutes. Solely on the basis of this fact, the one of the following which is the most reasonable inference is that in
(A) no case did a vehicle reach the scene of an emergency in less than M minutes
(B) no case did a vehicle reach the scene of an emergency in more than M minutes
(C) every case a vehicle reached the scene of an emergency in exactly M minutes
(D) some cases vehicles reached the scene of an emergency after M minutes had elapsed
(E) a majority of cases vehicles reached the scene of an emergency in a period of time equal to M divided by two.

52. "A proper record shall be kept of the dimension and capacity of each bin or space in quarters that is used for the storage of coal." Suppose that it is necessary to determine the capacity of a bin measuring 12 feet by 10 feet by 6 feet. The additional information required is
(A) the weight of a cubic foot of coal
(B) the volume of the bin
(C) the area of the base of the bin
(D) which dimension is the height
(E) the corresponding volume of coal required to fill the bin.

53. Suppose that the average number of violations per day during a period of P days is M. The total number of violations during the period of P days is expressed as
   (A) M
   (B) P
   (C) the product of P and M
   (D) the sum of M and P
   (E) the quotient M divided by P.

54. The fraction corresponding to the decimal .40 is
   (A) 1/25   (B) 1/4
   (C) 1/8   (D) 2/5
         (E) 1/40.

55. When 5.1 is divided by 0.017 the quotient is
   (A) 30   (B) 300
   (C) 3,000   (D) 30,000
         (E) 300,000.

56. One percent of $23,000 is
   (A) $.023   (B) $2.30
   (C) $23   (D) $230
         (E) $2,300.

57. The sum of $82.79; $103.06 and $697.88 is, most nearly,
   (A) $1628   (B) $791
   (C) $873   (D) $1395
         (E) $885.

58. A clerk is requested to file 800 cards. If he can file cards at the rate of 80 cards an hour, the number of cards remaining to be filed after 7 hours of work is
   (A) 40   (B) 140
   (C) 240   (D) 260
         (E) 560.

59. An officer's weekly salary is increased from $80.00 to $90.00. The per cent of increase is, most nearly,
   (A) 10 per cent   (B) 11-1/9 per cent
   (C) 12-1/2 per cent   (D) 14-1/7 per cent
         (E) 20 per cent.

60. If an engine pumps G gallons of water per minute, then the number of gallons pumped in half an hour may be found by
   (A) taking one-half of G
   (B) dividing 60 by G
   (C) multiplying G by 60 and then dividing the product by two
   (D) dividing 30 by G.

Correct Answers For The Foregoing Questions

(Please make every effort to answer the questions on your own before looking at these answers. You'll make faster progress by following this rule.)

1. B	9. D	17. D	24. C	31. A	38. B	45. A	53. C
2. D	10. D	18. A	25. A	32. C	39. B	46. B	54. D
3. C	11. B	19. C	26. D	33. B	40. A	47. D	55. B
4. D	12. C	20. D	27. B	34. A	41. B	48. B	56. D
5. A	13. A	21. A	28. D	35. A	42. B	49. C	57. E
6. C	14. D	22. B	29. C	36. B	43. A	50. B	58. C
7. D	15. B	23. C	30. A	37. D	44. D	51. D	59. C
8. A	16. B						60. C

GRAPH, CHART AND TABLE INTERPRETATION

The questions presented below on the interpretation of graphs and statistical tables have been compiled from previous examinations, and are designed to help you prepare for test questions which require reasoning and analytical ability.

GRAPH and table interpretation forms an important part of your examination. Many questions require the ability to read graphs and charts, or to make them up from a collection of data. You need a thorough understanding of their forms and meaning.

Wherever a question is based on a map, chart, graph or table, remember that it is important to answer it in the light of the information presented in the particular chart or table, without adding any ideas of your own. You are allowed to use scratch paper for computation while working on questions of this type.

DIRECTIONS FOR ANSWERING QUESTIONS. For each question, decide which is the best answer of the choices given. Note the capital letter preceding the best answer. On machine scored examinations you will be given an answer sheet and told to blacken the proper space on that answer sheet. Near the end of this book we have provided facsimiles of such answer sheets. Tear one out, and mark your answers on it, just as you would do on an actual exam.

A Sample Question Analyzed

CHART NO. I

Look at the two columns of data below:

Time sec.	Velocity ft./sec.
0	2
2	3
4	4
6	5
8	6
10	7

Which one of the lines on the graph at the right most closely represents the data in these two columns?

An examination of the graph shows that time values are indicated along the horizontal scale, and velocity values along the vertical scale. If we observe the velocity value at zero time, we see that the A line has a value of 0 velocity, and the C line a value of 2 ft./sec. No values are shown at 0 time for lines B and D. Hence line C is the only one which shows a velocity of 2 ft./sec. at 0 time.

Similarly at 2 sec. the velocity value for line B is 0, for line A is 2.5, and for line C, 3. Here again C is the only line which corresponds to the data in the table. At 4 sec. the velocity value for line D is 0, for line B is 1.9, for line C is 4, and for line A is 5. Here also line C is the only one that gives the value shown in the table. The same process can be repeated for time values 6, 8, and 10 sec., all of which show that line C is the only one corresponding to the values given in the table.

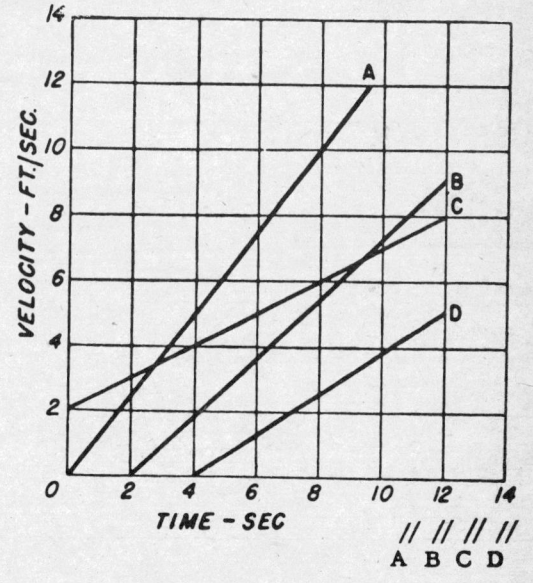

77

CHART NO. II

In the following graph the heavy curve represents postal receipts at St. Louis from 1930 to 1939. The light curve represents postal receipts at Detroit from 1930 to 1939.

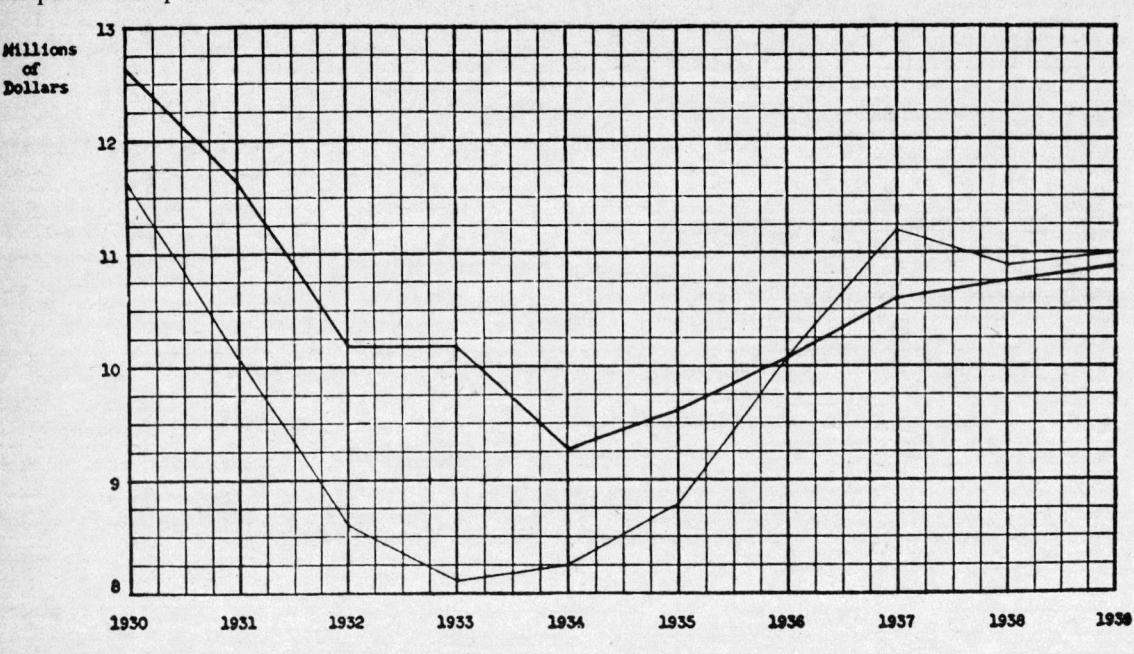

1. In 1937 the value of receipts in St. Louis was
   (A) 10,300,000 (B) 10,600,000
   (C) 11,100,000 (D) 11,200,000

2. Receipts were greatest in Detroit in
   (A) 1930 (B) 1933
   (C) 1937 (D) 1939

3. Detroit's and St. Louis' receipts were equal in
   (A) 1930 (B) 1933
   (C) 1936

4. Receipts in St. Louis were least in
   (A) 1932 (B) 1933
   (C) 1934 (D) 1937

5. In 1935 the ratio of the receipts in St. Louis to those in Detroit was
   (A) 2 to 1 (B) 5 to 3
   (C) 10 to 9 (D) 12 to 11

CHART NO. III

Answer Questions 6 to 10 on the basis of the following table:

VALUE OF PROPERTY STOLEN— 1963 and 1964
LARCENY

CATEGORY	1963 Number of Offenses	1963 Value of Stolen Property	1964 Number of Offenses	1964 Value of Stolen Property
Pocket - picking	20	$ 1,950	10	$ 950
Purse - snatching	175	5,750	120	12,050
Shoplifting	155	7,950	225	17,350
Automobile thefts	1040	127,050	860	108,000
Thefts of automobile accessories	1135	34,950	970	24,400
Bicycle thefts	355	8,250	240	6,350
All other thefts	1375	187,150	1300	153,150

6. Of the total number of larcenies reported for 1963, automobile thefts accounted for, most nearly,
   (A) 5%
   (B) 15%
   (C) 25%
   (D) 50%
   (E) 75%

7. The largest percentage decrease in the value of the stolen property from 1963 to 1964 was in the category of
   (A) bicycle thefts
   (B) automobile thefts
   (C) thefts of automobile accessories
   (D) pocket-picking
   (E) all other thefts

8. In 1964 the average amount of each theft was lowest for the category of
   (A) pocket-picking
   (B) purse-snatching
   (C) thefts of automobile accessories
   (D) shoplifting
   (E) bicycle thefts

9. The category which had the largest numerical reduction in the number of offenses from 1963 to 1964 was
   (A) pocket-picking
   (B) automobile thefts
   (C) thefts of automobile accessories
   (D) bicycle thefts
   (E) all other thefts

10. When the categories are ranked, for each year, according to the number of offenses committed in each category (largest number to rank first), the number of categories which will have the same rank in 1963 as in 1964 is
    (A) 3
    (B) 4
    (C) 5
    (D) 6
    (E) 7

11. For the two years combined (1963 and 1964), the average value of property stolen by pocket-picking was approximately
    (A) $25
    (B) $30
    (C) $150
    (D) $97
    (E) $74

Questions 12 through 16 are to be answered on the basis of the following graphs:

CHART NO. IV

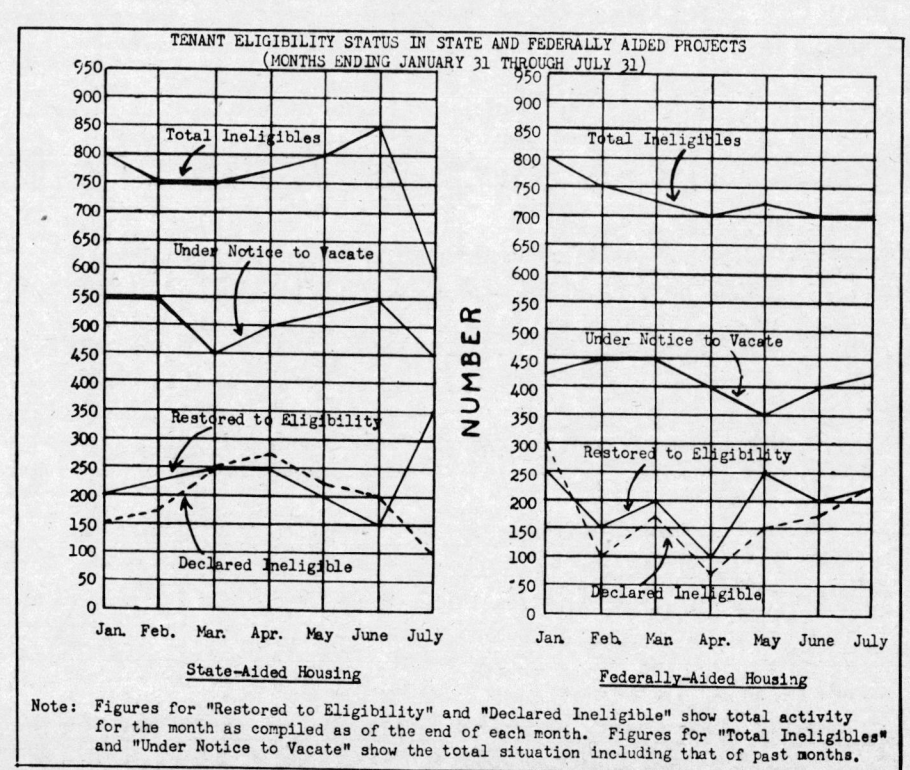

TENANT ELIGIBILITY STATUS IN STATE AND FEDERALLY AIDED PROJECTS
(MONTHS ENDING JANUARY 31 THROUGH JULY 31)

State-Aided Housing

Federally-Aided Housing

Note: Figures for "Restored to Eligibility" and "Declared Ineligible" show total activity for the month as compiled as of the end of each month. Figures for "Total Ineligibles" and "Under Notice to Vacate" show the total situation including that of past months.

12. In Federally-aided housing, the average number of tenants restored to eligibility during the first six months of the year is, most nearly
    (A) 100   (B) 192
    (C) 188   (D) 196
    (E) 200

13. For the months covered by the graphs, in State-aided housing, the ratio of the average number of total ineligibles to the average number under notice to vacate is, most nearly
    (A) 1:2   (B) 2:3
    (C) 3:2   (D) 2:1
    (E) 3:1

14. For State-aided housing, assume that it has been decided to predict figures for the end of August and the end of September on the basis that the number of tenants expected to be declared ineligible in each future month will be 30% less than the average for the previous three months. The number of tenants expected to be declared ineligible during the month of September is expected to be, most nearly,
    (A) 122   (B) 100
    (C) 141   (D) 158
    (E) 175

15. Of the four categories of tenant status in the graph, the number of categories in which, at the end of May as compared with the end of April, there was a greater *numerical* increase in State-aided housing as compared with the same category in Federally-aided housing, is
    (A) 1   (B) 0
    (C) 2   (D) 3
    (E) 4

16. Assume that, at the end of March, in State-aided housing, the total number of ineligibles was 10% greater than shown on the graph, and that this 10% increase was due entirely to a greater number of tenants being declared ineligible in that month than is shown on the graph. Under this assumption, the percentage increase in the number *declared ineligible,* as compared with the figure in the graph, would be, most nearly,
    (A) 3%   (B) 30%
    (C) 17%   (D) 23%
    (E) 10%

Questions 17 to 23 are to be answered on the basis of information contained in the chart and table below. The chart shows the percentage of annual expenditures for equipment, supplies, and salaries. The table shows the annual expenditures for each of the years 1957-1961.

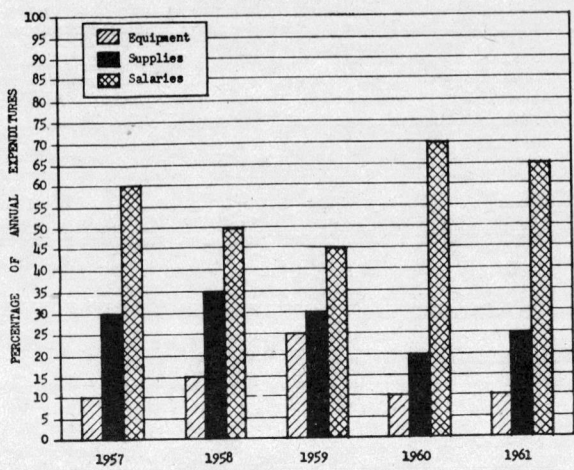

CHART NO. V

The bureau's annual expenditures for the years 1957-1961 are shown in the following table:

Year	Expenditures
1957	$ 800,000
1958	1,200,000
1959	1,500,000
1960	1,000,000
1961	1,200,000

Equipment, supplies, and salaries were the only three categories for which the bureau spent money.

17. The information contained in the chart and table is sufficient to determine the
    (A) average annual salary of an employee in the bureau in 1958
    (B) decrease in the amount of money spent on supplies in the bureau in 1957 from the amount spent in the preceding year
    (C) changes, between 1959 and 1960, in the prices of supplies bought by the bureau
    (D) increase in the amount of money spent on salaries in the bureau in 1961 over the amount spent in the preceding year

18. If the percentage of expenditures for salaries in one year is added to the percentage of expenditures for equipment in that year, a total of the two percentages for that year is obtained. The two years for which this total is the same are
    (A) 1958 and 1960   (B) 1957 and 1959
    (C) 1957 and 1960   (D) 1958 and 1961

19. On the following, the year in which the bureau spent the greatest amount of money on supplies was
    (A) 1961   (B) 1957
    (C) 1958   (D) 1959

Graph, Chart and Table Interpretation / 81

20. Of the following years, the one in which there was the greatest increase over the preceding year in the amount of money spent on salaries is
    (A) 1958   (B) 1961
    (C) 1960   (D) 1959

21. Of the bureau's expenditures for equipment in 1961, one-third was used for the purchase of mailroom equipment and the remainder was spent on miscellaneous office equipment. How much money did the bureau spend on miscellaneous office equipment in 1961?
    (A) $400,000   (B) $40,000
    (C) $800,000   (D) $80,000

22. If there were 120 employees in the bureau in 1960, then the average annual salary paid to the employees in that year was, most nearly,
    (A) $4,345   (B) $4,960
    (C) $5,835   (D) $8,080

23. In 1959 the bureau had 125 employees. If 20 of the employees earned an average annual salary of $8,000, then the average annual salary of the other 105 employees was, most nearly,
    (A) $6,400   (B) $4,900
    (C) $4,100   (D) $5,400

24. Assume that the bureau estimated that the amount of money it would spend on supplies in 1962 would be the same as the amount it spent on that category in 1961. Similarly, the bureau estimated that the amount of money it would spend on equipment in 1962 would be the same as the amount it spent on that category in 1961. However the bureau estimated that in 1962 the amount it would spend on salaries would be 10 per cent higher than the amount it spent on that category in 1961. The percentage of its annual expenditures that the bureau estimated it would spend on supplies in 1962 is most nearly
    (A) 27.5%   (B) 22.5%
    (C) 23.5%   (D) 25%

CHART NO. VI

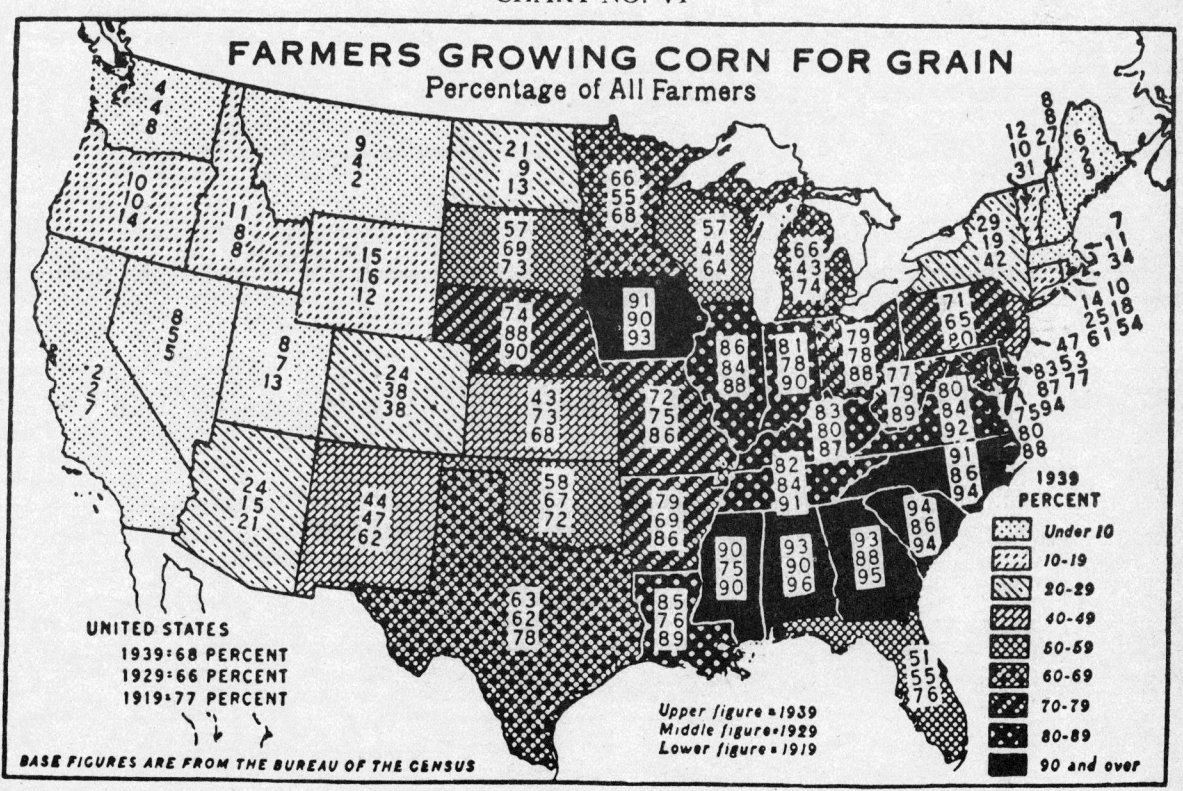

Answer the following by referring to the map above.

25. In what State(s) west of the Mississippi did 90% or more of the farmers raise corn for grain in 1919?
    (A) Minnesota and Kansas
    (B) Kansas and Nebraska
    (C) Missouri and Kansas
    (D) Nebraska and Iowa
    (E) Iowa

26. In 1939, how many States had the same percentage of farmers growing corn for grain as

Colorado had in 1919?
(A) 0   (B) 1
(C) 2   (D) 3
(E) Not answerable

27. What was the average percentage of Illinois farmers raising corn for grain for the three years referred to on the map?
(A) 77.7   (B) 83.0
(C) 86.0   (D) 91.25
(E) 129.0

28. The quantity of corn produced for grain was the same in Mississippi and Missouri in what year?
(A) 1919   (B) 1929
(C) 1935 (approximately)   (D) 1939
(E) Not answerable

29. What two States had the lowest proportion of farmers growing corn for grain in 1929?
(A) Washington and Montana
(B) Washington and California
(C) Maine and California
(D) Montana and Maine
(E) Montana and Nevada

30. In what two States east of the Missouri River did 60% to 69% of the farmers raise corn for grain in 1939?
(A) Illinois and Wisconsin
(B) Michigan and Minnesota
(C) Texas and Michigan
(D) Wisconsin and Minnesota
(E) Texas and Oklahoma

31. In Washington, Oregon, and California combined, the percentage of farmers growing corn for grain in 1929 exceeded the percentage in 1919 by approximately what percent?
(A) 0   (B) 13
(C) 8   (D) 6
(E) Not answerable

32. The proportion of farmers in New York growing corn for grain in 1919 was what percent greater than the proportion in North Dakota in 1939?
(A) 21   (B) 50
(C) 100   (D) 200
(E) Not answerable

33. The number of farmers in Vermont in 1939 was approximately 24,000 and in 1929 approximately 25,000. The number of farmers growing corn for grain in 1939 was an increase of approximately what percent over those in 1929?
(A) 2.0   (B) 13.3
(C) 15.2   (D) 20.0
(E) Not answerable

34. Based on the map and the table below, in which of the three states given was there an increase in farmers growing corn for grain between the 1929 and 1939 figures?
(A) Oregon
(B) Oregon and New Mexico
(C) Oregon and Texas
(D) Texas and New Mexico
(E) All three

TOTAL NUMBER OF FARMERS

	1929	1939
New Mexico	31,000	34,000
Oregon	55,000	62,000
Texas	495,000	418,000

35. Assuming that the number of farmers in the United States increased by 8% from 1919 to 1929, the number of farmers growing corn for grain decreased by what percent from 1919 to 1929?
(A) 3.0   (B) 11
(C) 10.1   (D) 11.9
(E) Not answerable

CHART NO. VII

Answer questions 36 to 40 on the basis of the chart following.

36. The one of the following years for which average employee production was LOWEST was
(A) 1941   (B) 1943
(C) 1945   (D) 1947
(E) 1949

37. The average annual employee production for the ten year period was, in terms of work units, most nearly
(A) 30   (B) 50
(C) 70   (D) 80
(E) 90

38. On the basis of the chart, it can be deduced

that personnel needs for the coming year are budgeted on the basis of

(A) workload for the current year
(B) expected workload for the coming year
(C) no set plan
(D) average workload over the five years immediately preceding the period
(E) expected workload for the five coming years

39. "The chart indicates that the operation is carefully programmed and that the labor force has been used properly." This opinion is

(A) supported by the chart; the organization has been able to meet emergency situations requiring much additional work without commensurate increases in staff
(B) not supported by the chart; the irregular work load shows a complete absence of planning
(C) supported by the chart; the similar shapes of the "Workload" and "Labor Force" curves show that these important factors are closely related
(D) not supported by the chart; poor planning with respect to labor requirements is obvious from the chart
(E) supported by the chart; the average number of units of work performed in any 5 year period during the 10 years shows sufficient regularity to indicate a definite trend.

40. "The chart indicates that the department may be organized in such a way as to require a permanent minimum staff which is too large for the type of operation indicated." This opinion is

(A) supported by the chart; there is indication that the operation calls for an irreducible minimum number of employees and application of the most favorable work production records show this to be too high for normal operation
(B) not supported by the chart; the absence of any sort of regularity makes it impossible to express any opinion with any degree of certainty
(C) supported by the chart; the expected close relationship between workload and labor force is displaced somewhat, a phenomenon which usually occurs as a result of a fixed minimum requirement
(D) not supported by the chart; the violent movement of the "Labor Force" curve makes it evident that no minimum requirements are in effect
(E) supported by the chart; calculation shows that the average number of employees was 84 with an average variation of 17.8 thus indicating that the minimum number of 60 persons was too high for efficient operation.

DEPARTMENT X
WORKLOAD AND LABOR FORCE
1940-1949

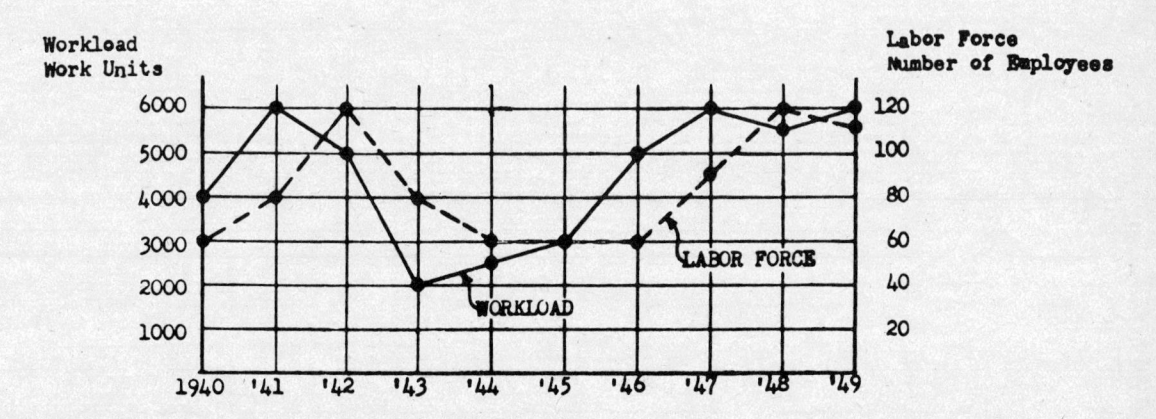

Questions 41 to 44 are to be answered on the basis of the following graph.

AVERAGE HOURLY INCIDENCE OF ARRESTS AND ACCIDENTS FOR COMMUNITY X FOR 1955

Note: Hourly figures represent total number of occurrences in the immediately preceding hour.

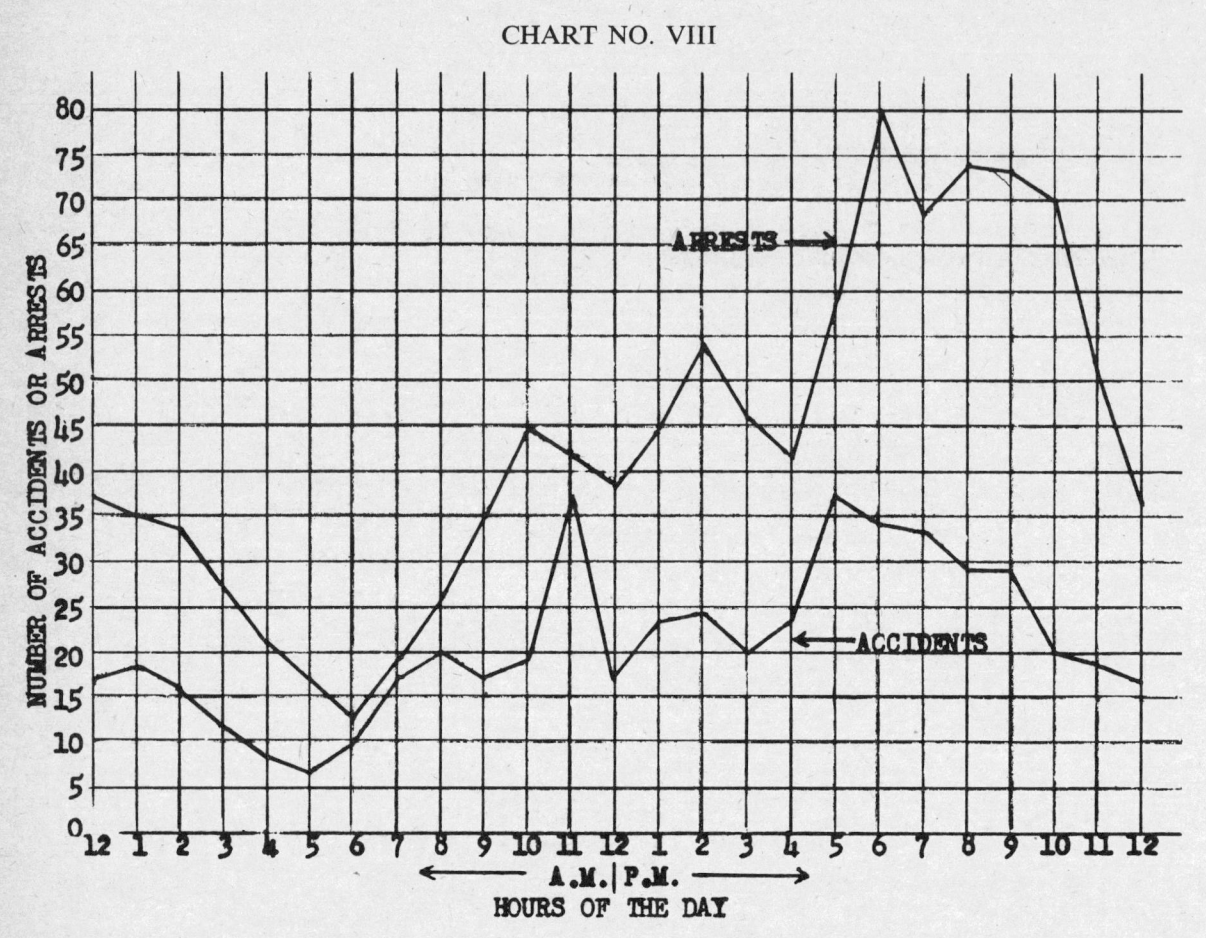

CHART NO. VIII

41. According to this graph, of the following hours of the day, the hour which shows the highest ratio of arrests to accidents is
    (A) 2 p.m.   (B) 6 p.m.
    (C) 8 p.m.   (D) 10 p.m.

42. According to the above graph, the *least* average hour-to-hour variation, during the following time periods, was in the number of
    (A) arrests during the 4 p.m. through 8 p.m. period
    (B) accidents during the 12 noon through 4 p.m. period
    (C) arrests during the 8 p.m. through 12 midnight period
    (D) accidents during the 8 a.m. through 12 noon period.

43. According to the above graph, of all the accidents occurring from 12 noon through midnight, the percentage which occurred from 12 noon through 4 p.m. was most nearly
    (A) 26%   (B) 30%
    (C) 34%   (D) 38%.

44. On the basis of the above graph
    (A) an equal number of accidents was recorded daily at 8 a.m. and 3 p.m.
    (B) on any given day, during the year covered, there were more arrests recorded at 2 p.m. than at 10 a.m.
    (C) the number of accidents entered in the first 12 o'clock column must always equal the number of accidents in the last 12 o'clock column
    (D) the wide variation in the number of arrests makes statistical interpretation of the figures unreliable.

Questions 45 through 54 are to be answered on the basis of Chart IX, Immigration.

Select the date which completes each of the following statements.

45. Emigration was 1/4 immigration in:
    (A) 1910   (B) 1913
    (C) 1920   (D) 1924

46. Immigration was 1/2 emigration in:
    (A) 1915   (B) 1921
    (C) 1932   (D) 1934

47. Emigration and immigration were equal in:
    (A) 1919   (B) 1922
    (C) 1931   (D) 1935

48. Emigration rose at the greatest rate between:
    (A) 1914 and 1915 (B) 1919 and 1920
    (C) 1922 and 1923 (D) 1931 and 1932

49. The excess of immigrants over emigrants was greatest in:
    (A) 1910   (B) 1914
    (C) 1921   (D) 1932

50. Immigration fell off at the greatest rate between:
    (A) 1914 and 1915
    (B) 1919 and 1920
    (C) 1924 and 1925
    (D) 1931 and 1932

51. There were fewest emigrants in:
    (A) 1917   (B) 1923
    (C) 1933   (D) 1935

52. The rate of change of net immigration was greatest between:
    (A) 1920 and 1921
    (B) 1925 and 1926
    (C) 1930 and 1931
    (D) 1932 and 1933

53. The rates of increase of emigrants and immigrants were most nearly equal between:
    (A) 1932 and 1933
    (B) 1925 and 1926
    (C) 1918 and 1919
    (D) 1913 and 1914

54. Immigration was lowest in:
    (A) 1918   (B) 1931
    (C) 1933   (D) 1935

CHART NO. IX

In the graph below, the heavy curve represents immigration from 1910-1935. The light curve represents emigration from 1910-1935.

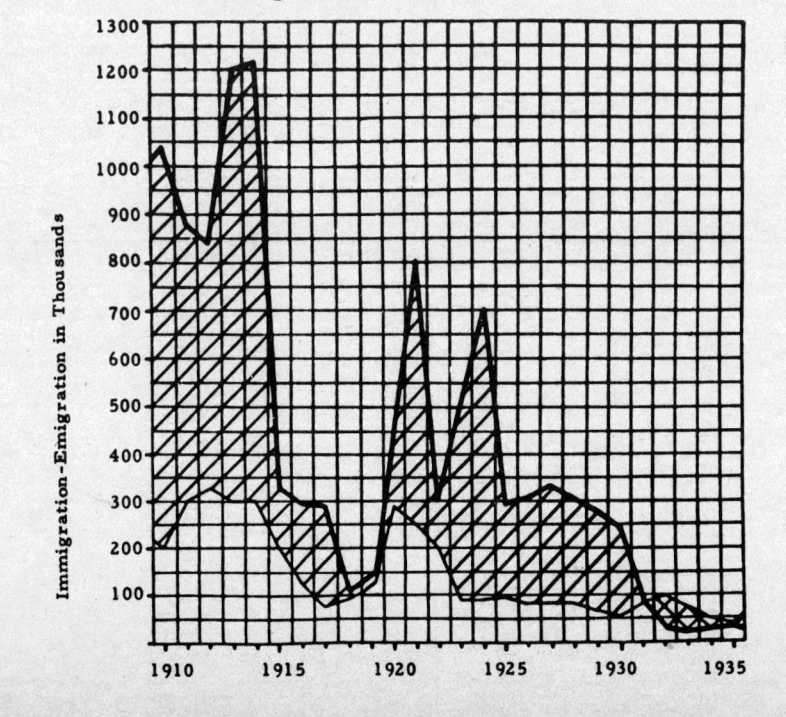

CHART NO. X

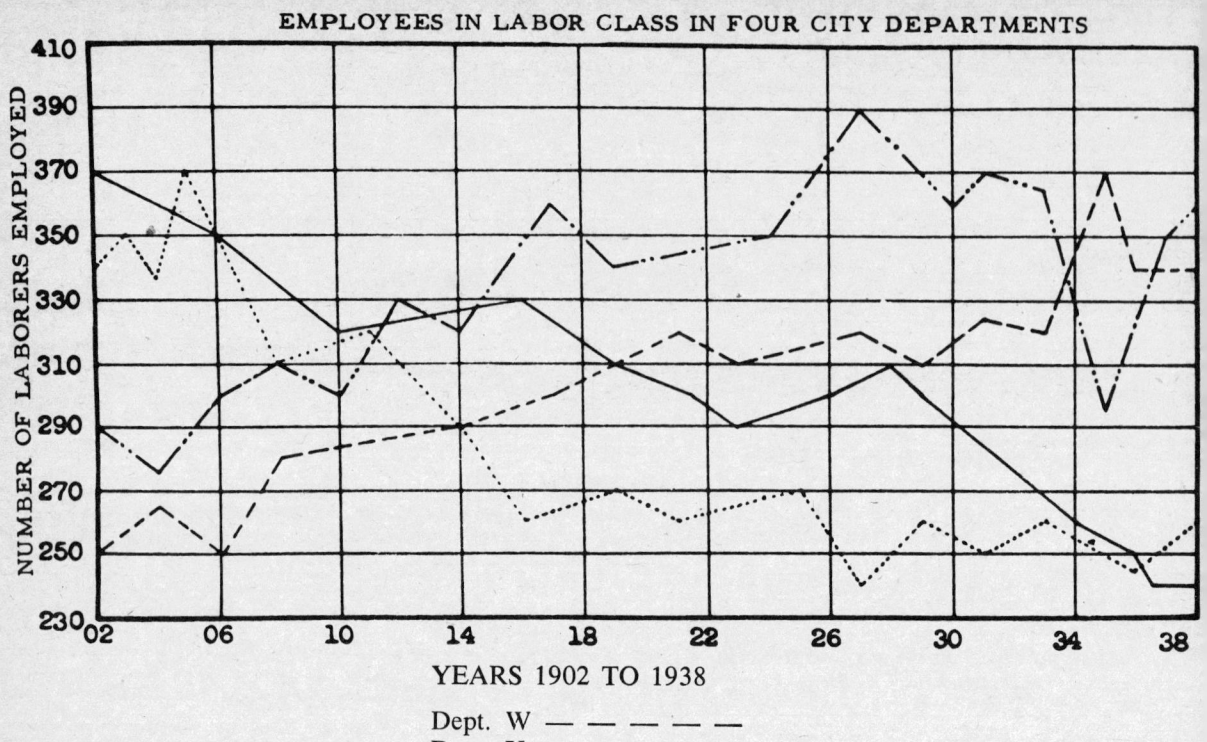

EMPLOYEES IN LABOR CLASS IN FOUR CITY DEPARTMENTS

YEARS 1902 TO 1938

Dept. W — — — — —
Dept. X ——————
Dept. Y ....
Dept. Z —··—··—··—

Items 55 to 64 are based on information contained in chart. No. X. Choose the letter which is the same as the answer which correctly completes the statement.

55. W had its largest number of laborers in
    (A) 1926 (B) 1914
    (C) 1935 (D) 1906
    (E) 1937

56. In 1919 the same number of laborers were employed in
    (A) W and Z (B) Y and Z
    (C) X and Y (D) W and X
    (E) X and Z

57. In the same year that Z reached its greatest peak, the lowest number of laborers was employed in
    (A) W and X (B) Y
    (C) W (D) X
    (E) W and Y

58. The department which showed the greatest increase of labor class employees in 1938 as compared to 1902 is
    (A) W (B) X
    (C) Y (D) Z
    (E) not determinable from graph

59. In 1930 Z showed a 20% increase over
    (A) 1910 (B) 1926
    (C) 1914 (D) 1934
    (E) 1938

60. W employed the same number of laborers in 1906 as X did in
    (A) 1913 (B) 1931
    (C) 1906 (D) 1927
    (E) 1936

61. The smallest number of laborers employed in 1914 was in
    (A) Z (B) Y and Z
    (C) W and Y (D) W and X
    (E) X and Z

62. Z in 1906 is to X in 1926 as Z in 1910 is to
    (A) Y in 1938 (B) W in 1921
    (C) Z in 1927 (D) Y in 1919
    (E) X in 1929

Graph, Chart and Table Interpretation / 87

. In 1935 W had .... times as many laborers as in 1906
(A) 2 (B) 2.22
(C) 1.48 (D) 1.50
(E) 1.65

64. Z in 1904 is to Y in 1931 as X in 1916 is to
(A) Y in 1919 (B) W in 1917
(C) Z in 1927 (D) Z in 1919
(E) W in 1923

CHART NO. XI

Answer questions 65 to 69 solely on the basis of the following table.

r of Persons Receiving Public Assistance and Cost of Public Assistance in 1961 and 1962

gory of stance	Monthly average number receiving assistance during		Total Cost for Year in Millions of Dollars		Cost Paid by New York City for Year in Millions of Dollars	
	1961	1962	1961	1962	1961	1962
	36,097	38,263	$19.2	$17.4	$9.7	$8.7
	6,632	5,972	2.5	1.6	1.3	.8
A	32,545	31,804	33.7	29.7	6.5	5.0
A	13,992	11,782	13.2	21.3	3.3	5.3
C	212,795	228,795	108.3	121.4	27.5	31.3

Assume that the *total* cost of the Home Relief program decreases by 10% each year for the next three years after 1962. Then the total cost of the Home Relief program for 1965 will be, most nearly,
(A) $11.5 million (C) $12.7 million
(B) $14.1 million (D) $14.5 million
(E) $36.0 million

The category for which New York City paid the smallest percentage of the total cost was
(A) O A A in 1961 (C) V A in 1961
(B) A D C in 1961 (D) O A A in 1962
(E) A D C in 1962

The *monthly* cost to the city for each person receiving MAA during 1962 was, most nearly,
(A) $18 more than in 1961
(B) $26 less than in 1961
(C) $20 more than in 1961
(D) $67 more than in 1961
(E) $18 less than in 1961

68. Assume that 40% of the number of persons receiving ADC in 1961 were adults caring for minor children, but the city's contribution towards maintaining these adults was only 36% of its total contribution to the ADC program in 1961, then the amount paid by the city for each adult per month in 1961 is, most nearly,
(A) $10 (B) $14 (C) $31 (D) $36
(E) $107

69. Assume that 10% of the persons receiving OAA in 1962 will be transferred to MAA in 1963, and 6% of the persons receiving MAA in 1962 will no longer need any public assistance in 1963, then the percentage change from 1962 to 1963 in the monthly average number receiving MAA would be, most nearly,
(A) an increase of 4%
(B) an increase of 27%
(C) a decrease of 6%
(D) an increase of 21%

Questions 70 to 79 are to be answered solely on the basis of Chart XII which relates to the Investigation Division of Department X. This chart contains four curves which connect the points that show for each year the variations in percentage deviation from normal in the number of investigators, the number of clerical employees, the cost of personnel, and the number of cases processed for the period 1942-1952 inclusive. The year 1942 was designated as the normal year. The personnel of the Investigation Division consists of investigators and clerical employees only.

CHART NO. XII
INVESTIGATION DIVISION, DEPARTMENT X
VARIATIONS IN NUMBER OF CASES PROCESSED, COST OF PERSONNEL NUMBER OF CLERICAL EMPLOYEES, AND NUMBER OF INVESTIGATORS FOR EACH YEAR FROM 1942 TO 1952 INCLUSIVE
(IN PERCENTAGES FROM NORMAL)

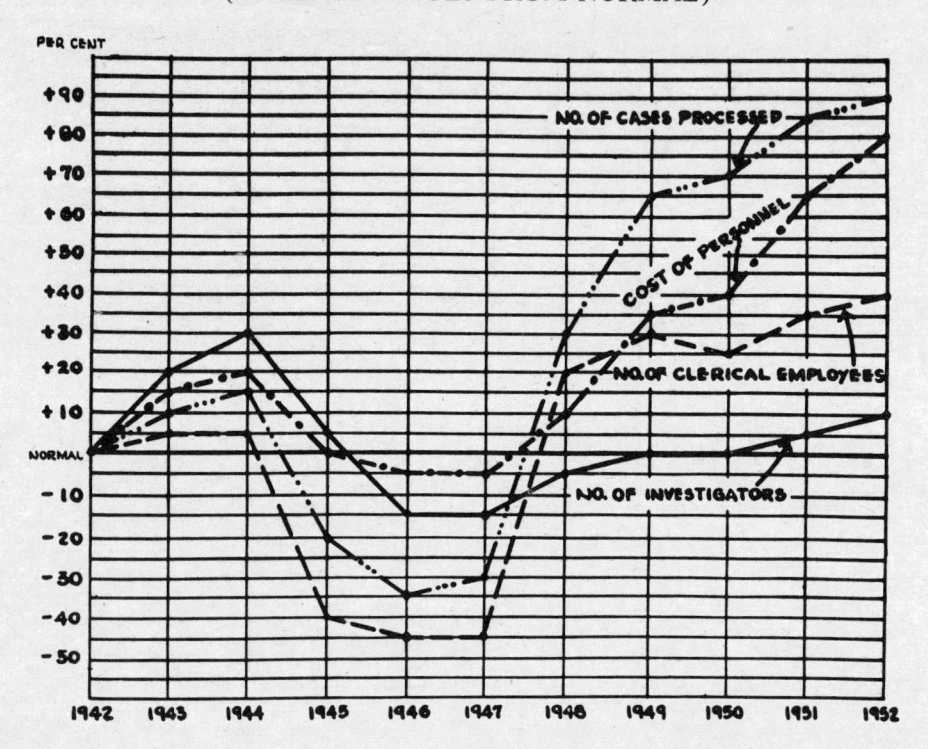

70. If 1300 cases were processed by the division in 1946, then the number of cases processed in 1942 was
    (A) 2000 (B) 1755
    (C) 2145 (D) 1650.

71. Of the following, the year in which there was no change in the size of the division's total staff from that of the preceding year is
    (A) 1945 (B) 1947
    (C) 1949 (D) 1951.

72. Of the following, the year in which the size of the division's total staff decreased most sharply from that of the preceding year is
    (A) 1945 (B) 1946
    (C) 1947 (D) 1948.

73. An inspection of the chart discloses that the curve that fluctuated *least,* as determined by the average deviation from normal, is the curve for the
    (A) number of cases processed
    (B) cost of personnel
    (C) number of clerical employees
    (D) number of investigators.

74. A comparison of 1946 with 1942 reveals an increase in 1946 in the
    (A) cost of personnel for the division
    (B) number of cases processed per investigator
    (C) number of cases processed per clerical employee
    (D) number of clerical employees per investigator.

75. If the personnel cost per case processed in 1942 was $12.30, then the personnel cost per case processed in 1952 was most nearly
    (A) $ 9.85   (B) $10.95
    (C) $11.65   (D) $13.85.

76. Suppose that there was a total of 108 employees in the division in 1942 and a total of 125 employees in 1950. On the basis of these figures, it is most accurate to state that the number of investigators employed in the division in 1950 was
    (A) 40   (B) 57
    (C) 68   (D) 85.

77. It is predicted that the number of cases processed in 1953 will exceed the number processed in 1952 by exactly the same quantity that the number processed in 1952 exceeded that processed in 1951. It is also predicted that the personnel cost in 1953 will exceed the personnel cost in 1952 by exactly the same amount that that the 1952 personnel cost exceeded that for 1951. On the basis of these predictions, it is most accurate to state that the personnel cost per case in 1953 will be
    (A) ten per cent less than the personnel cost in 1952
    (B) exactly the same as the personnel cost per case in 1952
    (C) twice as much as the personnel cost per case in 1942
    (D) exactly the same as the personnel cost per case in 1942.

78. The variation between the per cent of cases processed and the number of investigators of Department X was greatest in
    (A) 1949   (B) 1951
    (C) 1952   (D) 1944.

79. In 1950, the difference between two categories in Department X is equal to a third. The third is the
    (A) number of investigators
    (B) cost of personnel
    (C) number of clerical employees
    (D) number of cases processed.

CHART NO. XIII

NUMBER OF EMPLOYEES IN CIVIL SERVICE BETWEEN YEARS 1902 AND 1937

Year	Total Number (In Thousands)	Competitive Class (In Thousands)	Labor Class (In Thousands)	Non-Competitive Class (In Thousands)
1902	33	18	12	2
1906	43	24	16	2
1910	53	29	18	5
1914	56	31	18	6
1918	54	31	16	6
1922	60	35	17	7
1926	74	44	19	9
1930	90	52	24	12
1933	91	49	25	15
1937	107	63	27	17

Items 80 through 84 relate to the table above.

80. The greatest percentage increase in the competitive class occurred between the years of

    (A) 1933 and 1937
    (B) 1926 and 1930
    (C) 1922 and 1926
    (D) 1906 and 1910
    (E) 1902 and 1906

81. The smallest percentage of employees in the competitive class is found in the year
    (A) 1902   (B) 1910
    (C) 1914   (D) 1933
         (E) 1937

82. The greatest percentage of employees in the labor class is found in the year
    (A) 1902   (B) 1906
    (C) 1910   (D) 1930
         (E) 1937

83. The approximate ratio of 54%, 27%, and 16% for competitive, labor class and non-competitive employees respectively

    (A) never occurs
    (B) occurs once
    (C) occurs twice
    (D) occurs three times
    (E) occurs five times

84. The most accurate of the following statements regarding the interpretation of the table is that
    (A) the percentage of employees in the non-competitive class has been constantly increasing since the World War
    (B) the percentage of employees in the competitive class has never fallen below 55%
    (C) since 1926, employees in the labor class have been increasing at a faster rate than in the non-competitive class
    (D) the average number of employees in the competitive class between the years of 1922 and 1937 inclusive was greater than the average number of total employees between 1902 and 1922 inclusive
    (E) between 1933 and 1937, the percentage increase in the competitive class was more than 3 1/2 times the percentage increase in the labor class.

CHART NO. XIV

Carefully study the table below. You are to answer questions 85 through 89 solely on the basis of the data given in the table.

| YEAR | PRIVATELY FINANCED |||| Total publicly financed | TOTAL |
	1-family	2-family	Multi-family	Total		
1937	267,000	16,000	49,000	332,000	4,000	336,000
1938	316,000	18,000	65,000	399,000	7,000	406,000
1939	373,000	19,000	66,000	458,000	57,000	515,000
1940	448,000	26,000	56,000	530,000	73,000	603,000
1941	533,000	28,000	58,000	619,000	96,000	715,000
1942	252,000	18,000	31,000	301,000	196,000	497,000
1943	136,000	18,000	30,000	184,000	166,000	350,000
1944	115,000	11,000	13,000	139,000	30,000	169,000
1945	184,000	9,000	15,000	208,000	18,000	226,000
1946	590,000	24,000	48,000	662,000	114,000	776,000
1947	745,000	34,000	72,000	851,000	3,000	854,000

85. "Multi-family private dwellings have been built in greater numbers than 2-family private dwellings." For the years covered by the table, this statement
    (A) is true
    (B) is false
    (C) is partly true
    (D) cannot be determined from the table

86. Considering only the last ten years of the table, the number of years in which the number of 1-family private dwellings exceeded the number of publicly-financed dwellings is
    (A) 1   (B) 2
    (C) 9   (D) 10

87. The number of years during which the number of publicly-financed dwellings was more than half the number of privately-financed dwellings is
    (A) 1   (B) 2
    (C) 3   (D) 4.

88. The number of years during which privately-financed 1-family dwellings was less than half the total number of all dwellings is
    (A) 1   (B) 2
    (C) 3   (D) 4.

89. The number of years during which there was an increase of at least 10% in the number of private 2-family dwellings built is
    (A) 1   (B) 2
    (C) 3   (D) 4.

Questions 90 through 94 are to be answered on the basis of the following graph.

CHART NO. XV

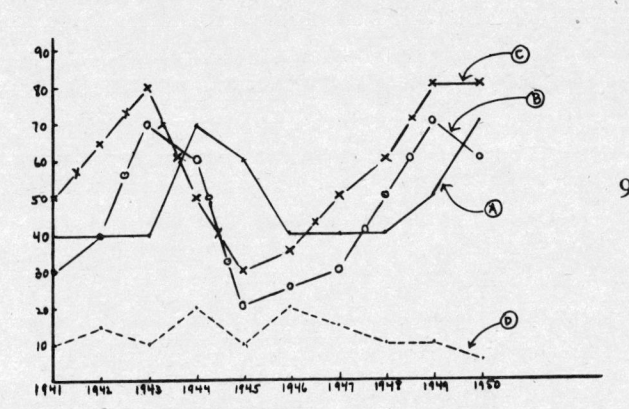

A. ———— total number of examiners employed during year
B. o-o-o-o total number of examinations held during year.
C. x-x-x-x total number of candidates tested during year in thousands.
D. - - - - total number of appeals from candidates who took an examination during year in tens.

90. The number of appeals from candidates who took an examination during any one year is apparently
   (A) directly related to the number of examiners employed during the year
   (B) directly related to the number of examinations held during the year
   (C) inversely related to the number of candidates tested during the year
   (D) unrelated to any of the other curves
   (E) inversely related to the average of the number of candidates tested and examiners employed during each year.

91. The total number of candidates tested during any one year is apparently
   (A) inversely related to the average of the number of tests given and the number of examiners employed during the year
   (B) completely unrelated to any of the other variables
   (C) inversely related to the number of examiners employed during the year
   (D) directly related to the number of appeals received during the year
   (E) directly related to the number of examinations held during that year.

92. It may be inferred that throughout the period covered the number of examinations for the coming year had been assumed to be
   (A) the same as that for the current year
   (B) unpredictable
   (C) the average of the number of examinations held in each of the past five years
   (D) approximately one per cent of the number of candidates in the current year
   (E) the average of the number of examinations and one per cent of the number of candidates for the past year.

93. The assumption that the average number of examinations completed by an examiner has remained constant during the ten year period is
   (A) inconsistent with the information given in the graph as the ratio between number of examiners employed during a year and the number of examinations given is not constant
   (B) not inconsistent with the information given in the graph if it is the case that after the examiners have completed the examinations to be given in any year they proceed at once to the preparation of examinations to be given in a future period
   (C) inconsistent with the information given as the sum of the deviations of the ratios between the number of examiners employed during a year and the number of examinations given during a year for all years from the mean of these ratios must be zero
   (D) not inconsistent with the information given as the sum of the deviations of the ratios between number of examiners employed during a year and the number of examinations given during the year for all years from the mean of these ratios is zero
   (E) inconsistent with the information given if we also assume that after the examiners have completed the examination to be given in any year, they proceed at once to the preparation of examinations to be given in a future period.

94. The one of the following years **during** which the average number of candidates on an examination was the least is
   (A) 1943   (B) 1944
   (C) 1945   (D) 1948
   (E) 1949.

Questions 95, 96, 97 and 98 are to be answered solely on the basis of the graph below.

CHART NO. XVI

AVERAGE MONTHLY DISTRIBUTION OF CRIMES AGAINST PROPERTY FOR COMMUNITY X   1951-1955

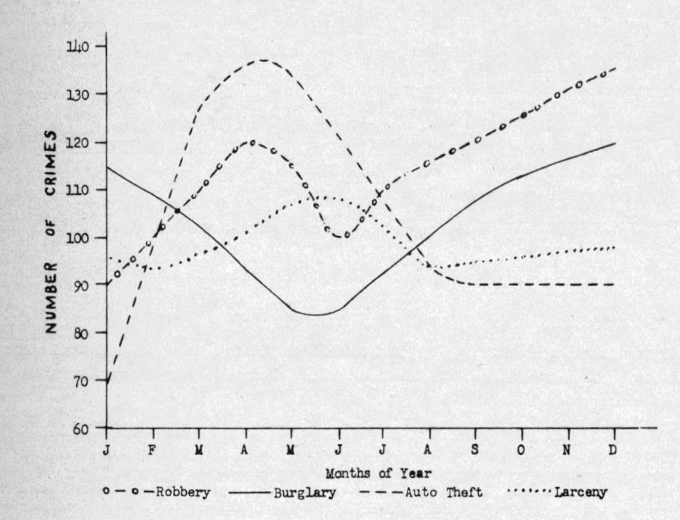

(A) January (B) June
(C) July (D) August
(E) September.

98. According to this graph, of the following crimes, the one which showed the *least* average month-to-month variation in the number of occurrences was
(A) automobile theft during the January through June period
(B) burglary during the January through June period
(C) burglary during the July through December period
(D) larceny during the July through December period
(E) robbery during the January through June period.

95. The above graph indicates that, during the entire five-year period covered,
(A) larceny showed the greatest variation
(B) more crimes against property were being committed at the end of the period than at the beginning
(C) robbery was becoming an increasingly serious police problem
(D) specific crimes against property follow no pattern
(E) there were seasonal variations in the number of burglaries.

96. If the population of this community averaged 150,000 during the period covered by this graph, then the crime rate for burglaries in December, computed in accordance with the F.B.I. method of crime reporting, was most nearly
(A) 50 (B) 80
(C) 110 (D) 140
(E) 170.

97. According to this graph, the month in which all crimes against property (total for the four crimes) were *least* frequently committed is

Correct Answers

1. B	13. C	25. D	37. B
2. A	14. B	26. A	38. A
3. C	15. A	27. C	39. C
4. C	16. B	28. B	40. A
5. C	17. D	29. C	41. D
6. C	18. B	30. B	42. B
7. D	19. D	31. B	43. B
8. C	20. A	32. C	44. C
9. B	21. D	33. A	45. B
10. C	22. C	34. B	46. D
11. D	23. B	35. B	47. C
12. B	24. C	36. B	48. B
49. B	61. C	73. D	85. A
50. A	62. E	74. C	86. C
51. D	63. C	75. C	87. B
52. A	64. B	76. A	88. A
53. C	65. C	77. D	89. D
54. C	66. D	78. C	90. D
55. C	67. A	79. B	91. E
56. D	68. A	80. E	92. A
57. B	69. D	81. D	93. B
58. A	70. A	82. B	94. B
59. A	71. B	83. B	95. E
60. E	72. A	84. E	96. B
			97. A
			98. D

AIR FORCE PLACEMENT TESTS

TOP SCORES ON VOCABULARY TESTS

Although questions on vocabulary may not actually appear on your test, it is advisable to practice with the kind of material you have in this chapter. Words and their meanings are quite important in pushing up your score on tests of reading, comprehension, effective writing and correct usage. By broadening your vocabulary, you will definitely improve your marks in these and similar subjects.

INCREASE YOUR VOCABULARY

How is your vocabulary? Do you know the meanings of just about every word you come upon in your reading—or do you find several words that stump you? You must increase your vocabulary if you want to read with understanding. Following are six steps that you can take in order to build up your word power:

(a) Read as much as you have the time for. Don't confine yourself to one type of reading either. Read all kinds of things—newspaper, magazines, books. Seek variety in what you read—different newspapers, several types of magazines, all types of books (novels, poetry, essays, plays, etc.). If you get into the habit of reading widely, your vocabulary will grow by leaps and bounds. You'll learn the meanings of words *by context*. That means that, very often, even though you may not know the meaning of a certain word in a sentence, the other words that you are familiar with will help you get the meaning of the hard word.

(b) Take vocabulary tests. There are many practice books which have word tests. We suggest one of these: *2300 Steps to Word Power*—$1.45 (Arco Publishing Co.). These tests are fun to take—and they will build up your vocabulary fast.

(c) Listen to lectures, discussions, and talks by people who speak well. There are some worthwhile TV programs that have excellent speakers. Listen to such people—you'll learn a great many words from them simply by listening to them.

(d) Use a dictionary. Whenever you don't know the meaning of a word, make a note of it. Then, when you get to a dictionary, look up the meaning of the word. Keep your own little notebook—call it "New Words." In a month or two, you will have added a great many words to your vocabulary. If you do not have a dictionary at home, you should buy one. It is just as important in your life as pots and pans, furniture, or a television set. A good dictionary is not expensive. Any one of the following is highly recommended—and costs about five or six dollars:

Standard College Dictionary (Funk and Wagnalls)

Seventh New Collegiate Dictionary (Merriam-Webster)

American College Dictionary (Random House)

You'll never regret buying a good dictionary for your home.

(c) Play word games. Have you ever played Anagrams or Scrabble? They're really interesting. Buy one of these at a stationery store. They are quite inexpensive but effective in building up your vocabulary. Crossword puzzles will teach you new words also. Practically every daily newspaper has a crossword puzzle.

(f) Learn stems, prefixes, and suffixes. It is very important that you know these.

BASIC LETTER COMBINATIONS

One of the most efficient ways in which you can build up your vocabulary is by a systematic study of the basic word and letter combinations which make up the greater part of the English language.

Etymology is the science of the formation of words, and this somewhat frightening-sounding science can be of great help to you in learning new words and identifying words which may be unfamiliar to you. You will also find that the progress you make in studying the following pages will help to improve your spelling.

A great many of the words which we use every day have come into our language from the Latin and Greek. In the process of being absorbed into English, they appear as parts of words, many of which are related in meaning to each other.

For your convenience, this material is presented in easy-to-study form. Latin and Greek syllables and letter-combinations have been categorized into three groups:

1. *Prefixes:* letter combinations which appear at the beginning of a word.

2. *Suffixes:* letter combinations which appear at the end of a word.

3. *Roots or stems:* which carry the basic meaning and are combined with each other and with prefixes and suffixes to create other words with related meanings.

With the prefixes and suffixes, which you should study first, we have given examples of word formation with meanings, and additional examples. If you find any unfamiliar words among the samples, consult your dictionary to look up their meanings.

The list of roots or stems is accompanied by words in which the letter combinations appear. Here again, use the dictionary to look up any words which are not clear in your mind.

Remember that this section is not meant for easy reading. It is a guide to a program of study that will prove invaluable if you do your part. Do not try to swallow too much at one time. If you can put in a half-hour every day, your study will yield better results.

After you have given this section your full attention, then try the Sample Vocabulary Questions. You will be surprised how many new words are at your command.

ETYMOLOGY - A KEY TO WORD RECOGNITION

PREFIXES

PREFIX	MEANING	EXAMPLE
ab, a	away from	absent, amoral
ad, ac, ag, at	to	advent, accrue, aggressive, attract
an	without	anarchy
ante	before	antedate
anti	against	antipathy
bene	well	beneficent
bi	two	bicameral
circum	around	circumspect
com, con, col	together	commit confound, collate
contra	against	contraband
de	from, down	descend
dis, di	apart	distract, divert
ex, e	out	exit, emit
extra	beyond	extracurricular
in, im, il, ir, un	not	inept, impossible, illicit
inter	between	interpose
intra, intro, in	within	intramural, introspective

PREFIX	MEANING	EXAMPLE
mal	bad	malcontent
mis	wrong	misnomer
non	not	nonentity
ob	against	obstacle
per	through	permeate
peri	around	periscope
poly	many	polytheism
post	after	post-mortem
pre	before	premonition
pro	forward	propose
re	again	review
se	apart	seduce
semi	half	semicircle
sub	under	subvert
super	above	superimpose
sui	self	suicide
trans	across	transpose
vice	instead of	vice-president

SUFFIXES

SUFFIX	MEANING	EXAMPLE
able, ible	capable of being	capable, reversible
age	state of	storage
ance	relating to	reliance
ary	relating to	dictionary
ate	act	confiscate
ation	action	radiation
cy	quality	democracy

SUFFIX	MEANING	EXAMPLE
ence	relating to	confidence
er	one who	adviser
ic	pertaining to	democratic
ious	full of	rebellious
ize	to make like	harmonize
ment	result	filament
ty	condition	sanity

LATIN AND GREEK STEMS

STEM	MEANING	EXAMPLE
ag, ac	do	agenda, action
agr	farm	agriculture
aqua	water	aqueous
cad, cas	fall	cadence, casual
cant	sing	chant
cap, cep	take	captive, accept
capit	head	capital
cede	go	precede
celer	speed	celerity
cide, cis	kill, cut	suicide, incision
clud, clus	close	include, inclusion
cur, curs	run	incur, incursion
dict	say	diction
duct	lead	induce
fact, fect	make	factory, perfect
fer, lat	carry	refer, dilate
fring, fract	break	infringe, fracture
frater	brother	fraternal
fund, fus	pour	refund, confuse
greg	group	gregarious
gress, grad	move forward	progress, degrade
homo	man	homicide
ject	throw	reject
jud	right	judicial
junct	join	conjunction
lect, leg	read, choose	collect, legend
loq, loc	speak	loquacious, interlocutory
manu	hand	manuscript
mand	order	remand
mar	sea	maritime
mater	mother	maternal
med	middle	intermediary
min	lessen	diminution
mis, mit	send	remit, dismiss
mort	death	mortician
mote, mov	move	remote, remove
naut	sailor	astronaut
nom	name	nomenclature
pater	father	paternity
ped, pod	foot	pedal, podiatrist
pend	hang	depend
plic	fold	implicate
port	carry	portable
pos, pon	put	depose, component
reg, rect	rule	regicide, direct
rupt	break	eruption
scrib, scrip	write	inscribe, conscription
anthrop	man	anthropology

STEM	MEANING	EXAMPLE
arch	chief, rule	archbishop
astron	star	astronomy
auto	self	automatic
biblio	book	bibliophile
bio	life	biology
chrome	color	chromosome
chron	time	chronology
cosmo	world	cosmic
crat	rule	autocrat
dent, dont	tooth	dental, indent
eu	well, happy	eugenics
gamos	marriage	monogamous
ge	earth	geology
gen	origin, people	progenitor
graph	write	graphic
gyn	women	gynecologist
homo	same	homogeneous
hydr	water	dehydrate
logy	study of	psychology
meter	measure	thermometer
micro	small	microscope
mono	one	monotony
onomy	science	astronomy
onym	name	synonym
pathos	feeling	pathology
philo	love	philosophy
phobia	fear	hydrophobia
phone	sound	telephone
pseudo	false	pseudonym
psych	mind	psychic
scope	see	telescope
soph	wisdom	sophomore
tele	far off	telepathic
theo	god	theology
thermo	heat	thermostat
sec	cut	dissect
sed	remain	sedentary
sequ	follow	sequential
spect	look	inspect
spir	breathe	conspire
stat	stand	status
tact, tang	touch	tactile, tangible
ten	hold	retentive
term	end	terminal
vent	come	prevent
vict	conquer	evict
vid, vis	see	video, revise
voc	call	convocation
volv	roll	devolve

VOCABULARY TEST QUESTIONS FOR PRACTICE

The following questions have been selected to give you as broad a sampling as possible of words which have appeared on previous tests. The ease or difficulty with which you answer these questions will indicate whether or not your word power is adequate for the test you are about to take.

YOU will find these questions divided into separate sub-tests of ten questions each. This division has been made for two reasons: (1) the average number of vocabulary questions on tests of this grade is ten: (2) by doing each sub-test separately, you are enabled to see your progress as you proceed from one test to the next.

You will note that following each test, space is provided for recording the time you took to do the test, and for recording the number of correct answers. By comparing the second test with the first, the third with the second, etc., you will be able to see whether or not you are improving your word power as you study. Successful study should result in speedier time on each successive test, accompanied by increasing accuracy. If this is not the case when you have completed all the tests, then you had better begin again until the desired results are obtained.

These tests, as you will see, take several forms. In general, they are multiple-choice type asking for a word's definition or its opposite. Some questions ask whether a word is used correctly or not, and require you to answer "True" if it is, and "False" if it isn't. You will find, however, that a majority of questions are of the former type. The number of questions in any one form reflects its frequency on actual exams.

Use a watch or clock to keep an accurate record of the time consumed by each test. Read the instructions which precede each test carefully. You may check your accuracy by referring to the answers at the end of the chapter. Do not refer to these answers until you have completed each test.

Sample Test Question Analyzed

The questions may appear in one of several forms, but one of the most numerous is that of choosing a word which is most nearly the same in meaning as the question word. The example below has been chosen because it will help to illustrate the way in which vocabulary questions are answered.

Blacken the appropriate space for the letter preceding the word which is most nearly the same in meaning as the *italicized* word in the sentence.

<u>Sample Question.</u>   One who is *garrulous* in his relations with others is, most nearly:

(A) complaining
(B) careless
(C) overly talkative
(D) defensive
(E) dishonest.

Notice that the instructions ask for the selection of the choice which is *most nearly* the same in meaning as the italicized word.

First, examine the italicized word. If you know its meaning, your task is fairly simple. But suppose you do not know what *garrulous* means. Perhaps we can eliminate some of the choices by analyzing them.

(A) Complaining: Does *complaining* have anything to do with *garrulous*? It might. However, a synonym for *complaining* is querulous. In this case, it is best to avoid *complaining* as a possibility, since it is probably there to confuse you.

(B) Careless: Most people know what careless means. Here again is a word which only sounds like the question word. You would not use *garrulous* to describe a neglectful person.

(C) Overly Talkative: There is nothing to indicate that this phrase is not a synonym for *garrulous*. Do not eliminate it as a possibility.

(D) Defensive: You can think of synonyms for this one, like protective, safe-guarding, and maybe even fortress and garrison may come to mind. In general, any word that sounds like the question word should be avoided. You would do well to eliminate *defensive* as a possibility.

(E) Dishonest: There is not much to indicate that this is not a synonym for *garrulous*, and none of the synonyms for *dishonest* sounds like the question word. It cannot be eliminated entirely.

The choice is now between (C) and (E); *overly talkative* and *dishonest*. If you have no idea at all regarding the meaning of *garrulous*, then you must guess. Since three of the choices have already been eliminated, you have a much better chance to guess correctly.

Garrulous: The dictionary defines *garrulous* as: "given to continual and tedious talking," "habitually loquacious," "chattering," "verbose." Therefore, (C) "overly talkative" is the correct answer.

Directions for answering questions. For each question, decide which is the best answer of the choices given. Note the capital letter preceding the best answer. On machine-scored examinations you will be given an answer sheet and told to blacken the proper space on that answer sheet. Near the end of this book we have provided facsimiles of such answer sheets. Tear one out, and mark your answers on it, just as you would do on an actual exam. In most machine-scored examinations, competitors are instructed to "place no marks whatsoever on the test booklet." In other examinations, competitors are instructed to mark the answers in the booklet, but they should be careful that no other marks interfere with the legibility of the answers. It is always best not to mark the booklet unless you are sure that it is permitted. It is most important that you learn to mark the answer sheet clearly.

Test No. 1

Directions: Questions 1 thru 10 consist of sentences which contain an *italicized* word. If the italicized word is used correctly in the sentence, encircle the "T" (True) to the right of the question. If the italicized word is used incorrectly, encircle the "F" (False) to the right of the question.

1. A *competent* employee is one who is slow and inefficient. T F
2. A person who commits *perjury* does not tell the truth. T F
3. The *prosecutor* in a criminal case is the lawyer who presents evidence against the defendant. T F
4. A *destitute* person has a large amount of money. T F
5. A person with a *florid* complexion has a pale face. T F
6. A noise that is *audible* is capable of being heard. T F
7. Anyone who is *agile* is quick and nimble. T F
8. An employee who gives information in a *curt* manner is sympathetic and courteous. T F
9. A person who is *prudent* is careless in his attention to duty. T F
10. If a person pays an *exorbitant* amount of money for an article, he is paying a fair price. T F

Time:_____ No. Correct:_____

Test No. 2

Directions: (These directions also apply to Test No. 3, which follows.) Below is a set of words containing ten words numbered 1 to 10, and twenty other words divided into five groups—Group A, Group B, Group C, Group D and Group E. For each of the ten numbered words, select the word in one of the five groups which is most nearly the same in meaning. The letter of that group is the answer for that item.

1. fiscal
2. deletion
3. equivocal
4. corroboration
5. tortuous
6. predilection
7. sallow
8. virtuosity
9. scion
10. tenuous

Group A
indication   ambiguous   excruciating   thin

Group B
confirmation   financial   phobia   erasure

Group C
fiduciary   similar   yellowish   skill

Group D
theft   winding   receive   procrastination

Group E
franchise   heir   hardy   preference

Time:_____ No. Correct:_____

Test No. 3

Directions: See Test No. 2.

1. prophylactic
2. palliation
3. redolent
4. indictment
5. misfeasance
6. holograph
7. ancillary
8. hectic
9. obsolescence
10. holocaust

Group A
ruddy   retribution   mitigation   decadence

Group B
dental   fragrant   accusation   symptom

Group C
preventive   destruction   aggravation   testimony

Group D
intimidation   subsidiary   feverish   trespass

Group E
consecration   excited   corpulence   handwritten

Time:_____   No. Correct:_____

Test No. 4

Directions: Below are 10 groups of paired words, numbered 1 thru 10. For each group, select the one pair of words lettered A, B, C, D, or E which is the *opposite* in meaning.

1. (A) wax-wane   (B) comfort-console   (C) exalt-rejoice   (D) enraged-angry   (E) tiny-minute.

2. (A) becoming-fit   (B) commodious-roomy   (C) lack-plenty   (D) beg-supplicate   (E) compromise-conciliation.

3. (A) certify-attest   (B) forbid-sanction   (C) kingly-regal   (D) quell-subdue   (E) quick-hasty.

4. (A) concede-assent   (B) condemn-spurn   (C) convey-carry   (D) lag-hasten   (E) contrast-differentiate.

5. (A) defer-postpone   (B) noble-base   (C) exigency-emergency   (D) fiery-ardent   (E) fault-flaw.

6. (A) formidable-invincible   (B) futile-unavailing   (C) genuine-real   (D) halt-stop   (E) recant-admit.

7. (A) alleviate-moderate   (B) apathy-unconcern   (C) turbid-clear   (D) arraign-charge   (E) austere-severe.

8. (A) robust-unhealthy   (B) impediment-obstruct   (C) insidious-cunning   (D) novice-beginner   (E) obscure-hidden.

9. (A) obstinate-stubborn   (B) pique-fret   (C) raze-destroy   (D) relinquish-renounce   (E) sinister-good.

10. (A) ruthless-merciless   (B) support-sustain   (C) valid-sound   (D) timid-daring   (E) zeal-ardor.

Time:_____   No. Correct:_____

Test No. 5

Directions: Below are 10 groups of paired words, numbered 1 thru 10. For each group, select the one pair of words lettered A, B, C, D, or E which is the *same* in meaning.

1. (A) transitory-permanent   (B) prohibit-allow   (C) beautiful-ugly   (D) broken-disunited   (E) ferocious-mild.

2. (A) elucidate-clarify   (B) recent-ancient   (C) enthusiasm-apathy   (D) equivocal-indubitable   (E) evade-acknowledge.

3. (A) extricate-imprison   (B) concur-endorse   (C) intimidate-assure   (D) lucid-obscure   (E) molest-comfort.

4. (A) abandon-hold   (B) awkward-skillful   (C) consistent-varying   (D) constrain-beseech   (E) tedious-tiresome.

5. (A) deficient-ample   (B) waste-conserve   (C) compromise-quarrel   (D) sanguine-optimistic   (E) desist-persevere.

6. (A) monotony-variety   (B) remote-near   (C) propitiate-appease   (D) many-few   (E) veracity-deception.

7. (A) fraud-honesty   (B) important-significant   (C) mollify-vex   (D) abate-maintain   (E) authorize-forbid.

8. (A) eradicate-destroy   (B) barbarous-humane   (C) compulsion-freedom   (D) concur-differ   (E) incite-quell.

9. (A) morose-cheerful   (B) munificent-penurious   (C) censorious-fault-finding   (D) predominate-subordinate   (E) extricate-bind.

10. (A) gratify-displease   (B) grudge-good will   (C) interpose-withdraw   (D) irresponsible-accountable   (E) augment-increase.

Time:_____   No. Correct:_____

Test No. 6

Directions: Following are ten pairs of words numbered 1 thru 10. A pair of words may be the same or nearly the same in meaning, or may be opposite or nearly opposite in meaning, or may be related to each other in neither way. Encircle "S" to the right of the question if a pair of words are the same or nearly the same; "O" if they are opposite or nearly opposite in meaning; and "N" if they are related to each other in neither way.

1. pertinent-irrelevant   S O N
2. condone-forgive   S O N
3. obdurate-yielding   S O N
4. allocation-assertion   S O N
5. summarize-recapitulate   S O N
6. intrinsic-real   S O N
7. innocuous-harmful   S O N
8. exigency-emergency   S O N
9. tantamount-urgent   S O N
10. temerity-rashness   S O N

Time:_____ No. Correct:_____

Test No. 7

Directions: Below are ten groups of words numbered 1 thru 10. For each group, select the word lettered A, B, C, or D that most nearly expresses the meaning of the word in capital letters.

1. EXPEDITE
   (A) obstruct
   (B) advise
   (C) accelerate
   (D) demolish.

2. COORDINATOR
   (A) enumerator
   (B) organizer
   (C) spokesman
   (D) advertiser.

3. REPRISAL
   (A) retaliation
   (B) advantage
   (C) warning
   (D) denial.

4. CAPITULATE
   (A) repeat
   (B) surrender
   (C) finance
   (D) retreat.

5. EXTENUATING
   (A) excusing
   (B) opposing
   (C) incriminating
   (D) distressing.

6. COLLUSION
   (A) decision
   (B) insinuation
   (C) connivance
   (D) conflict.

7. SUBVERSIVE
   (A) secret
   (B) foreign
   (C) evasive
   (D) destructive.

8. VACILLATING
   (A) changeable
   (B) decisive
   (C) equalizing
   (D) progressing.

9. ARBITRARY
   (A) responsible
   (B) despotic
   (C) conciliatory
   (D) argumentative.

10. AUSPICIOUS
    (A) questionable
    (B) well-known
    (C) free;
    (D) favorable.

Time:_____ No. Correct:_____

Test No. 8

Directions: For each question 1 thru 10, choose the letter which precedes the word or words which best complete the sentence.

1. An amendment is a
   (A) civic center
   (B) charter
   (C) penalty
   (D) change.

2. A quorum is a
   (A) minority
   (B) committee
   (C) majority
   (D) bicameral system.

3. Clearance refers to a
   (A) weight
   (B) hoistway
   (C) distance
   (D) cleaning process.

4. Pasteurized milk is milk that has been
   (A) watered
   (B) condemned
   (C) embargoed
   (D) purified.

5. Antitoxin is used in cases of
   (A) corrupt governmental officials
   (B) sanitary inspection
   (C) disease
   (D) elevator construction.

100 / Practice For Air Force Placement Tests

6. Libel refers to the
    (A) process of incurring financial liability
    (B) publication of a false statement which injures others
    (C) deportation of aliens
    (D) necessity for compulsory schooling.

7. Naturalization refers to the process of
    (A) becoming a civil service employee
    (B) being summoned to court
    (C) becoming a citizen
    (D) pledging allegiance to the American flag.

8. To comply with a rule means to
    (A) abide by a rule
    (B) abrogate a rule
    (C) dislike a rule
    (D) ignore a rule.

9. A budget is a
    (A) financial statement
    (B) method for training operators
    (C) device for insuring courtesy
    (D) means for selecting judges

10. A fulcrum is part of a
    (A) typewriter
    (B) lever
    (C) radio
    (D) lamp.

Time: _____ No. Correct: _____

Test No. 9

Directions: For each question 1 thru 5, select the word lettered A, B, C, or D which is most nearly *alike* in meaning to the word italicized in the sentence. For each question 6 thru 10, select the word lettered A, B, C, or D which is most nearly *opposite* in meaning to the word italicized in the sentence.

1. The attitude of the supervisor toward his staff was very *lenient*.
    (A) severe   (B) harsh
    (C) exacting   (D) easy-going.

2. Use of the premises for a public meeting was *prohibited*.
    (A) urged   (B) ordered
    (C) forbidden   (D) promised.

3. He *resolved* to act at once.
    (A) offered   (B) refused
    (C) hesitated   (D) determined.

4. He *predicted* the accident.
    (A) escaped   (B) described
    (C) foresaw   (D) feared.

5. Do not *abandon* me.
    (A) persecute   (B) desert
    (C) mock   (D) restrain.

6. The administration was *rigorous* in the enforcement of departmental rules and regulations.
    (A) determined   (B) resolute
    (C) harsh   (D) lenient.

7. The employee was asked to present the *transscripts* of the cases immediately.
    (A) originals   (B) copies
    (C) facts   (D) carbons.

8. The evidences of forgery were *apparent*.
    (A) discernible   (B) dubious
    (C) presumable   (D) unequivocal.

9. The employer was *friendly* to his employees.
    (A) amicable   (B) tender
    (C) accessible   (D) inimical.

10. He was *acquitted* of his role in the disturbance.
    (A) absolved   (B) vindicated
    (C) convicted   (D) exonerated.

Time: _____ No. Correct: _____

Test No. 10

Directions: (These directions also apply to Tests Nos. 11 through 20, which follow.) For each question 1 thru 10, select the appropriate letter preceding the word which is most nearly the *same* in meaning as the italicized word in each sentence.

1. The person who is *diplomatic* in his relations with others is, most nearly
    (A) well dressed   (B) very tactful
    (C) somewhat domineering (D) deceitful and tricky
    (E) verbose.

2. Action at this time would be *inopportune*. The word "inopportune" means most nearly
    (A) untimely   (B) premeditated
    (C) sporadic   (D) commendable
    (E) fortunate.

3. The word *appraise* means most nearly
    (A) consult   (B) attribute
    (C) manage   (D) honor
    (E) judge.

4. The word *cognizant* means most nearly
    (A) rare   (B) reluctant
    (C) aware   (D) haphazard
    (E) correlated.

5. *Probity* is an important requirement of many positions. The word "probity" means most nearly
   (A) analytical ability (B) vision
   (C) tried integrity (D) clear insight
   (E) perseverence.

6. The word *denote* means most nearly
   (A) encumber (B) evade
   (C) furnish (D) indicate
   (E) reduce in rank.

7. The competent employee should know that a method of procedure which is *expedient* is most nearly
   (A) unchangeable (B) based upon a false assumption
   (C) unduly harmful (D) difficult to work out
   (E) suitable to the end in view.

8. An incentive which is *potent* is most nearly
   (A) impossible (B) highly effective
   (C) not immediately (D) a remote possibility practicable
   (E) universally applicable.

9. An employer who is *judicious* is most nearly
   (A) domineering (B) argumentative
   (C) sincere (D) arbitrary
   (E) wise.

10. He presented a *controversial* plan. The word "controversial" means most nearly
    (A) subject to debate (B) unreasonable
    (C) complex (D) comparable
    (E) well formulated.

Time:_____ No. Correct:_____

Test No. 11

Directions: See Test No. 10.

1. A clerk who is asked to prepare an *abstract* should prepare
   (A) a verbatim record (B) an original essay
   (C) a translation which is non-technical
   (D) a summary of essential points
   (E) an extensive elaboration.

2. To say that the task assigned to a person is *exacting* means most nearly that the task is
   (A) brief (B) responsible
   (C) equivocal (D) arithmetical in nature
   (E) severe in its demands.

3. "Contributions to the employee welfare fund shall be prorated." The word *prorated* means most nearly
   (A) on a voluntary basis (B) divided
   (C) compulsory for all proportionately
   (D) regular in payment (E) audited.

4. "Complete cooperation by members of the staff is postulated." The word *postulated* means most nearly
   (A) encouraged (B) endangered
   (C) achieved (D) obviated
   (E) assumed.

5. To say that a person is *dynamic* means most nearly that he is
   (A) careful (B) stubborn
   (C) energetic (D) insubordinate
   (E) dutiful.

6. To say that someone *misconstrued* directions means most nearly that he has
   (A) followed directions implicitly
   (B) displayed commendable ingenuity
   (C) acted in a supervisory capacity
   (D) interpreted his assignment erroneously
   (E) listened carefully to his instructions.

7. "The supervisor advised his staff that the benefits of the proposed plan are likely to be transitory." The word *transitory* means most nearly
   (A) significant (B) temporary
   (C) obvious (D) cumulative
   (E) determinate.

8. An action which is *inexplicable* is
   (A) not explicit (B) incapable of being explained
   (C) ineffectual (D) inexpedient
   (E) inappropriate to the end in view.

9. To say that the circumstances surrounding an act were *extenuating* means most nearly that the circumstances
   (A) were stimulating (B) tended to be sustained
   (C) existed for a considerable period before the act
   (D) tended to excuse the act
   (E) were variable and inconsistent.

10. "In presenting his argument, the speaker should be careful lest his argument be specious." The word *specious* mean most nearly
    (A) showy (B) largely drawn
    (C) too detailed (D) inconsiderate
    (E) based on false premises.

Time:_____ No. Correct:_____

Test No. 12

Directions: See Test No. 10.

1. "He sent the irate employee to the personnel manager." The word *irate* means most nearly
   - (A) irresponsible
   - (B) untidy
   - (C) insubordinate
   - (D) angry.

2. An *ambiguous* statement is one which is
   - (A) forceful and convincing
   - (B) capable of being understood in more than one sense
   - (C) based upon good judgment and sound reasoning processes
   - (D) uninteresting and too lengthy.

3. To *extol* means most nearly to
   - (A) summon
   - (B) praise
   - (C) reject
   - (D) withdraw.

4. The word *proximity* means most nearly
   - (A) similarity
   - (B) exactness
   - (C) harmony
   - (D) nearness.

5. "His friends had a detrimental influence on him." The word *detrimental* means most nearly
   - (A) favorable
   - (B) lasting
   - (C) harmful
   - (D) short-lived.

6. "The chief inspector relied upon the veracity of his inspectors." The word *veracity* means most nearly
   - (A) speed
   - (B) assistance
   - (C) shrewdness
   - (D) truthfulness.

7. "There was much diversity in the suggestions submitted." The word *diversity* means most nearly
   - (A) similarity
   - (B) value
   - (C) triviality
   - (D) variety.

8. "The survey was concerned with the problem of indigence." The word *indigence* means most nearly
   - (A) poverty
   - (B) corruption
   - (C) intolerance
   - (D) morale.

9. "The investigator considered this evidence to be extraneous." The word *extraneous* means most nearly
   - (A) significant
   - (B) pertinent but unobtainable
   - (C) not essential
   - (D) inadequate.

10. "He was surprised at the temerity of the new employee." The word *temerity* means most nearly
    - (A) shyness
    - (B) enthusiasm
    - (C) rashness
    - (D) self-control.

Test No. 13

Directions: See Test No. 10.

1. The change in procedure *stimulated* the men
   - (A) rewarded
   - (B) antagonized
   - (C) gave an incentive to
   - (D) restricted the activities of
   - (E) lowered the efficiency of.

2. Courage is a trait difficult to *instill*. The word "instill" means most nearly
   - (A) measure exactly
   - (B) impart gradually
   - (C) predict accurately
   - (D) restrain effectively
   - (E) discuss meaningfully.

3. The vehicle was left *intact*. The word "intact" means most nearly
   - (A) a total loss
   - (B) unattended
   - (C) where it could be noticed
   - (D) undamaged
   - (E) repaired.

4. The witness was *recalcitrant*. The word "recalcitrant" means most nearly
   - (A) cooperative
   - (B) delirious
   - (C) highly excited
   - (D) accustomed to hard work
   - (E) stubbornly resistant.

5. A *conscientious* person is one who
   - (A) feels obligated to do what he believes right
   - (B) rarely makes errors
   - (C) frequently makes suggestions for procedural improvements
   - (D) has good personal relationships with others
   - (E) is consistent in his behavior.

6. It was reported that *noxious* fumes were escaping. The word "noxious" means most nearly
   - (A) concentrated
   - (B) gaseous
   - (C) greenish colored
   - (D) heavy
   - (E) harmful.

7. A person with a *sallow* complexion was seen near the scene. The word "sallow" means most nearly
   - (A) ruddy
   - (B) dark
   - (C) pale and yellowish
   - (D) highly freckled
   - (E) red and florid.

8. The word *cogent* means most nearly
   - (A) confused
   - (B) opposite
   - (C) unintentional
   - (D) convincing
   - (E) irrelevant.

9. The word *divergent* means most nearly
   - (A) simultaneous
   - (B) differing
   - (C) approaching
   - (D) parallel
   - (E) twisting.

10. The word *ostensibly* means most nearly
    - (A) undoubtedly
    - (B) infrequently
    - (C) powerfully
    - (D) apparently
    - (E) slowly.

Test No. 14

Directions: See Test No. 10.

1. To say that the work is *tedious* means, most nearly, that it is
   - (A) technical
   - (B) interesting
   - (C) tiresome
   - (D) confidential.

2. A *vivacious* person is one who is
   - (A) kind
   - (B) talkative
   - (C) lively
   - (D) well-dressed.

3. An *innocuous* statement is one which is
   - (A) forceful
   - (B) harmless
   - (C) offensive
   - (D) brief.

4. To say that the order was *rescinded* means, most nearly, that the order was
   - (A) revised
   - (B) canceled
   - (C) misinterpreted
   - (D) confirmed.

5. To say that the administrator *amplified* his remarks means, most nearly, that the remarks were
   - (A) shouted
   - (B) expanded
   - (C) carefully analyzed
   - (D) summarized briefly.

6. "Peremptory commands will be resented in any organization." The word *peremptory* means most nearly
   - (A) unexpected
   - (B) unreasonable
   - (C) military
   - (D) dictatorial.

7. A person should know the word *sporadic* means, most nearly
   - (A) occurring regularly
   - (B) sudden
   - (C) scattered
   - (D) disturbing.

8. To *oscillate* means, most nearly, to
   - (A) lubricate
   - (B) waver
   - (C) decide
   - (D) investigate.

9. A *homogeneous* group of persons is characterized by its
   - (A) similarity
   - (B) teamwork
   - (C) discontent
   - (D) differences.

10. A *vindictive* person is one who is
    - (A) prejudiced
    - (B) unpopular
    - (C) petty
    - (D) revengeful.

Time:_____ No. Correct:_____

Test No. 15

Directions: See Test No. 10.

1. "The visitor was *morose*." The word "morose" as used in this sentence means most nearly
   - (A) curious
   - (B) gloomy
   - (C) impatient
   - (D) timid.

2. "He was unwilling to *impede* the work of his unit." The word "impede" as used in this sentence means most nearly
   - (A) carry out
   - (B) criticize
   - (C) praise
   - (D) hinder.

3. "The *remuneration* was unsatisfactory." The word "remuneration" as used in this sentence means most nearly
   - (A) payment
   - (B) summary
   - (C) explanation
   - (D) estimate.

4. A *recurring* problem is one that
   - (A) replaces a problem that existed previously
   - (B) is unexpected
   - (C) has long been overlooked
   - (D) comes up from time to time.

5. "His subordinates were aware of this *magnanimous* act." The word "magnanimous" as used in this sentence means most nearly
   - (A) insolent
   - (B) shrewd
   - (C) unselfish
   - (D) threatening.

6. "The new employee is a *zealous* worker." The word "zealous" as used in this sentence means most nearly
   - (A) awkward
   - (B) untrustworthy
   - (C) enthusiastic
   - (D) skillful.

7. To *impair* means most nearly to
   - (A) weaken
   - (B) conceal
   - (C) improve
   - (D) expose.

8. "The unit head was in a *quandary*." The word "quandary" as used in this sentence means nearly
   - (A) violent dispute
   - (B) puzzling predicament
   - (C) angry mood
   - (D) strong position.

9. "His actions were *prudent*." The word "prudent" as used in this sentence means most nearly
   - (A) wise
   - (B) biased
   - (C) final
   - (D) limited.

10. "His report contained many *irrelevant* statements." The word "irrelevant" as used in this sentence means most nearly
    - (A) unproven
    - (B) not pertinent
    - (C) hard to understand
    - (D) insincere.

Time:_____ No. Correct:_____

Test No. 16

Directions: See Test No. 10.

1. "The supply of pamphlets has been *depleted*." The word "depleted" means most nearly
   - (A) exhausted
   - (B) delivered
   - (C) included
   - (D) rejected.

2. "They are discussing *trivial* matters." The word "trivial" means most nearly
   - (A) of a personal nature
   - (B) very significant
   - (C) interesting and educational
   - (D) of little importance.

3. To say that the information obtained was *meager* means most nearly that it was
   - (A) well received
   - (B) valuable
   - (C) long overdue
   - (D) scanty.

4. "Mr. Dorman asked for a *candid* opinion." The word "candid" means most nearly
   - (A) biased
   - (B) frank
   - (C) written
   - (D) confidential.

5. "He wishes to *terminate* the conversation." The word "terminate" means most nearly
   - (A) end
   - (B) postpone
   - (C) ignore
   - (D) continue.

6. A *futile* effort is one which is
   - (A) strong
   - (B) clumsy
   - (C) useless
   - (D) sincere.

7. "Miss Fulton showed her *reluctance* to serve as relief operator." The word "reluctance" means most nearly
   - (A) eagerness
   - (B) unreliability
   - (C) ability
   - (D) unwillingness.

8. "This equipment is *obsolete*." The word "obsolete" means most nearly
   - (A) complicated
   - (B) out of date
   - (C) highly suitable
   - (D) reliable.

9. "He had a *prior* appointment with the manager." The word "prior" means most nearly
   - (A) private
   - (B) later
   - (C) definite
   - (D) previous.

10. "The operator was commended for her *dexterity*. The word "dexterity" means most nearly
    - (A) skill
    - (B) courtesy
    - (C) punctuality
    - (D) cooperation.

Time: _____ No. Correct: _____

Test No. 17

Directions: See Test No. 10.

1. Employees are directed to exercise *vigilance*. The word "vigilance" means most nearly
   - (A) strict discipline
   - (B) routine precaution
   - (C) systematic practice
   - (D) alert watchfulness.

2. To say that a man's knowledge of the law is *extensive* means most nearly that his knowledge is
   - (A) factual
   - (B) sufficient
   - (C) broad
   - (D) hypothetical.

3. An action which is *commendable* is most nearly
   - (A) premeditated
   - (B) praiseworthy
   - (C) broad
   - (D) hypothetical.

4. A regulation which is *rigid* is most nearly
   - (A) precisely stated
   - (B) strictly enforced
   - (C) clearly expressed
   - (D) rarely applied.

5. The reasons for the man's behavior were *obscure*. The word "obscure" means
   - (A) vague
   - (B) rational
   - (C) debatable
   - (D) foolish.

6. The driver *conceded* that he was at fault. The word "conceded" means most nearly
   - (A) denied
   - (B) explained
   - (C) implied
   - (D) admitted.

7. A recommendation was made to *apportion* the work. The word "apportion" means most nearly to
   - (A) divide in some manner
   - (B) increase in significance
   - (C) complete quickly
   - (D) postpone for a given period.

8. The injured man's story was *incoherent*. The word "incoherent" means most nearly
   - (A) obviously untrue
   - (B) not very long
   - (C) not logically connected
   - (D) inconsistent with the known facts.

9. *Indolence* is a habit which cannot be excused. The word "indolence" means most nearly
   - (A) flagrant carelessness
   - (B) unnecessary caution
   - (C) constant fault-finding
   - (D) habitual idleness.

10. A person who is *slovenly* is, most nearly
    - (A) neat and well dressed
    - (B) eager and ambitious
    - (C) lazy and slipshod
    - (D) aggressive and resentful.

Time: _____ No. Correct: _____

Test No. 18

Directions: See Test No. 10.

1. "He was asked to *pacify* the visitor." The word "pacify" means most nearly
   - (A) escort
   - (B) interview
   - (C) calm
   - (D) detain.

2. To say that a certain document is *authentic* means most nearly that it is
   - (A) fictitious
   - (B) well written
   - (C) priceless
   - (D) genuine.

3. A person who is *meticulous* in performing his work is one who is
   - (A) alert to improved techniques
   - (B) likely to be erratic and unpredictable
   - (C) excessively careful of small details
   - (D) slovenly and inaccurate.

4. A pamphlet which is *replete* with charts and graphs is one which
   - (A) deals with the construction of charts and graphs
   - (B) is full of charts and graphs
   - (C) substitutes illustrations for tabulated data
   - (D) is in need of charts and graphs.

5. "His former secretary was *diligent* in carrying out her duties." The word "diligent" means most nearly
   - (A) incompetent
   - (B) cheerful
   - (C) careless
   - (D) industrious.

6. To *supersede* means most nearly to
   - (A) take the place of
   - (B) come before
   - (C) be in charge of
   - (D) divide into equal parts.

7. "He was given considerable *latitude* in setting up the procedures for the new unit." The word "latitude" as used in this sentence means most nearly
   - (A) advice and encouragement
   - (B) assistance and cooperation
   - (C) cause for annoyance
   - (D) freedom from restriction.

8. "He said that this was an *expedient* method of performing the job." The word "expedient" as used in this sentence means most nearly
   - (A) inconvenient and ineffective
   - (B) effective but expensive
   - (C) practical and efficient
   - (D) convenient but time consuming.

9. "The men refused to give up their *prerogatives* without a struggle." The word "prerogatives" as used in this sentence means most nearly
   - (A) ideals
   - (B) demands
   - (C) rights
   - (D) advantages.

10. A *prolific* writer is one who is
    - (A) productive
    - (B) popular
    - (C) richly talented
    - (D) forward-looking.

Time: _____ No. Correct: _____

Test No. 19

Directions: See Test No. 10.

1. "He was not present at the *inception* of the program." The word "inception" as used in this sentence means most nearly
   - (A) beginning
   - (B) discussion
   - (C) conclusion
   - (D) rejection
   - (E) finale.

2. The word *solicitude* means most nearly
   - (A) request
   - (B) isolation
   - (C) seriousness
   - (D) concern
   - (E) recluse.

3. A man who performs his work with *discernment* is
   - (A) deliberative
   - (B) constructive
   - (C) unruffled
   - (D) discriminating
   - (E) capricious.

4. Everyone should know that the word *increment* means most nearly
   - (A) improvise
   - (B) account
   - (C) predict
   - (D) specify
   - (E) increase.

5. "The precise method to be employed is immaterial." The word *immaterial* means most nearly
   - (A) unclear
   - (B) unpredictable
   - (C) unimportant
   - (D) not debatable
   - (E) unknown.

6. He felt as though he were *groping* in the dark.
   (A) lying (B) feeling his way
   (C) running (D) screaming
   (E) digging a tunnel
7. "The supervisor *admonished* the clerk for his tardiness." The word "admonished" means most nearly
   (A) reproved (B) excused
   (C) transferred (D) punished
   (E) dismissed.
8. A *homogeneous* group of persons is characterized by its
   (A) similarity (B) teamwork
   (C) discontent (D) differences
   (E) harmony.
9. To *vacillate* means, most nearly, to
   (A) lubricate (B) waver
   (C) decide (D) investigate
   (E) implicate.
10. A clerk should know that the word *sporadic* means, most nearly
    (A) occurring regularly (B) sudden
    (C) scattered (D) disturbing
    (E) invariable.

Time: _____ No. Correct: _____

Test No. 20

Directions: See Test No. 10.

1. I could plainly hear the *clamor* of the crowd.
   (A) murmur (B) noise
   (C) questions (D) singing
   (E) arrival
2. The wind blew *incessantly* across the island.
   (A) occasionally (B) disagreeably
   (C) constantly (D) icily
   (E) noisily
3. They were surprised by the *solidity* of the ice.
   (A) unevenness (B) smoothness
   (C) firmness (D) clearness
   (E) color
4. The soldiers *repelled* the attackers.
   (A) fled from (B) surrendered to
   (C) forced back (D) caught sight of
   (E) joined with
5. The *solitude* of the sod hut depressed him.
   (A) loneliness (B) coldness
   (C) crudeness (D) poverty
   (E) smallness
6. He *declined* our offer of help.
   (A) suspected (B) misunderstood
   (C) consented to (D) refused
   (E) was annoyed by
7. He tried hard to *avert* the accident.
   (A) describe (B) prevent
   (C) forget (D) make light of
   (E) pay for
8. They discovered that the doctor was *an impostor*.
   (A) a specialist (B) a foreigner
   (C) an inventor (D) a pretender
   (E) a magician
9. Many *calamities* can be traced to simple causes.
   (A) joys (B) disasters
   (C) expenses (D) peaceful moments
   (E) loud noises
10. The knight came upon his *adversary* in the forest.
    (A) servant (B) sweetheart
    (C) leader (D) enemy
    (E) relative

Time: _____ No. Correct: _____

Test No. 21

Directions: For each question 1 thru 10, select the **appropriate** letter preceding the word which best *completes the* meaning of each sentence.

1. Many secretaries fail because they are not
   - (A) voracious
   - (B) vivacious
   - (C) vindictive
   - (D) versatile.

2. During the questioning of the witness, some unexpected information was
   - (A) elicited
   - (B) eliminated
   - (C) illicit
   - (D) illegitimate.

3. Enclosed please find our new manual of procedure, by which you will note that our instructions of May 10 have been entirely
   - (A) supplemented
   - (B) superimposed
   - (C) superseded
   - (D) suppressed.

4. In his ability to determine new policy, Mr. Smith seems to be particularly
   - (A) diffident
   - (B) decorous
   - (C) difficult
   - (D) decisive.

5. The information contained in this report has no bearing on production records; it is, in fact, distinctly
   - (A) irresponsible
   - (B) irrelevant
   - (C) irrevocable
   - (D) irrespective.

6. If an indelible ink had been used, these messages would not have been
   - (A) obliterated
   - (B) obligated
   - (C) obviated
   - (D) observed.

7. At the present time, we question whether such a policy would be
   - (A) exacted
   - (B) expressed
   - (C) expedient
   - (D) expendable.

8. The insurance adjuster was convinced that the driver had been
   - (A) negative
   - (B) neglected
   - (C) negligent
   - (D) negligible.

9. Some organizations hold meetings at which a nonmember may be admitted as a
   - (A) promoter
   - (B) proxy
   - (C) protege
   - (D) partner.

10. People invest money unwisely because they are too
    - (A) credible
    - (B) creditable
    - (C) credulous
    - (D) critical.

Time: _____ No. Correct: _____

Test No. 22

Directions: (Same Directions apply for Test No. 23) For each question 1 thru 10, select the two appropriate letters preceding the two words that are the *same* in meaning.

1. (A) more   (B) fewer   (C) equal   (D) distant   (E) less.

2. (A) fault   (B) bill   (C) via   (D) express   (E) way.

3. (A) droll   (B) piercing   (C) sorrowful   (D) ludicrous   (E) slack.

4. (A) verdict   (B) reception   (C) transcript   (D) copy   (E) sentence.

5. (A) expunge   (B) analyze   (C) correct   (D) erase   (E) use.

6. (A) legible   (B) sizable   (C) feasible   (D) remarkable   (E) plausible.

7. (A) derision   (B) mimicry   (C) photography   (D) ridicule   (E) imitation.

8. (A) synopsis   (B) nerves   (C) summary   (D) system   (E) bonus.

9. (A) corruption   (B) sheen   (C) soot   (D) luster   (E) disgrace.

10. (A) noxious   (B) prolific   (C) relic   (D) evasive   (E) offensive.

Time: _____ No. Correct: _____

Test No. 23

Directions: See Test No. 22

1. (A) penurious (B) dangerous (C) shameless (D) stingy (E) rich.
2. (A) affiliate (B) recede (C) veto (D) accede (E) consent.
3. (A) frenzy (B) interpretation (C) list (D) disbursement (E) expenditure.
4. (A) reconcile (B) compute (C) recruit (D) recover (E) adjust.
5. (A) garble (B) mutilate (C) hedge (D) associate (E) plan.
6. (A) foolish (B) contentious (C) quarrelsome (D) energetic (E) obsolete.
7. (A) stipulation (B) lien (C) lease (D) covenant (E) check.
8. (A) refrain (B) accommodate (C) increase (D) trace (E) oblige.
9. (A) nimble (B) natural (C) dominant (D) prevailing (E) floating.
10. (A) accessible (B) tenable (C) unexpected (D) approachable (E) cautious.

Time:_____ No. Correct:_____

Test No. 24

Directions: For each question 1 through 10, select the appropriate letter preceding the word that is *opposite* in meaning to the capitalized word.

1. PERTINENT
    (A) inappropriate (B) prudent (C) truthful (D) applicable (E) careful
2. DOGMATIC
    (A) bovine (B) canine (C) yielding (D) unprincipled (E) opinionated
3. INTREPID
    (A) fearful (B) cowardly (C) fanciful (D) fearless (E) willing
4. TENACITY
    (A) firmness (B) sagacity (C) temerity (D) discouragement (E) thinness
5. STERILE
    (A) antique (B) unclean (C) germ-proof (D) austere (E) artistic
6. CREDIBLE
    (A) believable (B) intelligent (C) correct (D) suitable (E) unbelievable
7. MORTGAGER
    (A) lender (B) giver (C) receiver (D) reckoner (E) dictator
8. IGNOMINY
    (A) fame (B) ill luck (C) disgrace (D) despair (E) illiteracy
9. PRODIGAL
    (A) wasteful (B) marvelous (C) ominous (D) harmless (E) thrifty
10. VOLUBLE
    (A) bulky (B) glib (C) desirable (D) reticent (E) fat

Time:_____ No. Correct:_____

Test No. 25

Directions: (These directions also apply to Tests Nos. 26 through 30, which follow.) For each question 1 thru 10, select the appropriate letter preceding the word which is most nearly the *same* in meaning as the capitalized word.

1. FACTIOUS
   - (A) truthful
   - (B) loyal
   - (C) quarrelsome
   - (D) conspiring

2. DISPARAGE
   - (A) praise
   - (B) belittle
   - (C) importune
   - (D) adulate

3. TURGID
   - (A) tubular
   - (B) hollowed
   - (C) swollen
   - (D) troubled

4. TIMBRE
   - (A) wood
   - (B) tone
   - (C) timing
   - (D) fear

5. SERRATED
   - (A) sawtoothed
   - (B) stretched
   - (C) dehydrated
   - (D) intensified

6. VOCIFEROUS
   - (A) energetic
   - (B) musical
   - (C) clamorous
   - (D) calmly

7. CRYPTIC
   - (A) overt
   - (B) burned
   - (C) adroit
   - (D) secret

8. CONTENTIOUS
   - (A) disputatious
   - (B) ingenious
   - (C) temperate
   - (D) appeasing

9. RECANT
   - (A) intone
   - (B) disavow
   - (C) relate
   - (D) evaluate

10. NEFARIOUS
    - (A) greedy
    - (B) holy
    - (C) needy
    - (D) wicked

Time: _____   No. Correct: _____

Test No. 26

Directions: See Test No. 25.

1. FUNDAMENTAL
   - (A) adequate
   - (B) essential
   - (C) official
   - (D) truthful.

2. SUPPLANT
   - (A) approve
   - (B) displace
   - (C) satisfy
   - (D) vary.

3. OBLITERATE
   - (A) erase
   - (B) demonstrate
   - (C) review
   - (D) detect.

4. ANTICIPATE
   - (A) foresee
   - (B) approve
   - (C) annul
   - (D) conceal.

5. EXORBITANT
   - (A) priceless
   - (B) extensive
   - (C) worthless
   - (D) excessive.

6. RELUCTANT
   - (A) anxious
   - (B) constant
   - (C) drastic
   - (D) hesitant.

7. PREVALENT
   - (A) current
   - (B) permanent
   - (C) durable
   - (D) temporary.

8. AUGMENT
   - (A) conclude
   - (B) suggest
   - (C) increase
   - (D) unite.

9. FRUGAL
   - (A) friendly
   - (B) thoughtful
   - (C) hostile
   - (D) economical.

10. AUSTERITY
    - (A) priority
    - (B) severity
    - (C) anxiety
    - (D) solitude.

Time: _____   No. Correct: _____

Test No. 27

Directions: See Test No. 25.

1. CORROBORATION
   - (A) expenditure
   - (B) compilation
   - (C) confirmation
   - (D) reduction.

2. IMPERATIVE
   - (A) impending
   - (B) impossible
   - (C) compulsory
   - (D) logical.

3. FEASIBLE
   - (A) simple
   - (B) practicable
   - (C) visible
   - (D) lenient.

4. SALUTARY
   - (A) popular
   - (B) urgent
   - (C) beneficial
   - (D) forceful.

5. ACQUIESCE
   - (A) endeavor
   - (B) discharge
   - (C) agree
   - (D) inquire.

6. DIFFIDENCE
   - (A) shyness
   - (B) distinction
   - (C) interval
   - (D) discordance.

7. HEINOUS
   - (A) flagrant
   - (B) habitual
   - (C) awful
   - (D) Hellenic.

8. ACCESS
   - (A) too much
   - (B) extra
   - (C) admittance
   - (D) arrival.

9. SUBSEQUENT
   - (A) preceding
   - (B) early
   - (C) following
   - (D) winning.

10. HERITAGE
    - (A) will
    - (B) unbeliever
    - (C) legend
    - (D) inheritance.

Time: _____   No. Correct: _____

Test No. 28

Directions: See Test No. 25.

1. PLAINT
   - (A) retribution
   - (B) easily bent
   - (C) lament
   - (D) fish.

2. IMPETUS
   - (A) excitable
   - (B) impulse
   - (C) vigor
   - (D) prevention.

3. DISSENT
   - (A) approve
   - (B) depart
   - (C) disagree
   - (D) protest.

4. FACILITY
   - (A) happiness
   - (B) willingness
   - (C) ease
   - (D) desirability.

5. LAUDABLE
   - (A) opium
   - (B) distasteful
   - (C) praiseworthy
   - (D) salable.

6. RECUMBENT
   - (A) cumbersome
   - (B) recurrent
   - (C) reclining
   - (D) occupant.

7. RAZE
   - (A) clear
   - (B) scrape
   - (C) demolish
   - (D) erect.

8. HALLOW
   - (A) consecrate
   - (B) scoop out
   - (C) buy
   - (D) call.

9. PLAUSIBLE
   - (A) stop
   - (B) true
   - (C) spacious
   - (D) specious.

10. PARTISAN
    - (A) soldier
    - (B) adherent
    - (C) mechanic
    - (D) division.

Time: _____   No. Correct: _____

Test No. 29

Directions: See Test No. 25.

1. COHERENT
   - (A) not clear
   - (B) logically related
   - (C) intelligible
   - (D) courteous.

2. OBESITY
   - (A) bestial
   - (B) corpulence
   - (C) obstinacy
   - (D) instrument.

3. MAIL
   - (A) armor
   - (B) seaside
   - (C) rapid travel
   - (D) wool.

4. PROXIMITY
   - (A) nearness
   - (B) declivity
   - (C) worldliness
   - (D) adherence.

5. HAGGLE
   - (A) dicker
   - (B) nag
   - (C) quarrel
   - (D) buy.

6. AMENABLE
   - (A) pleasant
   - (B) tractable
   - (C) amiable
   - (D) bloodless.

7. PALPABLE
   - (A) savory
   - (B) obvious
   - (C) paltry
   - (D) easy.

8. FLORID
   - (A) seedy
   - (B) flowery
   - (C) ruddy
   - (D) overflowing.

9. FALLACIOUS
   - (A) faltering
   - (B) stumbling
   - (C) deceptive
   - (D) foolish.

10. DOGMA
    - (A) canine
    - (B) creed
    - (C) truth
    - (D) prophecy.

Time: _____   No. Correct: _____

Test No. 30

Directions: See Test No. 25.

1. ANATHEMA
   - (A) curse
   - (B) blessing
   - (C) hymn
   - (D) benison.

2. VULNERABLE
   - (A) sacred
   - (B) dangling
   - (C) vaulting
   - (D) weak.

3. ACCENTUATE
   - (A) emphasize
   - (B) abbreviate
   - (C) acclaim
   - (D) assess.

4. ZEALOUS
   - (A) lazy
   - (B) enthusiastic
   - (C) envious
   - (D) careless.

5. VESTIGE
   - (A) design
   - (B) strap
   - (C) trace
   - (D) bar.

6. YEARN
   - (A) crave
   - (B) gape
   - (C) feel sleepy
   - (D) feel bored.

7. VETERINARY
   - (A) retired soldier
   - (B) civil servant
   - (C) hospital
   - (D) animal doctor.

8. STUPEFY
   - (A) subjugate
   - (B) stun
   - (C) resect
   - (D) imprecate.

9. WAXY
   - (A) large
   - (B) serious
   - (C) cereus
   - (D) seric.

10. TRYST
    - (A) meeting
    - (B) trick
    - (C) drama
    - (D) trifle.

Time: _____   No. Correct: _____

Correct Answers For The Foregoing Questions

(Please make every effort to answer the questions on your own before looking at these answers. You'll make faster progress by following this rule.)

Test 1
1. F 2. T 3. T 4. F 5. F
6. T 7. T 8. F 9. F 10. F

Test 2
1. B 2. B 3. A 4. B 5. D
6. E 7. C 8. C 9. E 10. A

Test 3
1. C 2. A 3. B 4. B 5. D
6. E 7. D 8. D 9. A 10. C

Test 4
1. A 2. C 3. B 4. D 5. B
6. E 7. C 8. A 9. E 10. D

Test 5
1. D 2. A 3. B 4. E 5. D
6. C 7. B 8. A 9. C 10. E

Test 6
1. O 2. S 3. O 4. N 5. S
6. S 7. O 8. S 9. N 10. S

Test 7
1. C 2. B 3. A 4. B 5. A
6. C 7. D 8. A 9. B 10. D

Test 8
1. D 2. C 3. C 4. D 5. C
6. B 7. C 8. A 9. A 10. B

Test 9
1. D 2. C 3. D 4. C 5. B
6. D 7. A 8. B 9. D 10. C

Test 10
1. B 2. A 3. E 4. C 5. C
6. D 7. E 8. B 9. E 10. A

Test 11
1. D 2. E 3. B 4. E 5. C
6. D 7. B 8. B 9. D 10. A

Test 12
1. D 2. B 3. B 4. D 5. C
6. D 7. D 8. A 9. C 10. C

Test 13
1. C 2. B 3. D 4. E 5. A
6. E 7. C 8. D 9. B 10. D

Test 14
1. C 2. C 3. B 4. B 5. B
6. D 7. C 8. B 9. A 10. D

Test 15
1. B 2. D 3. A 4. D 5. C
6. C 7. A 8. B 9. A 10. B

Test 16
1. A 2. D 3. D 4. B 5. A
6. C 7. D 8. B 9. D 10. A

Test 17
1. D 2. C 3. B 4. B 5. A
6. D 7. A 8. C 9. D 10. C

Test 18
1. C 2. D 3. C 4. B 5. D
6. A 7. D 8. C 9. C 10. A

Test 19
1. A 2. D 3. D 4. E 5. C
6. B 7. A 8. A 9. B 10. C

Test 20
1. B 2. C 3. C 4. C 5. A
6. D 7. B 8. D 9. B 10. D

Correct Answers For The Foregoing Questions

(Please make every effort to answer the questions on your own before looking at these answers. You'll make faster progress by following this rule.)

Test 21

1. D   2. A   3. C   4. B   5. B
6. A   7. C   8. C   9. B   10. C

Test 22

1. B & E   2. C & E   3. A & D   4. C & D
5. A & D   6. C & E   7. B & E or A & D
8. A & C   9. B & D   10. A & E

Test 23

1. A & D   2. D & E   3. D & E   4. A & E
5. A & B   6. B & C   7. A & D   8. B & E
9. C & D   10. A & D

Test 24

1. A   2. C   3. B   4. D   5. B
6. E   7. C   8. A   9. E   10. D

Test 25

1. C   2. B   3. A   4. B   5. A
6. C   7. D   8. A   9. B   10. D

Test 26

1. B   2. B   3. A   4. A   5. D
6. D   7. A   8. C   9. D   10. B

Test 27

1. C   2. C   3. B   4. C   5. C
6. A   7. A   8. C   9. C   10. D

Test 28

1. C   2. B   3. C   4. C   5. C
6. C   7. C   8. A   9. D   10. B

Test 29

1. B   2. B   3. A   4. A   5. A
6. B   7. B   8. C   9. C   10. B

Test 30

1. A   2. D   3. A   4. B   5. C
6. A   7. D   8. B   9. C   10. A

AIR FORCE PLACEMENT TESTS

CLERICAL SPEED AND APTITUDE

According to our information, your test will almost certainly be concerned with your clerical aptitude. This means that they will want to discover your chances of success in the job or in any clerical training they may find it necessary to give you. This section will familiarize you with clerical aptitude test questions. Read on.

An aptitude test is one used to predict success in some occupation or course of training. Thus, in addition to tests of clerical aptitude, there are tests of musical aptitude, engineering aptitude, aptitude for algebra, and so forth. Aptitude tests are not really different in form from other types of tests: for example, proficiency tests or achievement tests. Thus, a clerical aptitude test might include sections measuring general mental ability, proficiency in word usage or arithmetic. A proficiency test measures your ability to perform some task which is significant in its own right: typing, filing, taking dictation or writing a letter. Since one of the chief uses of a proficiency test is to evaluate performance of people who have already received training in a task, they are often called achievement tests. Such tests are used to examine your success in past study. An aptitude test, however, is used to forecast your success in some future course or job.

Examiners are fond of saying that you cannot prepare for an aptitude test because it does not depend on your training or knowledge, but rather on your innate ability. That may be true theoretically, but it also stands to reason that familiarity with the kind of question that will be asked, and practice with that kind of question can yield notable improvements in your score. We propose to provide that kind of familiarity and practice. Many of your competitors may already have gotten this advantage. We think it only fair that you be not asked to start with a handicap.

Tests designed to measure clerical aptitude usually emphasize your ability to understand a task and do it speedily. Your score will depend mostly on your speed. Naturally, you'll be penalized for errors, but our advice in all this practice is that you concentrate on working fast. We have found that many careful people obtain low scores on clerical ability tests because they proceed carefully in order to avoid errors. By contrast, the person who emphasizes speed at the expense of accuracy will complete many more items and will be penalized only a few points as a result of errors. You should understand that these are very simple tasks. Once you've gotten the idea and realize that it's quite difficult to err . . . then go.

AIR FORCE PLACEMENT TESTS

ADDRESS CHECKING

This is a sample of a clerical aptitude test in which you will be given addresses to compare.

DIRECTIONS: This is a test of your speed and accuracy in comparing addresses. For Part I of the test, blacken the proper space under A in the Answer Sheet if the two addresses are exactly alike in every way. Blacken B if they are not alike in every way. For Part II of the test, go back to number 1 on the Answer Sheet. But this time blacken the space under D if the two addresses are exactly alike in every way. Blacken the space under E if they are not exactly alike in every way. Allow exactly five minutes.

When you have finished the test, you should have marks in Columns A and B filled in for Part I and columns D and E filled in for Part II. There should be no marks in Column C. The answers to these sample questions are shown on the Sample Answer Sheet at the right.

TWO TEST QUESTIONS ANALYZED

Part I

1. 5164 South 60th St.   5164 North 60th St.

Since these two addresses are different, B is marked on the answer sheet.

Part II

2. 4616 Michael Lane   4616 Michael Lane

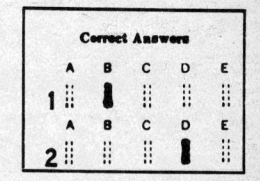

Since these two addresses in Part II are exactly alike the Sample Answer Sheet is marked D. Did you notice that you had a little difficulty remembering what to mark for Part I and Part II? Remember this difficulty and concentrate on the actual test. Memorize simple details like these. They are very important on clerical ability exams.

To assist you in scoring yourself we have provided Correct Answers alongside your Answer Sheet. May we therefore suggest that while you are doing the test you cover the Correct Answers with a sheet of white paper.....to avoid temptation and to arrive at an accurate estimate of your ability and progress.

ADDRESS CHECKING TEST ONE

DIRECTIONS: This is a test of your speed and accuracy in comparing addresses. For Part I of the test, blacken the proper space under A in the Answer Sheet if the two addresses are exactly alike in every way. Blacken B if they are not alike in every way. For Part II of the test, go back to number 1 on the Answer Sheet. But this time blacken the space under D if the two addresses are exactly alike in every way. Blacken the space under E if they are not exactly alike in every way. Allow exactly five minutes.

PART I

1.	2121 South Drive	2121 South Drive
2.	6354 Forest Ave.	6543 Forest Ave.
3.	Tuckahoe, N.Y.	Tuckahoe, New York
4.	140 Bay State Road	140 Bay State Road
5.	5689 Park Place	5689 Park Place
6.	6709 Dewey Ave.	6709 Dewey Ave.
7.	Eastern Parkway	Easten Parkway
8.	6790 Beekman	6709 Beekman
9.	4786 Catalana Dr.	4786 Catalina Dr.
10.	Stuyvesant Town	Stuyvesant Town
11.	Newport, Va.	Newport, R.I.
12.	Woodmere, L.I.	Woodmere, L.I.
13.	7809 Greer Garden	7890 Greer Garden
14.	334 N.W. Lane	334 N.W. Lake
15.	195 Craig St.	195 Craigie St.
16.	Brunswick, Maine	Brunswick, Maine
17.	7543 Stevens Ave.	7435 Stevens Avenue

PART II

1.	248 Love Lane	248 Love Lane
2.	Niagra Falls	Niagra Falls
3.	5329 Jefferson Ave.	5392 Jefferson Ave.
4.	7809 Windy Way	7809 Windy Way
5.	8218 Bedel St.	8218 Bedel St.
6.	3090 Catherine Road	3090 Catherine Road
7.	Cape Porpoise	Cape Porpose
8.	9669 Wrange Rd.	9669 Wrange Rd.
9.	418 N. Wallace St.	418 N. Wallace St.
10.	2144 W. Tenth Ave.	2144 W. Tenth Ave.
11.	1618 N. Tecumseh	1618 N. Tecumseh
12.	5856 S. Pershing Rd.	5866 S. Pershing Rd.
13.	4231 Kealing Ave. N.	4231 Kelling Ave. N.
14.	6349 Ewing Ave.	349 Ewing Ave.
15.	1322 E. Hampton Dr.	1322 E. Hampton St.
16.	3343 London Rd. N.E.	3343 London Pl. N.E.
17.	Paoli, Ill.	Paoli, Ind.

ADDRESS CHECKING TEST TWO

DIRECTIONS: This is a test of your speed and accuracy in comparing addresses. For Part I of the test, blacken the proper space under A in the Answer Sheet if the two addresses are exactly alike in every way. Blacken B if they are not alike in every way. For Part II of the test, go back to number 1 on the Answer Sheet. But this time blacken the space under D if the two addresses are exactly alike in every way. Blacken the space under E if they are not exactly alike in every way. Allow exactly five minutes.

PART I

1.	418 N. Wallac St.	418 N. Wallace St.
2.	2144 W. Tenth Ave.	144 W. Tenth Ave.
3.	1618 N. Tecumseh	1618 N. Tecumse
4.	5856 S. Pershing Rd.	5866 S. Pershing
5.	4231 Kealing Ave. N.	4231 Keeling Ave. N.
6.	6349 Ewing Ave.	6349 Ewing Ave.
7.	132 E. Hampton Dr.	1322 E. Hampton St.
8.	3343 London Rd. N.E.	334 London Pl. N.E.
9.	Paoli, Ill.	Poli, Ind.
10.	6892 Beech Grove Ave.	6892 Beech Grove Ave.
11.	2939 E. Division	2939 E. Diversey
12.	1066 Goethe Sq. S.	1096 Goethe Sq. S.
13.	1108 Lyndhurst Dr.	1108 Lyndhurst Dr.
14.	Berne, Wyo.	Berne, Wis.
15.	1468 Woodruff Pl.	1468 Woodruff Pl.
16.	992 S. Highland Ave.	992 S. Highland Ave.
17.	2478 Berkeley Rd.	2478 Barclay Rd.

PART II

1.	4718 N. Central St.	4718 S. Central St.
2.	1118 W. Jerriman	1218 W. Jerriman
3.	2541 Appleton St.	2541 Appleton St.
4.	6439 Kessler Blvd. S.	6439 Kessler Blvd. S.
5.	928 Miramar Rd.	928 Miramar Bldg.
6.	1929 Connecticut Ave. N.E.	1929 Connecticut Ave. N.E.
7.	9452 N. Gale St.	9452 N. Gale St.
8.	1815 Ridgewood Dr.	1815 Ridgewood Dr.
9.	25 92nd Elm	25 97th Elm
10.	389 Woodward Hts.	389 Woodward Ave.
11.	7718 Lincoln Pkwy.	7718 Lincoln Blvd.
12.	5798 Gd. Central Dr.	5798 Gd. Central Dr.
13.	108-46 159 Ave.	108-36 159 Ave.
14.	5 Willow Rd.	5 Willow Rd.
15.	3213 Brookhaven	3213 Brookhale
16.	186 Fr. Meadows	186 Fr. Meadows
17.	1109 Liberty Ave.	1109 Liberty St.

ADDRESS CHECKING TEST THREE

DIRECTIONS: This is a test of your speed and accuracy in comparing addresses. For Part I of the test, blacken the proper space under A in the Answer Sheet if the two addresses are exactly alike in every way. Blacken B if they are not alike in every way. For Part II of the test, go back to number 1 on the Answer Sheet. But this time blacken the space under D if the two addresses are exactly alike in every way. Blacken the space under E if they are not exactly alike in every way. Allow exactly five minutes.

PART I

1.	2439 Langston Ave.	2449 Langston Ave.
2.	408 W. Hamilton Dr.	408 E. Hamilton Dr.
3.	20 Hammerly Sq.	20 Hammerly Sq.
4.	193-08 50th Ave.	193-05 50th Ave.
5.	8949 Astoria Blvd.	8949 Astoria Pl.
6.	155 S.W. Flushing	155 S.W. Flusher
7.	4319 S. Elmont Rd.	4319 S. Elmont Rd.
8.	64 Woodbourne Ave.	64 Woodburn Ave.
9.	1421 N. 38th Ave.	1421 N. 38th Ave.
10.	289 Continental Pl.	289 Continental Pl.
11.	1654 Putnam St.	1644 Putnam St.
12.	1610 Mott Haven	1610 Mott Ave.
13.	4335 W. 167 Ave.	4335 W. 267 Ave.
14.	4192 N.W. Illinois	4192 N.W. Illinois
15.	3374 Ashburne House	3374 Adbourne House
16.	1719 Pleasant Run Blvd.	1719 Pleasant Run Blvd.
17.	3857 S. Morris St.	3857 S. Morris St.

PART II

1.	Bradford, O.	Bradford, O.
2.	2131 W. 18th Dr.	2131 W. 18th Dr.
3.	Townley, Texas	Townley, Tenn.
4.	2525 Wavecrest Ave.	2825 Wavecrest Dr.
5.	123 Linden Pl.	123 Linton Pl.
6.	5929 Washington Blvd.	5929 Washington Blvd.
7.	4628 Park Ave. N.	4628 Park Ave. E.
8.	1235 Meridian St.	1235 Meridian St.
9.	7832 Ruckle Pl. S.W.	7832 Ruckle Pl. S.W.
10.	3422 E. Tenth St.	3422 E. Tenth St.
11.	629 Beveridge Cir.	621 Beveridge Cir.
12.	6888 Forster Ave. W.	6888 Forester Ave. W.
13.	4531 E. 59th St.	4531 E. 59th St.
14.	Melrose Park Mich.	Melray Park Mich.
15.	1871 De Quincey Blvd.	1871 DeQuincy Blvd.
16.	2436 Massachusetts Ave.	2436 Massachusetts Ave.
17.	3951-D 29th St. E.	3951-D 29th St. E.

AIR FORCE PLACEMENT TESTS

MATCHING LETTERS AND NUMBERS

DIRECTIONS: In this test of clerical ability, Column I consists of sets of numbered questions which you are to answer one at a time. Column II consists of possible answers to the set of questions in Column I. Select from Column II the one possible answer which contains only the numbers and letters, regardless of their order, which appear in the question in Column I. If none of the four possible answers is correct, mark "E" on your answer sheet.

A SAMPLE QUESTION EXPLAINED

COLUMN I:
Set of Questions

1. 2-Q-P-5-T-G-4-7

COLUMN II:
Possible Answers

(A) 5-G-8-P-4-Q

(B) P-R-7-Q-4-2

(C) Q-5-P-9-G-2

(D) 4-2-5-P-7-Q

(E) None of these.

The Correct Answer to the Sample Question is (D). How did we arrive at that solution? First, remember that the instructions tell you to select as your answer the choice that contains only the numbers and letters, regardless of their order, which appear in the question. The answer choice in Column II does not have to contain all of the letters and numbers that appear in the question. But the answer cannot contain a number or letter that does not appear in the question. Thus, begin by checking the numbers and letters that appear in Answer (A). You will note that while 5-G-P-4-Q all appear in the Sample Question, the number 8, which is included in Answer (A), does not appear in the question. Answer (A) is thus incorrect. Likewise, Answer (B) is incorrect as the letter R does not appear in the Sample Question; Answer (C) is incorrect as the number 9 does not appear in the question. In checking Answer (D), however, one notes that 4-2-5-P-7-Q all appear in the Sample Question. (D) is therefore the correct choice. Answer (E) is obviously eliminated.

Now proceed to answer the following test questions on the basis of the instructions given above.

MATCHING LETTERS AND NUMBERS TEST

TIME: 10 Minutes

The following are representative examination type questions. They should be carefully studied and completely understood.

DIRECTIONS: In this test of clerical ability, Column I consists of sets of numbered questions which you are to answer one at a time. Column II consists of possible answers to the set of questions in Column I. Select from Column II the one possible answer which contains only the numbers and letters, regardless of their order, which appear in the question in Column I. If none of the four possible answers is correct, mark "E" on your answer sheet.

Correct key answers to all these test questions will be found at the end of the test.

COLUMN I:
Set of Questions

COLUMN II:
Possible Answers

1. 6-4-T-G-9-K-N-8
2. K-3-L-6-Z-7-9-T
3. N-8-9-3-K-G-7-Z
4. L-Z-G-6-4-9-K-3
5. 9-T-K-8-3-7-N-Z

(A) Z-8-K-G-9-7
(B) 7-N-Z-T-9-8
(C) L-3-Z-K-7-6
(D) 4-K-T-G-8-6
(E) None of these.

Set of Questions

Possible Answers

6. 2-3-P-6-V-Z-4-L
7. T-7-4-3-P-Z-9-G
8. 6-N-G-Z-3-9-P-7
9. 9-6-P-4-N-G-Z-2
10. 4-9-7-T-L-P-3-V

(A) 3-6-G-P-7-N
(B) 3-7-P-V-4-T
(C) 4-6-V-Z-2-L
(D) 4-7-G-Z-T-3
(E) None of these.

Clerical Speed and Aptitude / 121

COLUMN I: Set of Questions	COLUMN II: Possible Answers
11. Q-1-6-R-L-9-7-V	(A) F-3-N-K-J-4
12. 8-W-2-Z-P-4-H-O	(B) Q-H-4-O-5-M
13. N-J-3-T-K-5-F-M	(C) O-W-2-Z-4-8
14. 5-T-H-M-O-4-Q-J	(D) R-9-V-1-Q-6
15. 4-Z-X-8-W-O-2-L	(E) None of these.

Set of Questions	Possible Answers
16. S-2-L-8-U-Q-7-P	(A) 9-Q-T-K-2-7
17. 4-M-O-6-T-F-W-1	(B) F-O-1-4-W-M
18. J-M-4-X-W-Z-5-8	(C) U-2-8-P-Q-S
19. H-Q-2-9-T-I-K-7	(D) Z-M-4-5-8-Q
20. 8-M-Z-V-4-P-5-Q	(E) None of these.

CONSOLIDATE YOUR KEY ANSWERS HERE

Correct Answers For The Foregoing Questions

(Please make every effort to answer the questions on your own before looking at these answers. You'll make faster progress by following this rule.)

SCORE 1
........%
NO. CORRECT
NO. OF QUESTIONS ON THIS TEST

1. D	6. C	11. D	16. C
2. C	7. D	12. C	17. B
3. A	8. A	13. E	18. E
4. E	9. E	14. B	19. A
5. B	10. B	15. C	20. D

SCORE 2
........%
NO. CORRECT
NO. OF QUESTIONS ON THIS TEST

AIR FORCE PLACEMENT TESTS

CLASSIFICATION-CODING ABILITY

DIRECTIONS: In this test of clerical speed and accuracy you are asked to classify each of the items in Column I according to the following code of classifications:

Column I: ITEMS	Column II: CLASSIFICATIONS
Cloth	1
Metal	2
Liquid	3
Fruit	4
Vegetable	5
Bird	6
Tree	7
Fish	8
Gas	9
Animal	10

In Column II you are to write the Numerical Classification for each Item in Column I.

SAMPLE QUESTIONS AND EXPLANATIONS

	Column I: ITEMS	Column II: CLASSIFICATIONS
1.	chickadee	_____
2.	balsam	_____
3.	copper	_____
4.	leek	_____

The correct answer for question #1 is 6. A chickadee is in the bird family, and the corresponding numerical classification in Column II is 6. For question #2, the correct answer is 7. A balsam is in the tree family. The correct answers for questions #3 and 4 are 2 and 5 respectively. Copper is a metal and is coded as 2 in Column II. Likewise, a leek is a vegetable in the onion family, and is classified numerically as 5 in Column II.

Now proceed to answer the following test questions on the basis of the instructions given above. The Correct Answers appear at the end of each test.

CLASSIFICATION-CODING ABILITY TEST

TIME: 15 Minutes

DIRECTIONS: In this test of clerical speed and accuracy you are asked to classify each of the items in Column I according to the following code of classifications:

Column I: ITEMS	Column II: CLASSIFICATIONS
Cloth	1
Metal	2
Liquid	3
Fruit	4
Vegetable	5
Bird	6
Tree	7
Fish	8
Gas	9
Animal	10

In Column II you are to write the Numerical Classification for each Item in Column I.

	Column I: ITEMS	Column II: CLASSIFICATIONS		Column I: ITEMS	Column II: CLASSIFICATIONS
1.	lemur	_____	11.	turnip	_____
2.	hydrogen	_____	12.	oak	_____
3.	swallow	_____	13.	hare	_____
4.	radish	_____	14.	bronze	_____
5.	velvet	_____	15.	pear	_____
6.	apple	_____	16.	nitrogen	_____
7.	honey	_____	17.	satin	_____
8.	zinc	_____	18.	robin	_____
9.	poplar	_____	19.	peroxide	_____
10.	flounder	_____	20.	perch	_____

	Column I: ITEMS	Column II: CLASSIFICATIONS		Column I: ITEMS	Column II: CLASSIFICATIONS
21.	lemon	_____	45.	shark	_____
22.	lion	_____	46.	madras	_____
23.	oxygen	_____	47.	pine	_____
24.	tin	_____	48.	spaniel	_____
25.	cotton	_____	49.	carrot	_____
26.	tuna	_____	50.	lark	_____
27.	spinach	_____	51.	maple	_____
28.	fir	_____	52.	alcohol	_____
29.	peacock	_____	53.	leopard	_____
30.	lettuce	_____	54.	antimony	_____
31.	crow	_____	55.	banana	_____
32.	methane	_____	56.	dacron	_____
33.	starling	_____	57.	sateen	_____
34.	zebra	_____	58.	nickel	_____
35.	hickory	_____	59.	benzene	_____
36.	vinegar	_____	60.	grapes	_____
37.	peach	_____	61.	okra	_____
38.	fluke	_____	62.	gull	_____
39.	lead	_____	63.	fir	_____
40.	tweed	_____	64.	carp	_____
41.	calcium	_____	65.	chlorine	_____
42.	turtle	_____	66.	otter	_____
43.	persimmon	_____	67.	gingham	_____
44.	hawk	_____	68.	milk	_____

Column I: ITEMS	Column II: CLASSIFICATIONS		Column I: ITEMS	Column II: CLASSIFICATIONS
69. orange	_____		75. felt	_____
70. oriole	_____		76. iron	_____
71. willow	_____		77. molasses	_____
72. scrod	_____		78. currant	_____
73. argon	_____		79. chard	_____
74. elk	_____		80. turkey	_____

Correct Answers For The Foregoing Questions

(Please try to answer the questions on your own before looking at our answers. You'll do much better on your test if you follow this rule.)

1.10	11.5	21.4	31.6	41.2	51.7	61.5	71.7
2.9	12.7	22.10	32.9	42.10	52.3	62.6	72.8
3.6	13.10	23.9	33.6	43.4	53.10	63.7	73.9
4.5	14.2	24.2	34.10	44.6	54.2	64.8	74.10
5.1	15.4	25.1	35.7	45.8	55.4	65.9	75.1
6.4	16.9	26.8	36.3	46.1	56.1	66.10	76.2
7.3	17.1	27.5	37.4	47.7	57.1	67.1	77.3
8.2	18.6	28.7	38.8	48.10	58.2	68.3	78.4
9.7	19.3	29.6	39.2	49.5	59.3	69.4	79.5
10.8	20.8	30.5	40.1	50.6	60.4	70.6	80.6

SCORE 1	.... %
NO. CORRECT ÷	
NO. OF QUESTIONS ON THIS TEST	

SCORE 2	.... %
NO. CORRECT ÷	
NO. OF QUESTIONS ON THIS TEST	

AIR FORCE PLACEMENT TESTS

CODING SPEED

This is a test of clerical speed and accuracy. It involves matching code numbers to code words in accordance with a Code Identification Key. The idea is to complete as many questions as you can in the time allowed. Work as quickly and accurately as possible.

DIRECTIONS: The Code Identification Key contains a group of words with a Code Number beside each word. Each test question consists of one of the words from the Key followed by five possible Code Numbers arranged in columns labelled A, B, C, D and E. Choose the one Code Number for each word that corresponds to the number given in the Code Identification Key. On your answer sheet, blacken the letter of the column in which the correct Code Number appears.

SAMPLE QUESTIONS AND EXPLANATIONS

CODE IDENTIFICATION KEY

candy........2067	letter........4895	car..........6239
bear..........8473	pencil.........9723	basket........1546

QUESTIONS	A	B	C	D	E
1. candy	1546	8473	6239	9723	2067
2. bear	1546	8473	4895	9723	2067
3. car	1546	8473	6239	9723	4895
4. letter	1546	8473	6239	9723	4895
5. basket	1546	4895	6239	9723	2067
6. pencil	1546	4895	6239	9723	2067
7. letter	1546	4895	8473	9723	2067
8. bear	1546	4895	8473	9723	2067
9. candy	1546	6239	8473	9723	2067
10. car	1546	6239	8473	9723	2067

Notice that each of the questions is a word chosen from the Code Identification Key followed by five possible Code Numbers. The Code Word in question 1 is "candy." Looking at the Key, we can see that the code number for candy is 2067. Since 2067 is found in column E, the correct answer to the first sample question is "E."

CORRECT ANSWERS TO SAMPLE QUESTIONS

| 1. e | 3. c | 5. a | 7. b | 9. e |
| 2. b | 4. e | 6. d | 8. c | 10. b |

CODING SPEED TEST

TIME: 7 Minutes

DIRECTIONS: The Code Identification Key contains a group of words with a Code Number beside each word. Each test question consists of one of the words from the Key followed by five possible Code Numbers arranged in columns labelled A, B, C, D and E. Choose the one Code Number for each word that corresponds to the number given in the Code Identification Key. On your answer sheet, blacken the letter of the column in which the correct Code Number appears.

CODE IDENTIFICATION KEY

foreman.......1068	radiator......4341	tugboat.......3117
trooper.......5624	livestock.....8578	broadcast.....1499
lathe.........7690	insurance.....5742	engineer......2305
	photograph....2848	

QUESTIONS	A	B	C	D	E
1. foreman	4341	7690	2305	1068	5742
2. broadcast	3117	1499	1068	5624	4341
3. livestock	8578	1068	2848	5742	2305
4. lathe	1068	3117	7690	1499	8578
5. radiator	5624	2848	5742	8578	4341
6. tugboat	2305	3117	1068	2848	5742
7. engineer	1499	7690	5624	2305	3117
8. trooper	7690	8578	5624	1068	4341
9. insurance	5742	2305	1068	4341	8578
10. photograph	2305	2848	1499	5624	5742
11. radiator	1499	5742	8578	7690	4341
12. engineer	2848	3117	1499	2305	7690
13. tugboat	5624	8578	3117	1068	2848
14. insurance	5742	2305	7690	5624	8578
15. broadcast	7690	1499	2305	5742	4341
16. foreman	5624	2848	4341	8578	1068
17. photograph	4341	1068	2848	3117	2305
18. lathe	3117	4341	1068	7690	1499
19. livestock	7690	8578	2305	1499	5624
20. trooper	2848	5624	8578	1068	4341
21. insurance	1499	2305	3117	8578	5742
22. tugboat	3117	8578	2305	1068	7690
23. radiator	1068	5624	4341	3117	2305
24. livestock	5742	8578	1499	5624	4341
25. lathe	2305	1499	5624	7690	3117

CODE IDENTIFICATION KEY

fertilizer....1796	college.......2389	machinery.....6895
invention.....4760	ambulance.....9331	rocket........3942
actress.......5915	lumber........2194	newspaper.....7291
	plastics......0840	

QUESTIONS	A	B	C	D	E
26. actress	0840	5915	4760	9331	2389
27. college	2389	9331	3942	1796	5915
28. machinery	2194	7291	6895	0840	3942
29. fertilizer	7291	4760	5915	9331	1796
30. plastics	1796	3942	0840	2194	6895
31. rocket	5915	6895	7291	3942	4760
32. lumber	9331	2194	4760	5915	0840
33. newspaper	4760	7291	5915	1796	9331
34. invention	4760	5915	0840	3942	2389
35. ambulance	2194	2389	3942	9331	0840
36. lumber	3942	0840	2389	1796	2194
37. actress	0840	1796	5915	2194	6895
38. machinery	1796	2194	6895	0840	7291
39. plastics	0840	6895	9331	7291	2389
40. newspaper	4760	2389	0840	3942	7291
41. fertilizer	6895	4760	5915	1796	7291
42. college	9331	2389	2194	7291	1796
43. ambulance	2194	2389	9331	1796	4760
44. rocket	7291	3942	1796	9331	2194
45. invention	3942	2194	7291	6895	4760
46. newspaper	7291	3942	1796	4760	0840
47. machinery	2389	9331	0840	6895	5915
48. college	9331	1796	7291	3942	2389
49. plastics	2194	0840	4760	2389	5915
50. lumber	1796	2389	2194	7291	0840

CODE IDENTIFICATION KEY

tractor.......0919	detective.....3293	routine.......4018
inventory.....1563	music.........5680	chef..........2579
physics.......8921	recipes.......5734	tenant........9263
	operation.....0217	

QUESTIONS	A	B	C	D	E
51. music	0919	3293	2579	5680	9263
52. inventory	1563	9263	2579	0217	4018
53. chef	5734	2579	0217	1563	3293
54. physics	3293	8921	4018	5734	0217
55. tractor	8921	5734	0217	9263	0919
56. recipes	5680	0217	5734	4018	9263
57. detective	1563	5680	0919	3293	2579
58. tenant	0919	2579	9263	0217	8921
59. routine	4018	0919	1563	2579	5734
60. operation	2579	1563	4018	5734	0217
61. chef	9263	2579	8921	0217	3293
62. tractor	8921	0919	3293	9263	5734
63. detective	0919	8921	5734	3293	0217
64. tenant	9263	0217	0919	4018	5680
65. recipes	1563	9263	5680	5734	8921
66. inventory	8921	5734	9263	0217	1563
67. music	0919	3293	5680	2579	0217
68. physics	1563	8921	4018	9263	5734
69. operation	5680	0919	5734	0217	3293
70. routine	4018	5680	0919	1563	8921
71. recipes	0217	4018	5734	1563	9263
72. physics	1563	2579	5680	0217	8921
73. music	3293	9263	0217	2579	5680
74. tenant	0919	5734	2579	9263	1563
75. routine	2579	4018	9263	3293	0919

CODE IDENTIFICATION KEY

television....7562	foreign.......3580	dispatcher....3791
secretary.....1507	assembly......0469	library.......9616
factory.......6946	negatives.....2115	circuits......0323
	emergency.....4786	

QUESTIONS	A	B	C	D	E
76. circuits	4786	7562	0323	1507	6946
77. factory	3580	6946	9616	4786	0469
78. negatives	2115	0469	4786	7562	3580
79. library	1507	2115	3791	9616	7562
80. emergency	3791	9616	0469	4786	0323
81. foreign	7562	0469	4786	9616	3580
82. secretary	9616	1507	6946	0323	4786
83. television	6946	2115	7562	4786	9616
84. assembly	0469	3580	0323	2115	7562
85. dispatcher	1507	6946	3580	3791	0469
86. assembly	6946	0469	9616	4786	0323
87. factory	1507	2115	3791	0469	6946
88. foreign	4786	9616	0323	3791	3580
89. circuits	0323	7562	1507	6946	2115
90. dispatcher	2115	3791	4786	9616	1507
91. television	7562	2115	0323	3791	1507
92. library	6946	0469	4786	7562	9616
93. negatives	1507	3580	6946	2115	7562
94. secretary	3580	7562	1507	6946	0323
95. emergency	0469	4786	3791	0323	6946
96. library	1507	0323	9616	2115	4786
97. factory	7562	2115	4786	6946	0469
98. circuits	3580	0323	1507	3791	6946
99. foreign	0469	6946	3791	7562	3580
100. secretary	4786	9616	1507	0469	2115

CONSOLIDATE YOUR KEY ANSWERS HERE

Correct Answers For The Foregoing Questions

To assist you in scoring yourself we have provided Correct Answers alongside your Answer Sheet. May we therefore suggest that while you are doing the test you cover the Correct Answers with a sheet of white paper.....to avoid temptation and to arrive at an accurate estimate of your ability and progress.

1. D	14. A	27. A	40. E	53. B	65. D	77. B	89. A
2. B	15. B	28. C	41. D	54. B	66. E	78. A	90. B
3. A	16. E	29. E	42. B	55. E	67. C	79. D	91. A
4. C	17. C	30. C	43. C	56. C	68. B	80. D	92. E
5. E	18. D	31. D	44. B	57. D	69. D	81. E	93. D
6. B	19. B	32. B	45. E	58. C	70. A	82. B	94. C
7. D	20. B	33. B	46. A	59. A	71. C	83. C	95. B
8. C	21. E	34. A	47. D	60. E	72. E	84. A	96. C
9. A	22. A	35. D	48. E	61. B	73. E	85. D	97. D
10. B	23. C	36. E	49. B	62. B	74. D	86. B	98. B
11. E	24. B	37. C	50. C	63. D	75. B	87. E	99. E
12. D	25. D	38. C	51. D	64. A	76. C	88. E	100. C
13. C	26. B	39. A	52. A				

AIR FORCE PLACEMENT TESTS
HIDDEN FIGURES

This spatial relations test, sometimes called an "embedded figures test," presents a simple geometric pattern and requires the candidate to find it in a larger, more complete pattern which is sometimes a three-dimensional figure.

In some versions of the test the background is colored irregularly to increase confusion. We have not attempted here to increase your confusion.

In this Practice Chapter you are provided with a set of five simple figures labelled A, B, C, D and E. Then you will find a number of more complex figures which are numbered beginning with one. Next to each figure you are to write the letter of the simple figure which is found hidden or embedded in the more complex figure.................................Each test consists of facing pages, so that in answering questions the simple figures are constantly before you.

HIDDEN FIGURES TEST I

Simple Figures

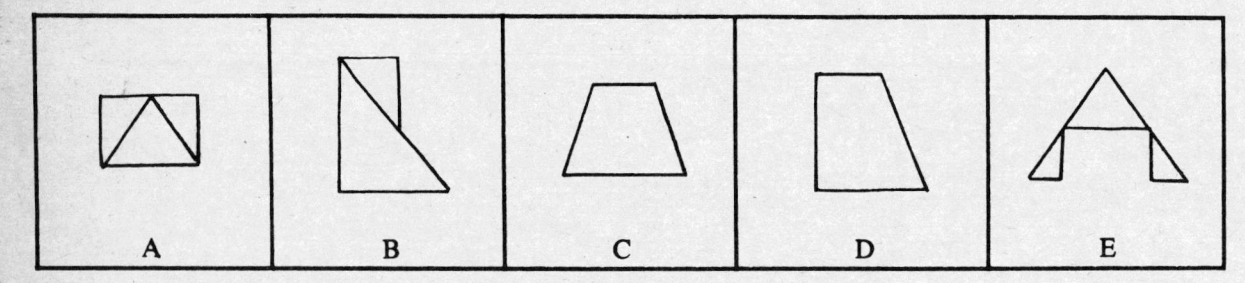

Find The Simple Figures Hidden In These More Complex Figures.

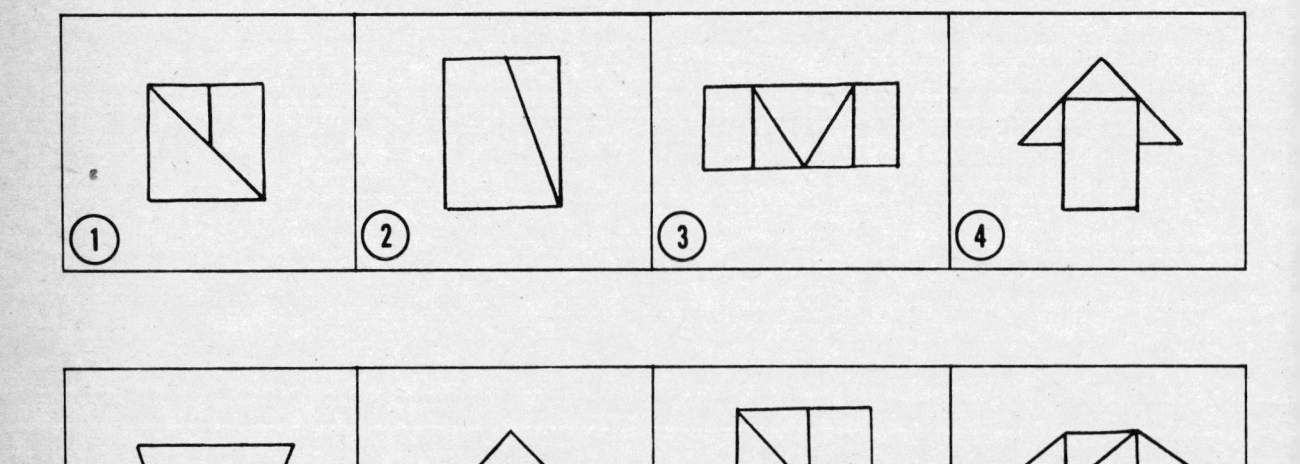

132

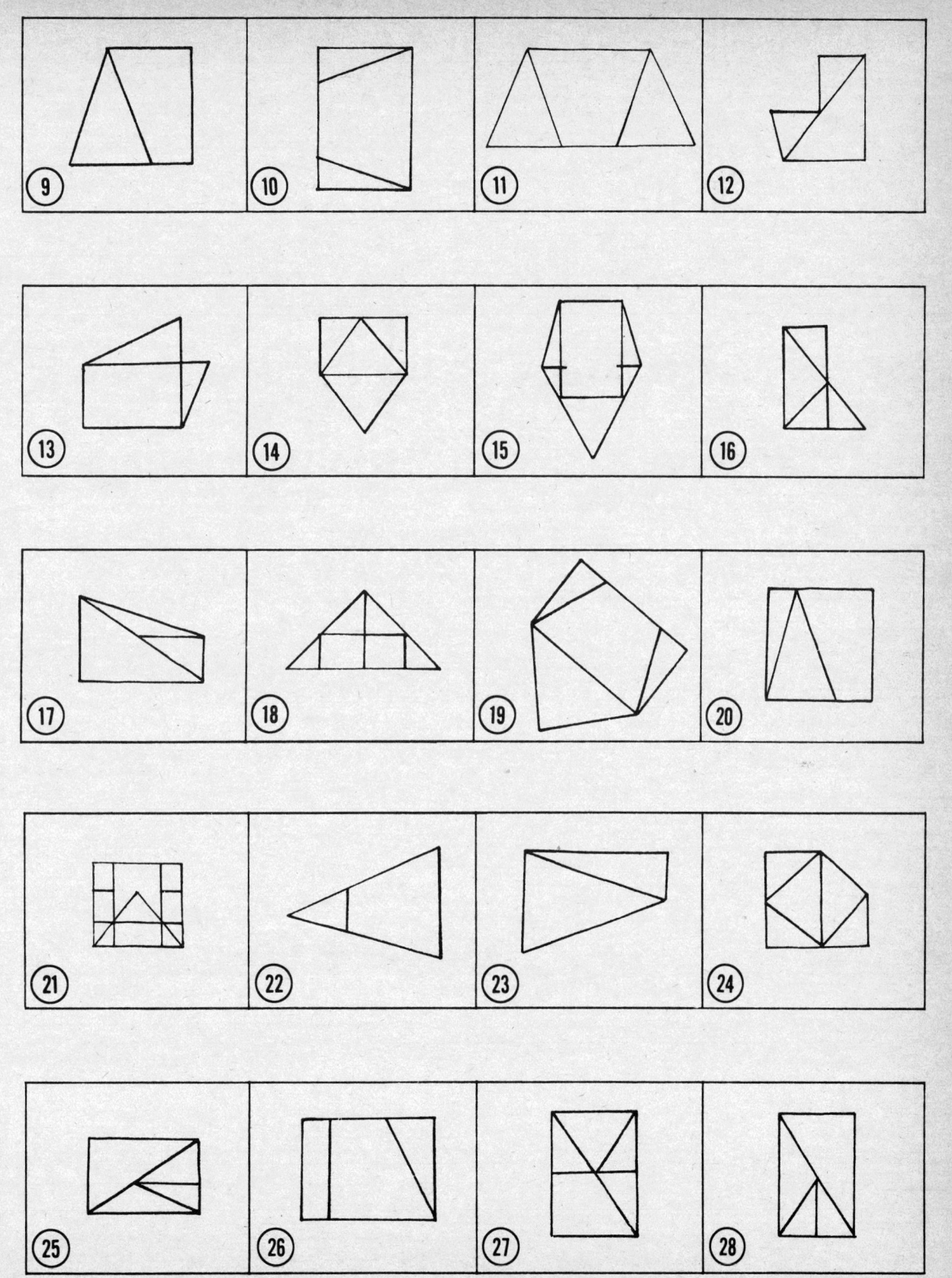

Hidden Figures / 133

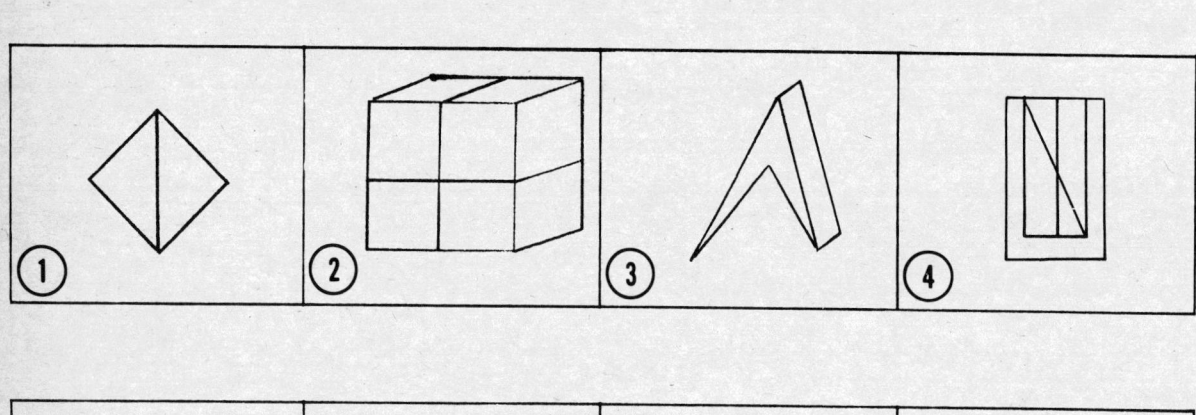

HIDDEN FIGURES TEST II

Simple Figures

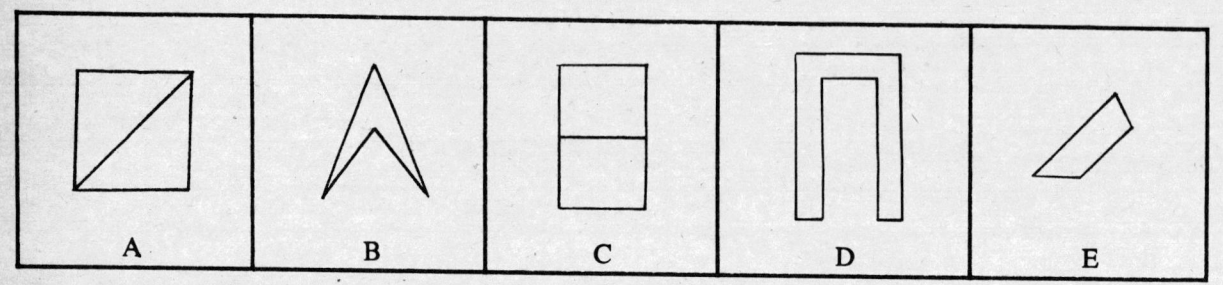

A B C D E

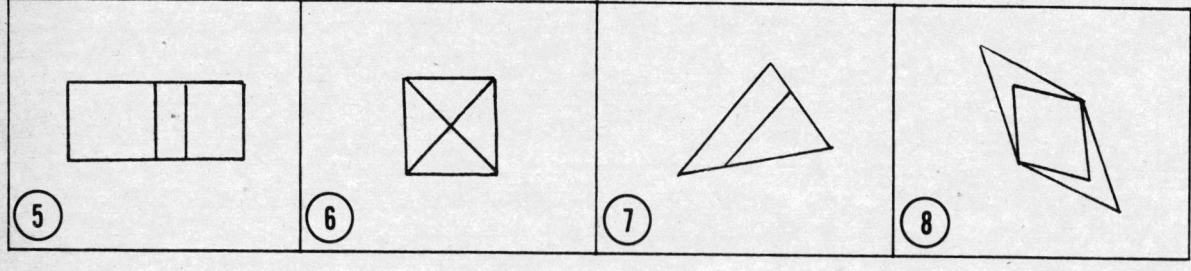

Find The Simple Figures Hidden In These More Complex Figures.

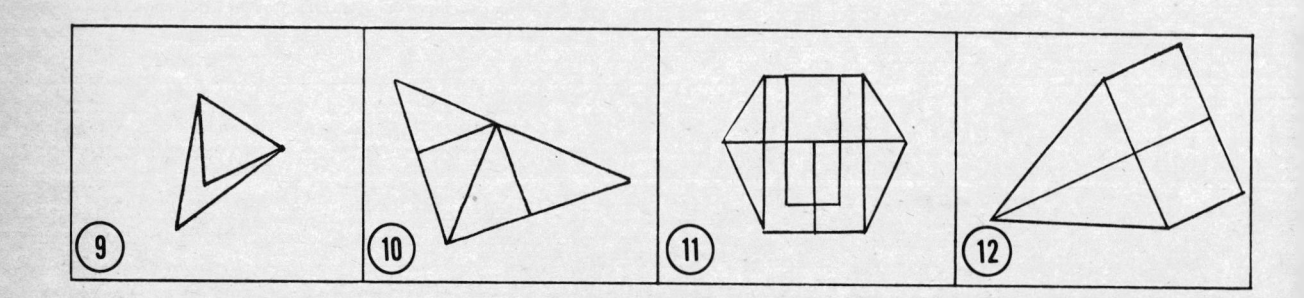

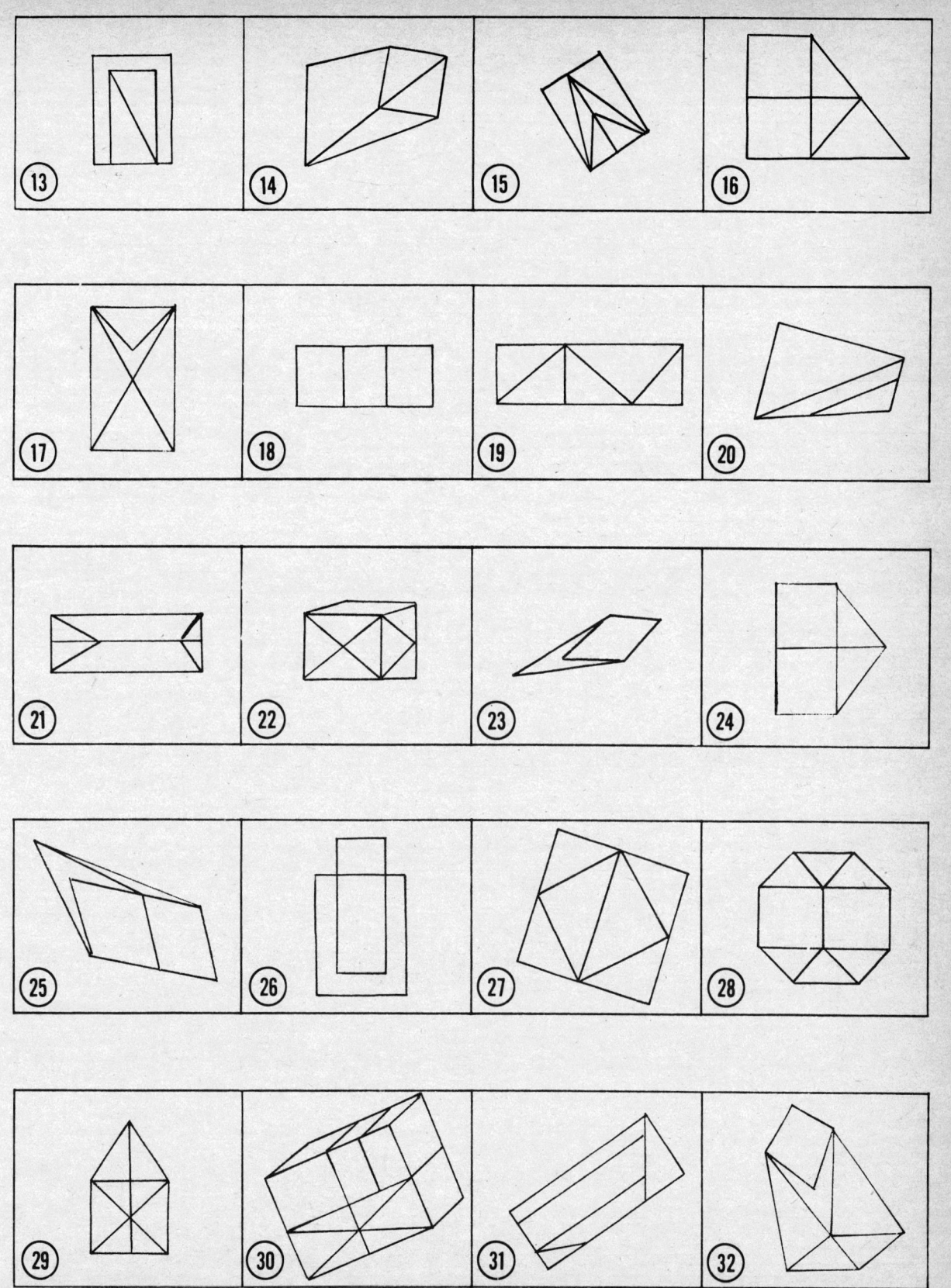

Hidden Figures / 135

HIDDEN FIGURES TEST III

Simple Figures

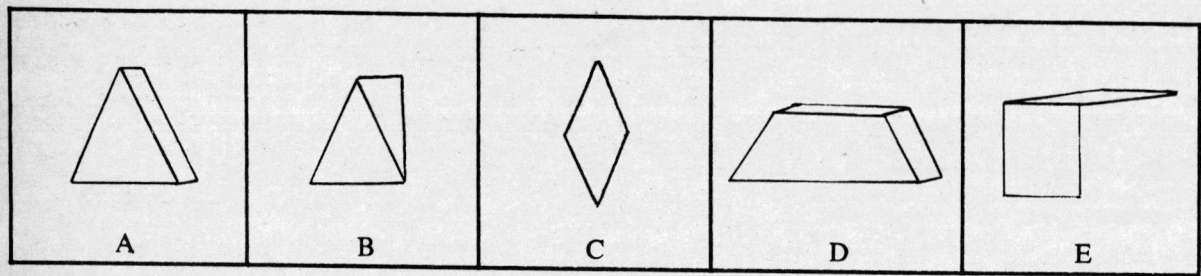

| A | B | C | D | E |

Find The Simple Figures Hidden In These More Complex Figures.

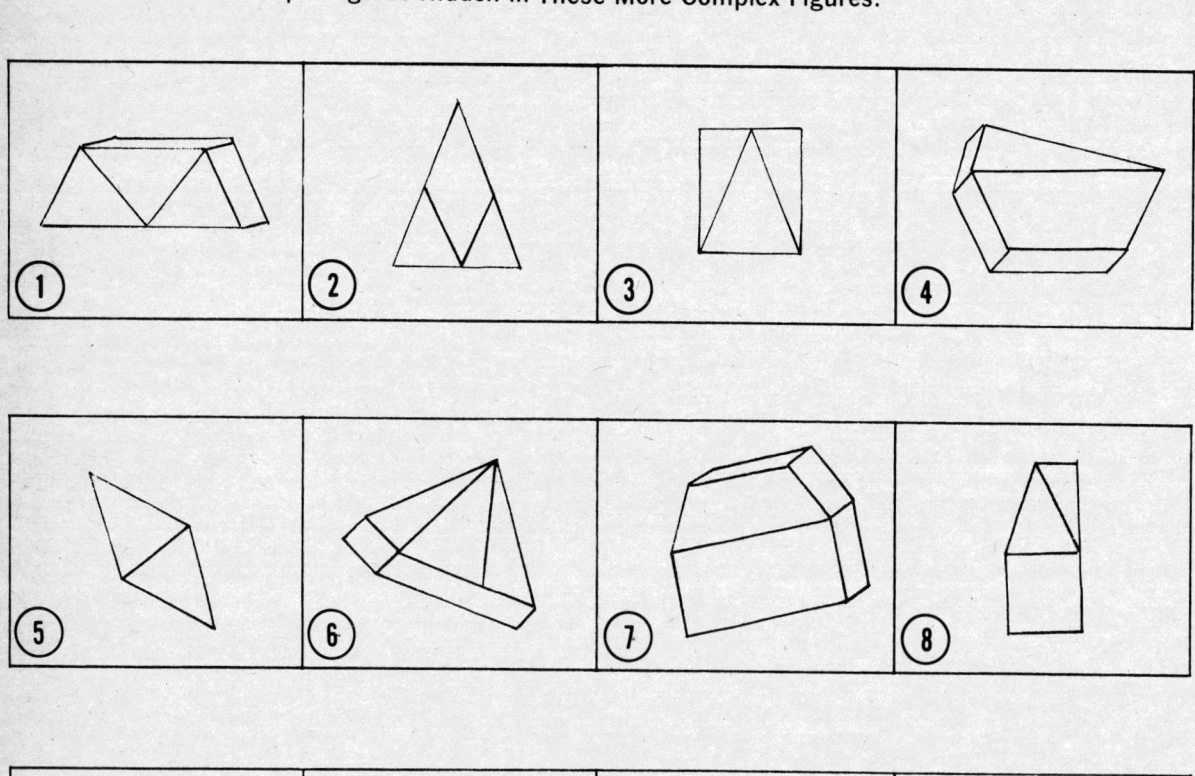

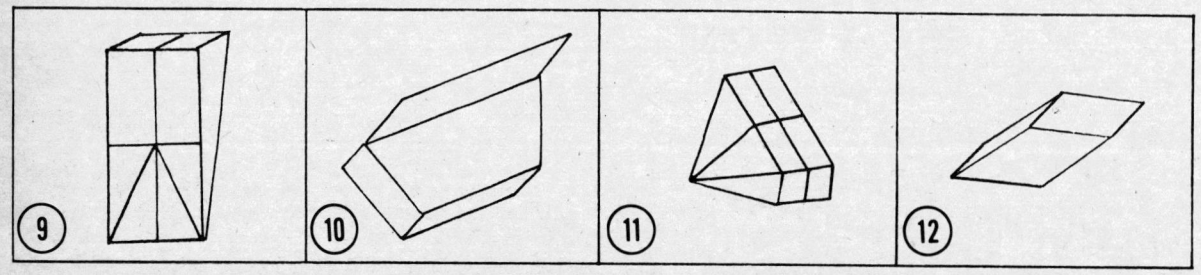

Hidden Figures / 137

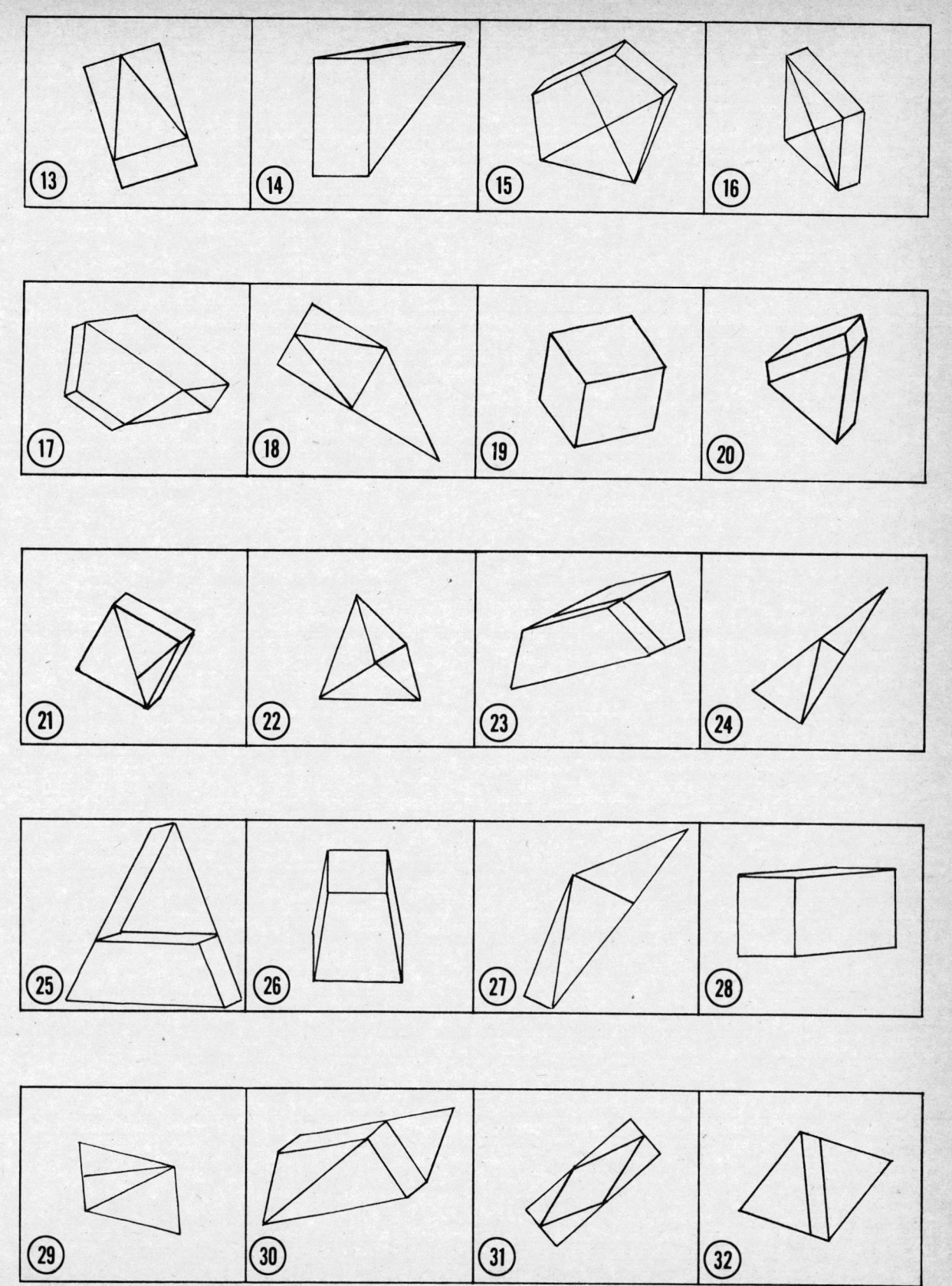

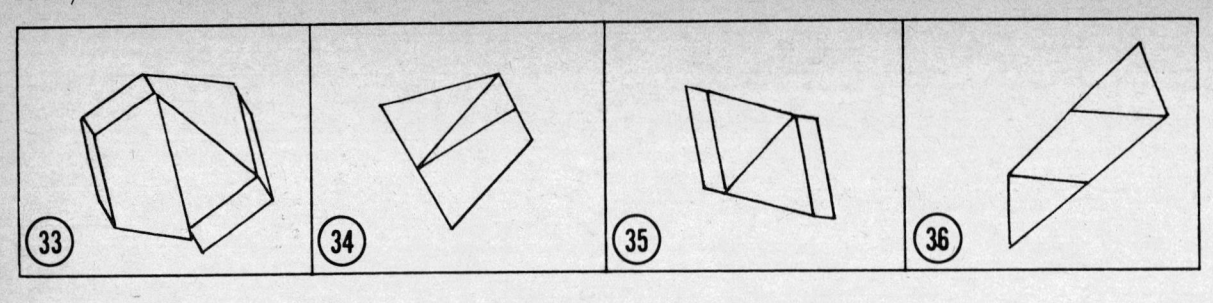

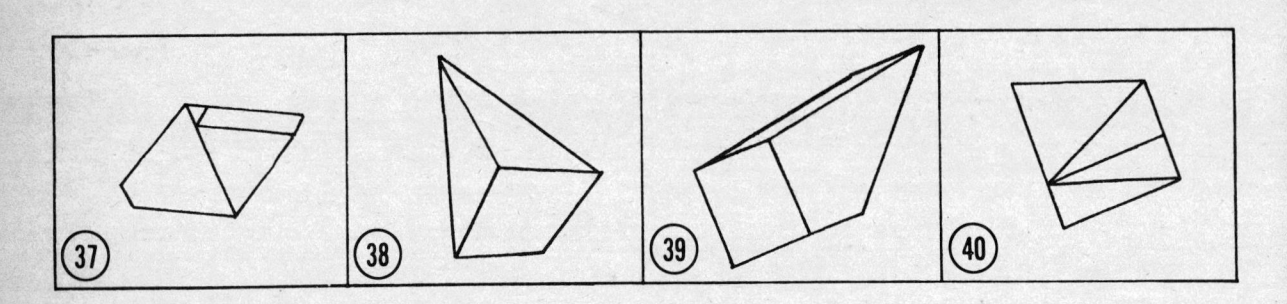

CORRECT ANSWERS FOR THE FOREGOING QUESTIONS

(Please try to answer the questions on your own before looking at our answers. You'll do much better on your test if you follow this rule.)

TEST I

1. B
2. D
3. A
4. E
5. C
6. E
7. B
8. A
9. D
10. C
11. C
12. B
13. D
14. A
15. E
16. B
17. B
18. E
19. C
20. D
21. E
22. C
23. D
24. A
25. B
26. D
27. A
28. B

TEST II

1. A
2. C
3. B
4. D
5. C
6. A
7. E
8. B
9. B
10. A
11. D
12. C
13. D
14. A
15. B
16. C
17. B
18. C
19. A
20. E
21. E
22. A
23. B
24. C
25. B
26. D
27. A
28. C
29. A
30. C
31. E
32. B

TEST III

1. A
2. C
3. B
4. D
5. C
6. A
7. D
8. B
9. B
10. D
11. A
12. C
13. B
14. E
15. D
16. C
17. D
18. B
19. C
20. A
21. A
22. C
23. D
24. D
25. D
26. E
27. B
28. E
29. B
30. D
31. C
32. A
33. D
34. B
35. A
36. C
37. A
38. C
39. E
40. B

AIR FORCE PLACEMENT TESTS

PATTERN ANALYSIS AND COMPREHENSION

17 practice exercises. Important variations on a significant test theme in spatial relations and aptitude exams.

Visualizing Figures

IN questions like these, which are given on tests like yours, you are required to select one of the drawings of objects (A), (B), (C), or (D) below, that could be made from the flat piece drawn at the left, if this flat piece were folded on the dotted lines shown in the drawing.

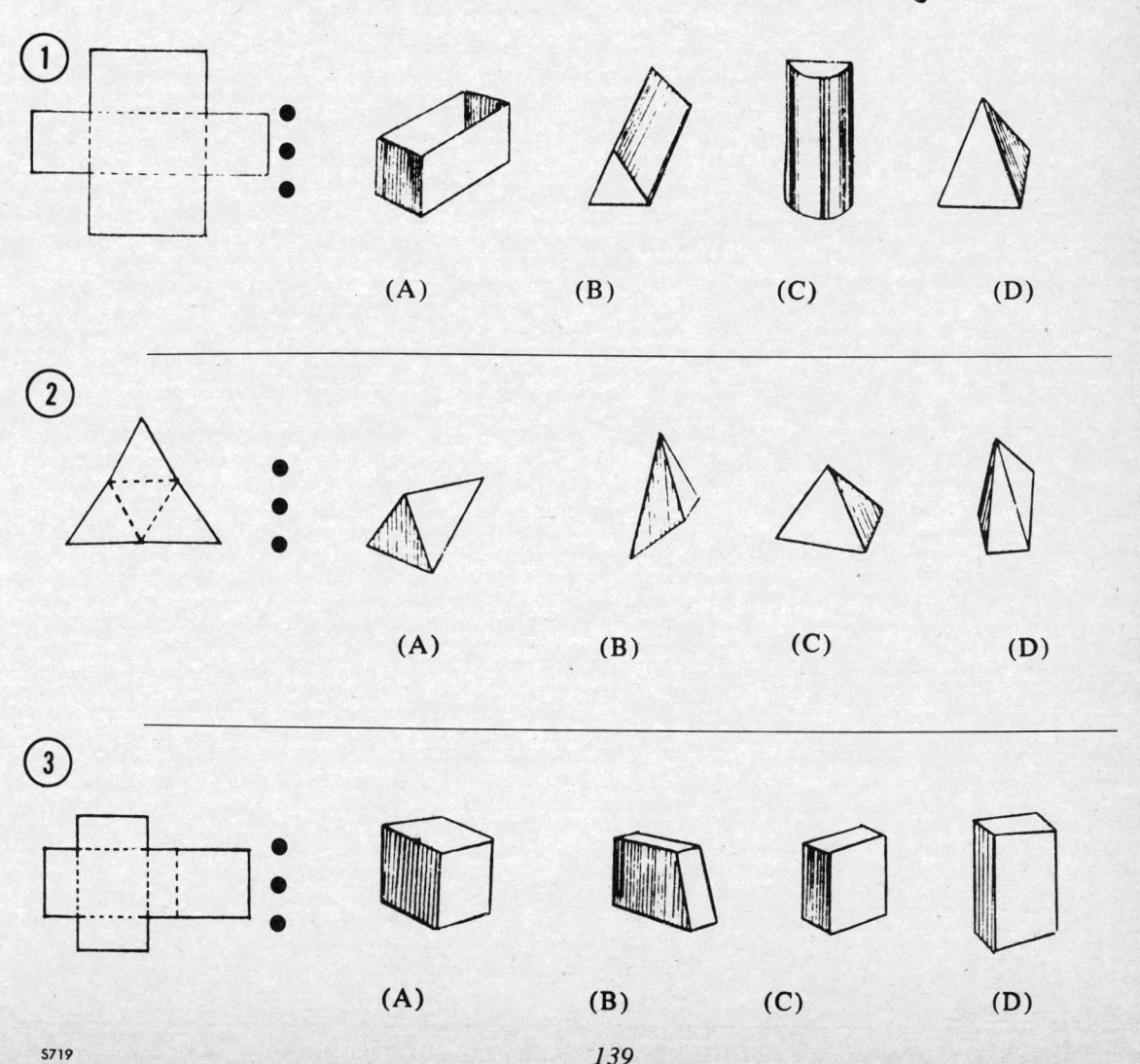

(1)

(A) (B) (C) (D)

(2)

(A) (B) (C) (D)

(3)

(A) (B) (C) (D)

140 / *Practice For Air Force Placement Tests*

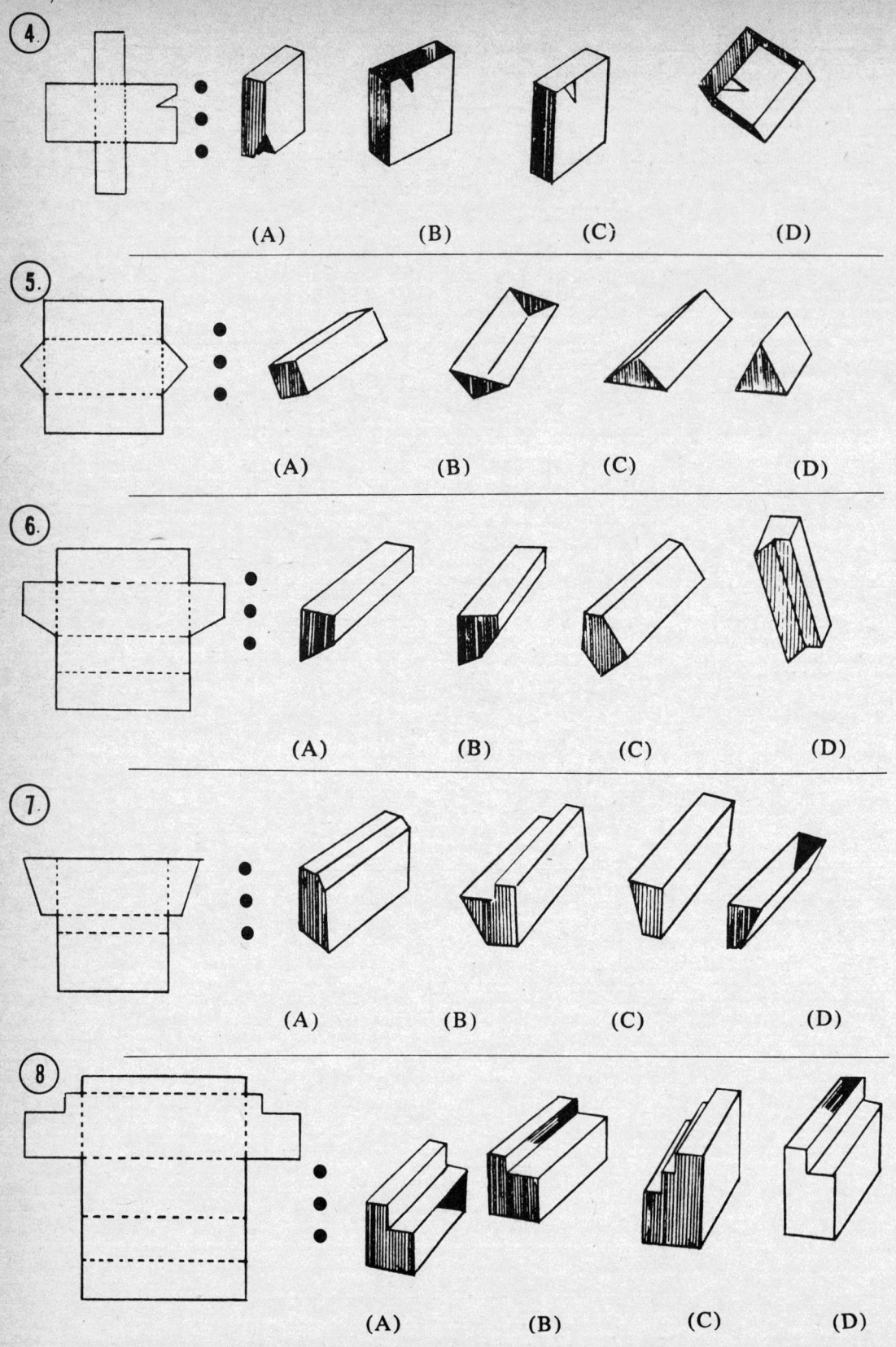

4. (A) (B) (C) (D)

5. (A) (B) (C) (D)

6. (A) (B) (C) (D)

7. (A) (B) (C) (D)

8. (A) (B) (C) (D)

Visualizing Figures / 141

⑨ (A) (B) (C) (D)

⑩ (A) (B) (C) (D)

⑪ (A) (B) (C) (D)

⑫ (A) (B) (C) (D)

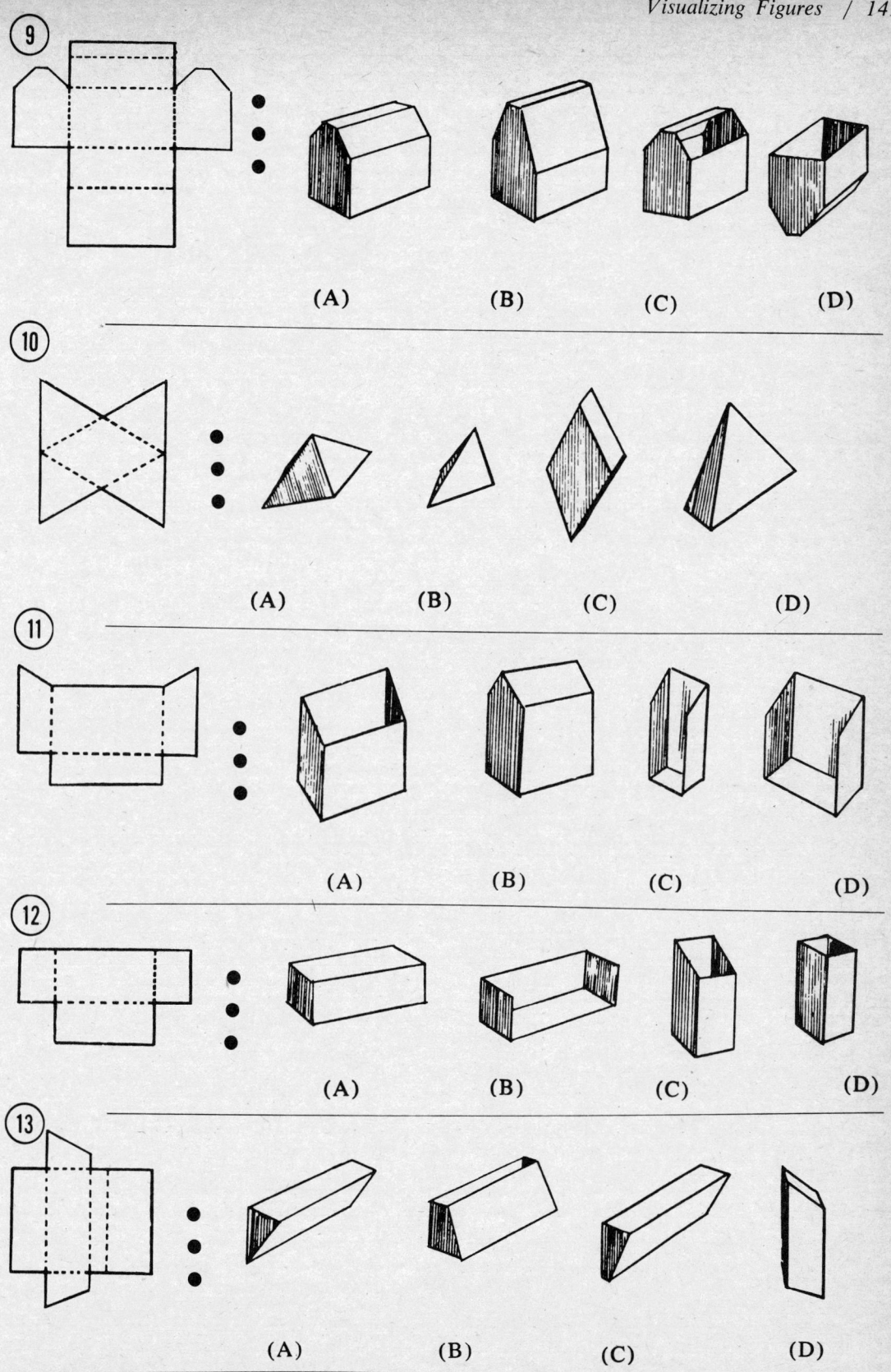

⑬ (A) (B) (C) (D)

142 / *Practice For Air Force Placement Tests*

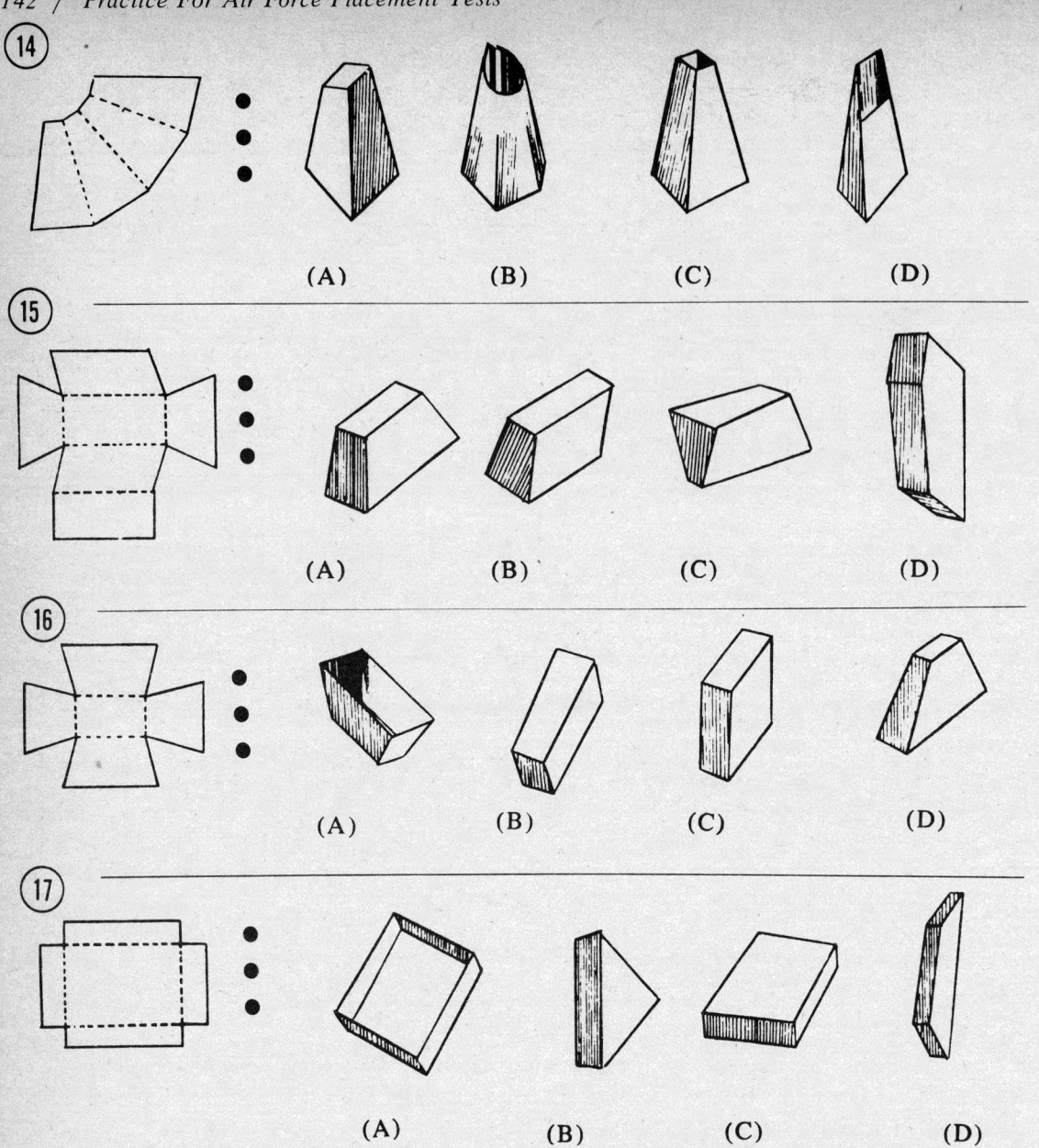

(14) (A) (B) (C) (D)

(15) (A) (B) (C) (D)

(16) (A) (B) (C) (D)

(17) (A) (B) (C) (D)

Correct Answers

(You'll learn more by writing your own answers before comparing them with these.)

1. A	5. C	9. C	13. C
2. C	6. A	10. A	14. C
3. C	7. D	11. D	15. B
4. B	8. B	12. B	16. A
			17. A

Practice For View Questions

In View Questions, you are faced again with fairly simple questions which any intelligent person can answer, given sufficient time. But on your test, you probably won't be given sufficient time. That causes you to rush along faster than you are able to do, and as a result, you make errors. By practicing with the scientific selection of questions in this chapter, you will noticeably increase your speed, your skill and your accuracy in answering questions of this type. On your test, you will find that you are familiar with them and that they offer you little difficulty.

DIRECTIONS

In these View Questions, you are asked to select one of the drawings of objects lettered (A), (B), (C), or (D), which would have the top, front and side views as shown in the drawing at the left. For each of the 18 questions that follow, work as quickly and accurately as you can in choosing your answers. Then compare them with those given at the end of the chapter.

EIGHTEEN EXERCISES IN ANALYSIS AND COMPREHENSION

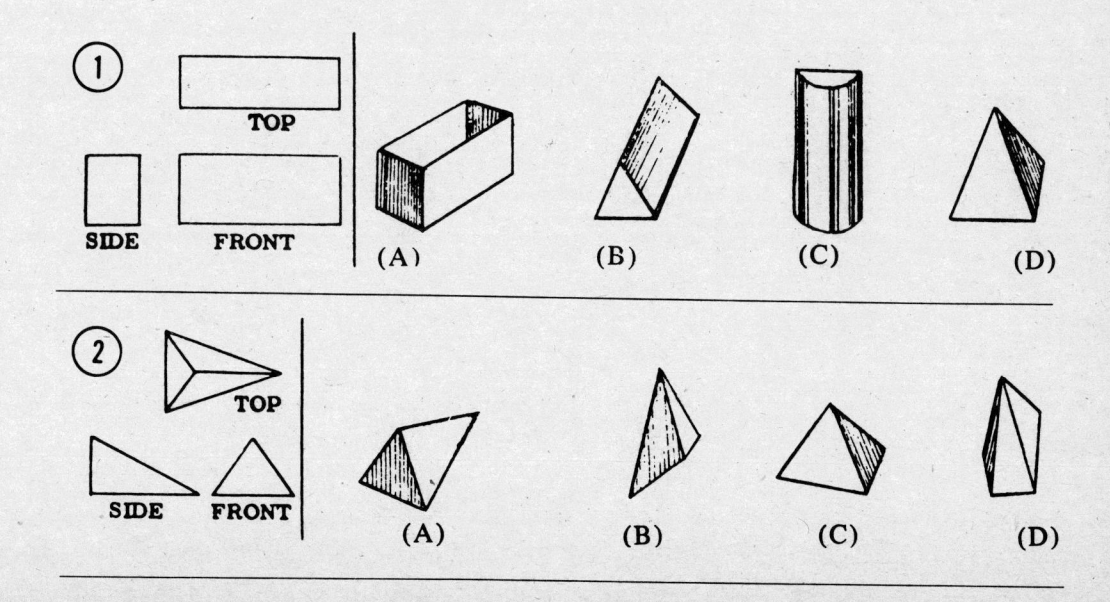

144 / *Practice For Air Force Placement Tests*

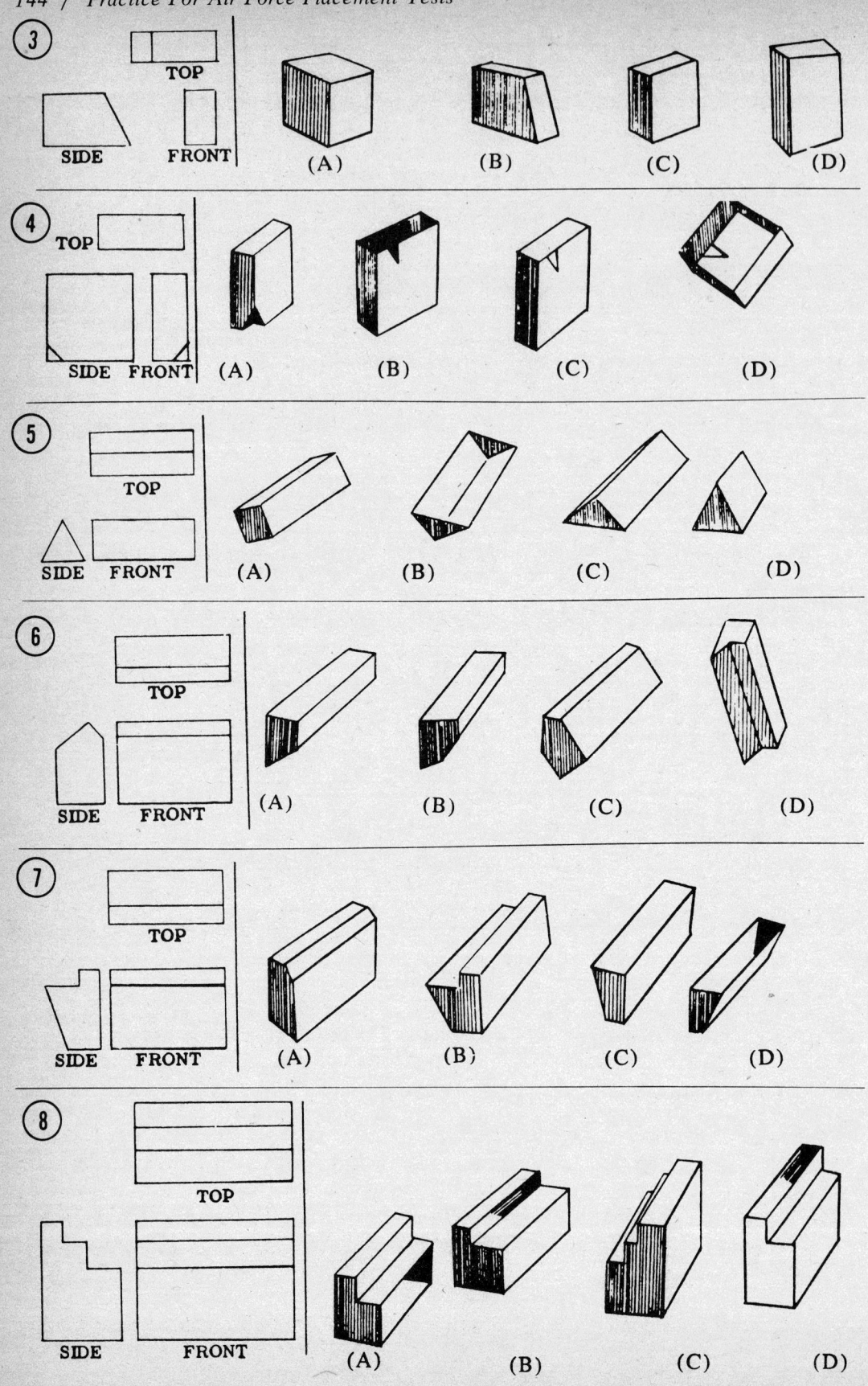

Practice For View Questions / 145

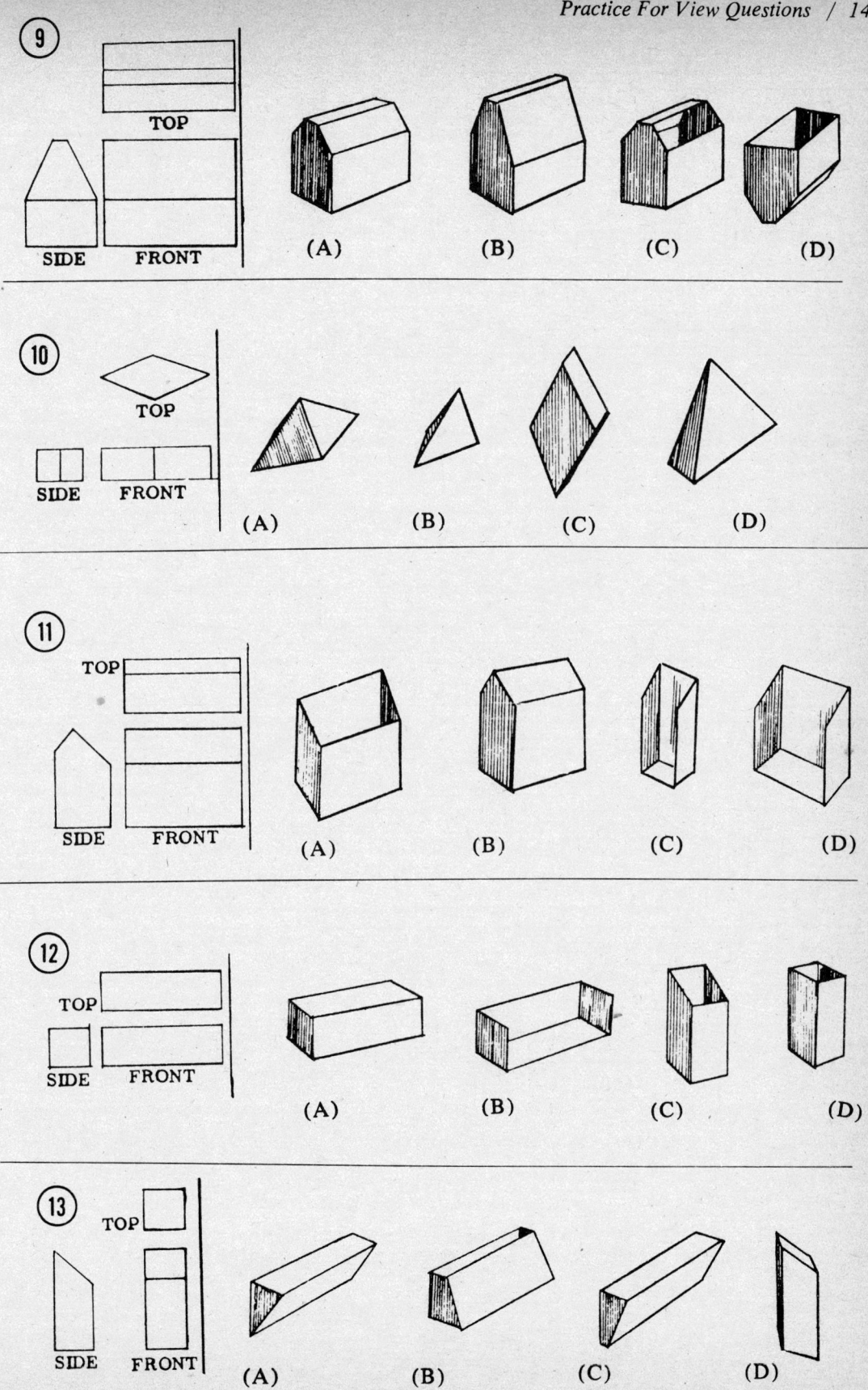

146 / *Practice For Air Force Placement Tests*

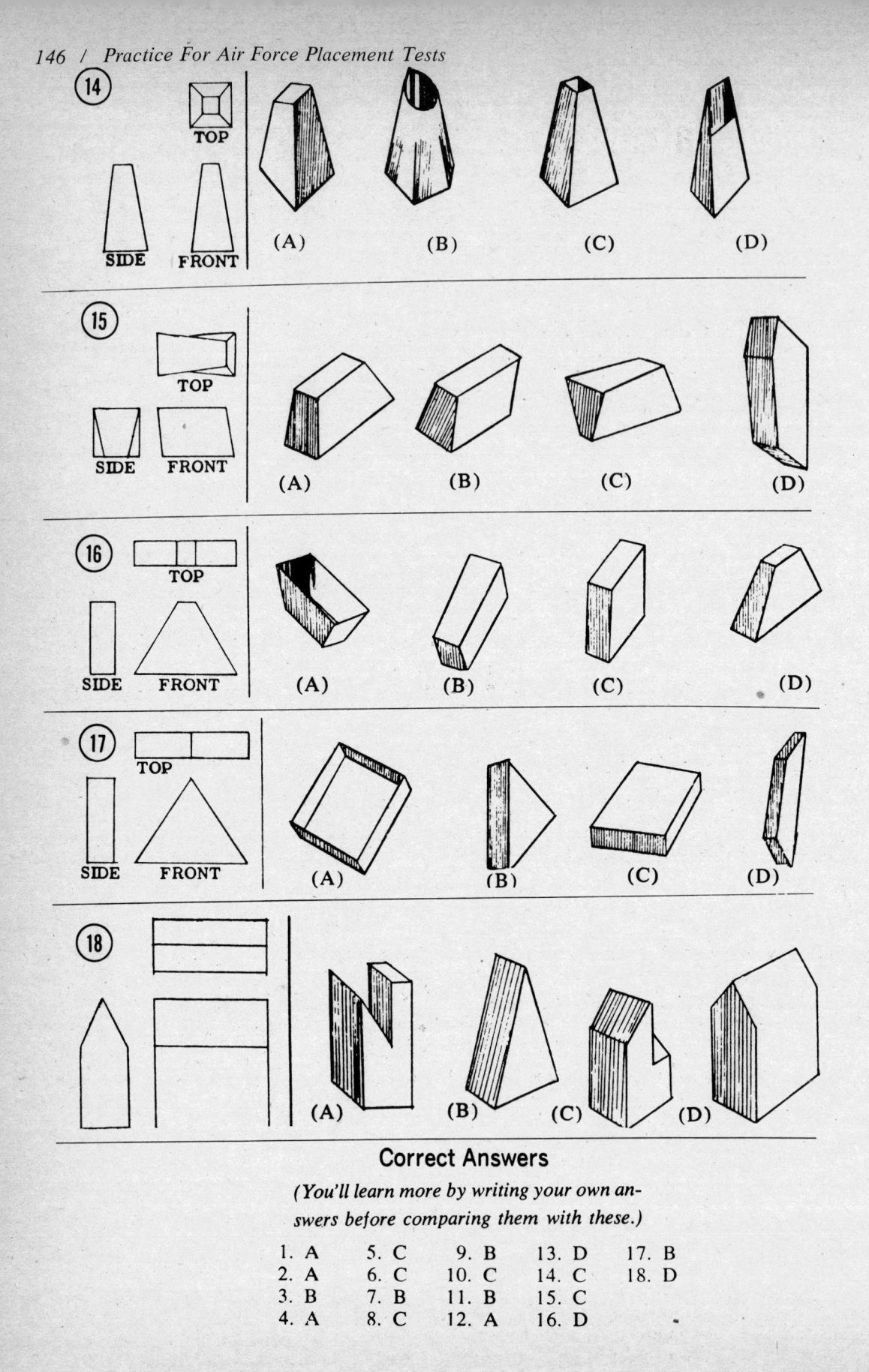

Correct Answers

(You'll learn more by writing your own answers before comparing them with these.)

1. A	5. C	9. B	13. D	17. B
2. A	6. C	10. C	14. C	18. D
3. B	7. B	11. B	15. C	
4. A	8. C	12. A	16. D	

Matching Parts and Figures

These questions on matching parts and figures test your understanding of spatial relations. They also present the type of problems found in making templates and patterns.

THE first two questions show, at the left side, two or more flat pieces. In each question select the arrangement lettered A, B, C, or D that shows how these pieces can be fitted together without gaps or overlapping. The pieces may be *turned around* or *turned over* in any way to make them fit together.

From these pieces

①

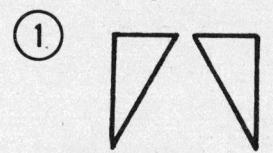

which one of these arrangements can you make?

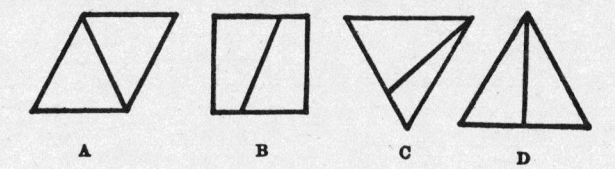

A   B   C   D

From these pieces

②

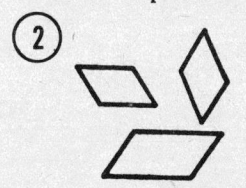

which one of these arrangements can you make?

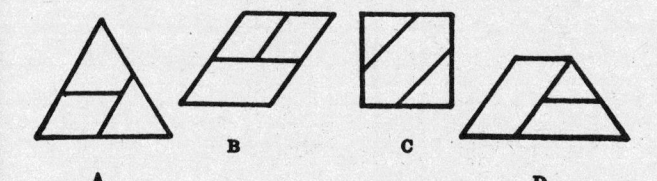

A   B   C   D

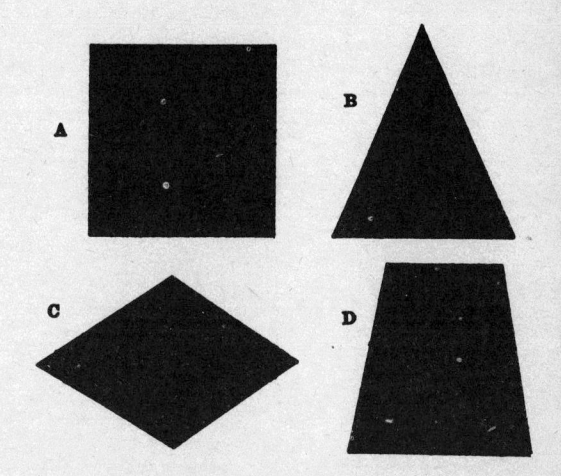

Look at sample question 3. If the two pieces were fitted together they would make pattern D. The piece on the left fits at the bottom of pattern D, and the piece at the right is turned around and over to make the top of the pattern.

③

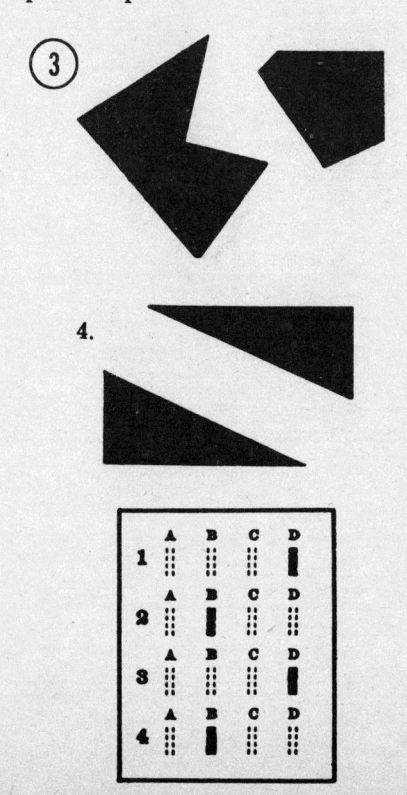

4.

The next questions are based on the four solid patterns shown.

Each of the questions shows *one* of these four patterns cut up into pieces. For each question, decide which one of the four patterns could be made by fitting *all of the pieces* together without having any edges overlap and without leaving any space between pieces. Some of the pieces may need to be *turned around* or *turned over* to make them fit. The pattern must be made in its exact size and shape.

148 / *Practice For Air Force Placement Tests*

TEST QUESTIONS FOR PRACTICE

Each of the following items numbered 1 to 46 is followed by a group of five figures lettered A, B, C, D, and E. Two of these lettered figures, when put together, make the drawing marked with the item number. Choose the letters of the two figures, which, when put together, are most nearly the same as the design marked with the item number. In writing answers, place the capital letters in alphabetical order.

Samples: The answer to Item IV is A and D; the answer to Item V is B and C.

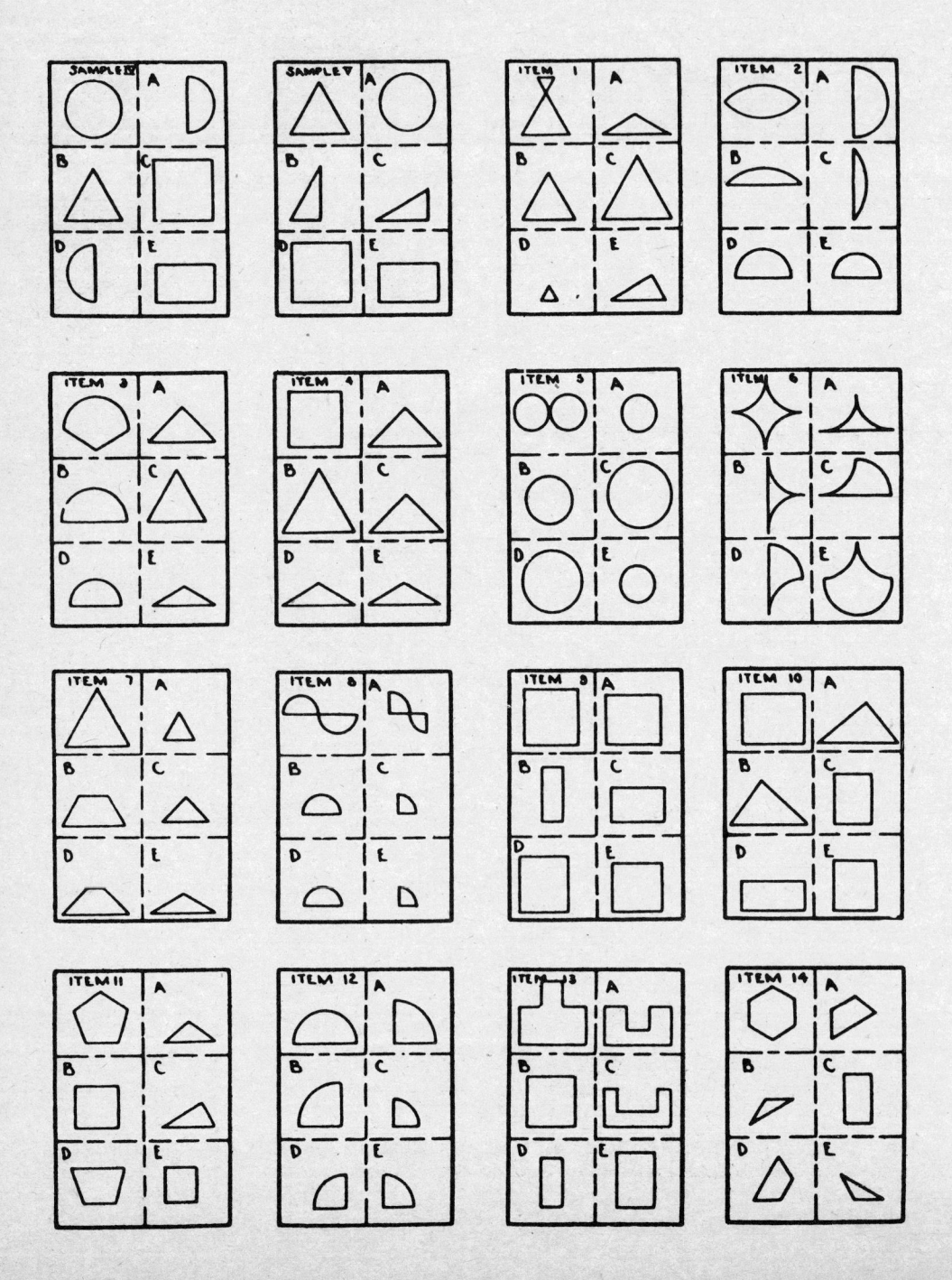

Matching Parts and Figures / 149

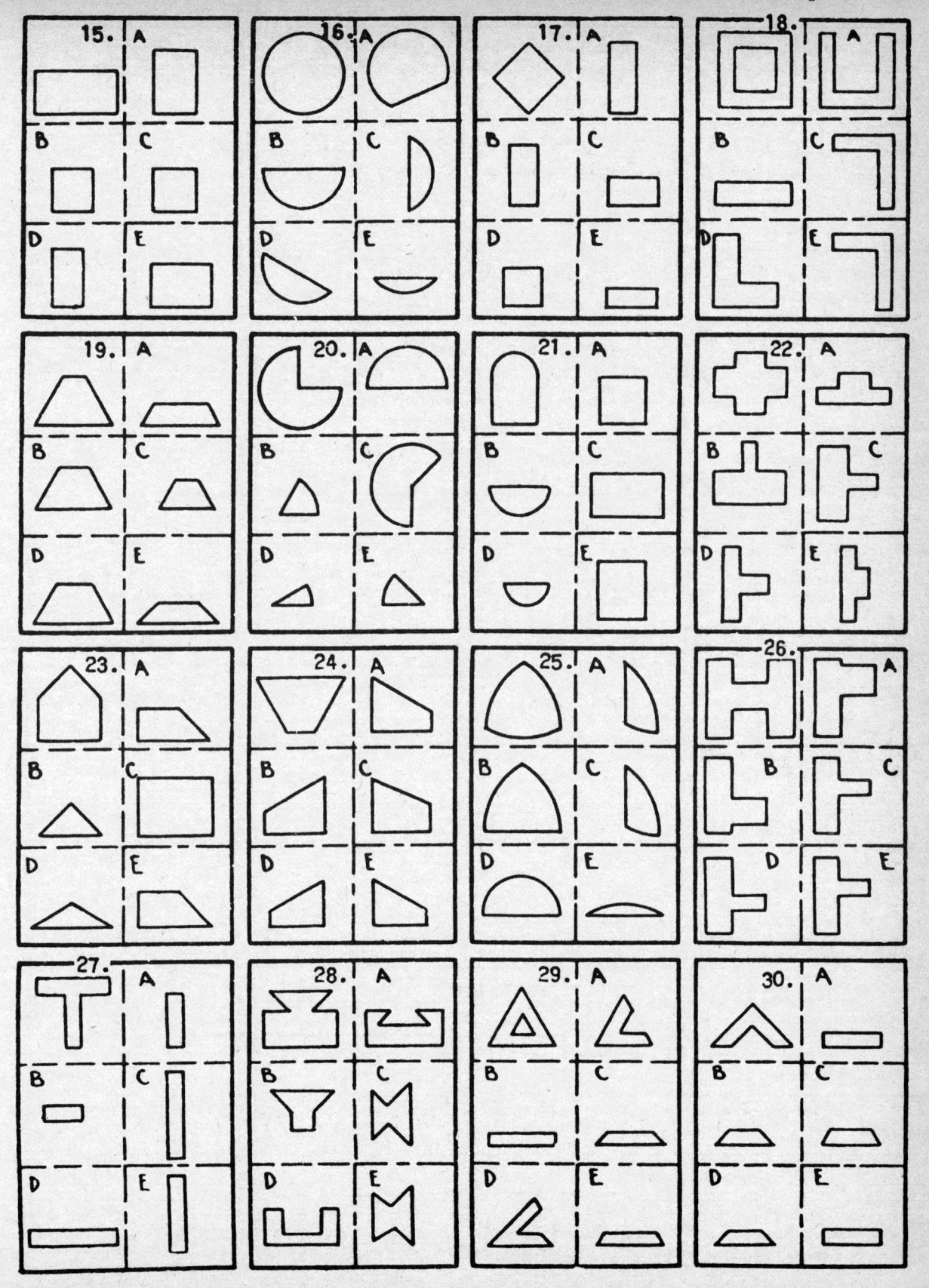

150 / *Practice For Air Force Placement Tests*

Matching Parts and Figures / 151

(47) Fitting Angles (Spatial Relations):
Which form is made from A?

(1)

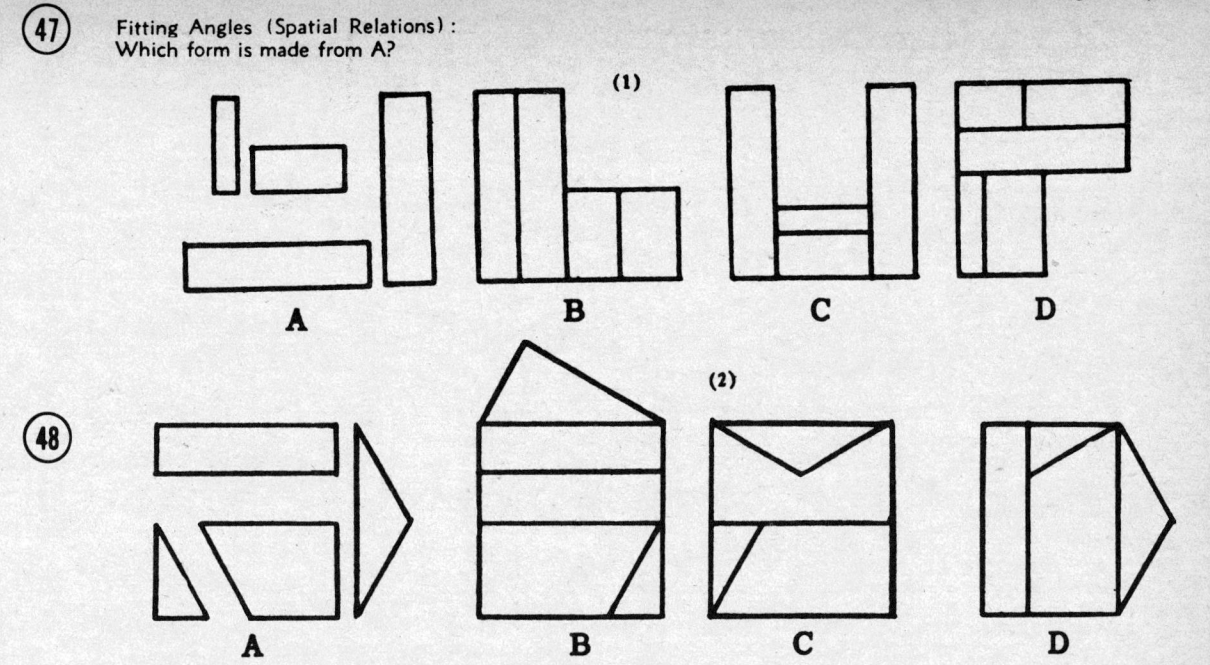

A   B   C   D

(2)

A   B   C   D

PAPER FORMS—1ST GROUP

In the diagrams below choose the form B, C, or D, made up only and entirely of the parts shown in A.

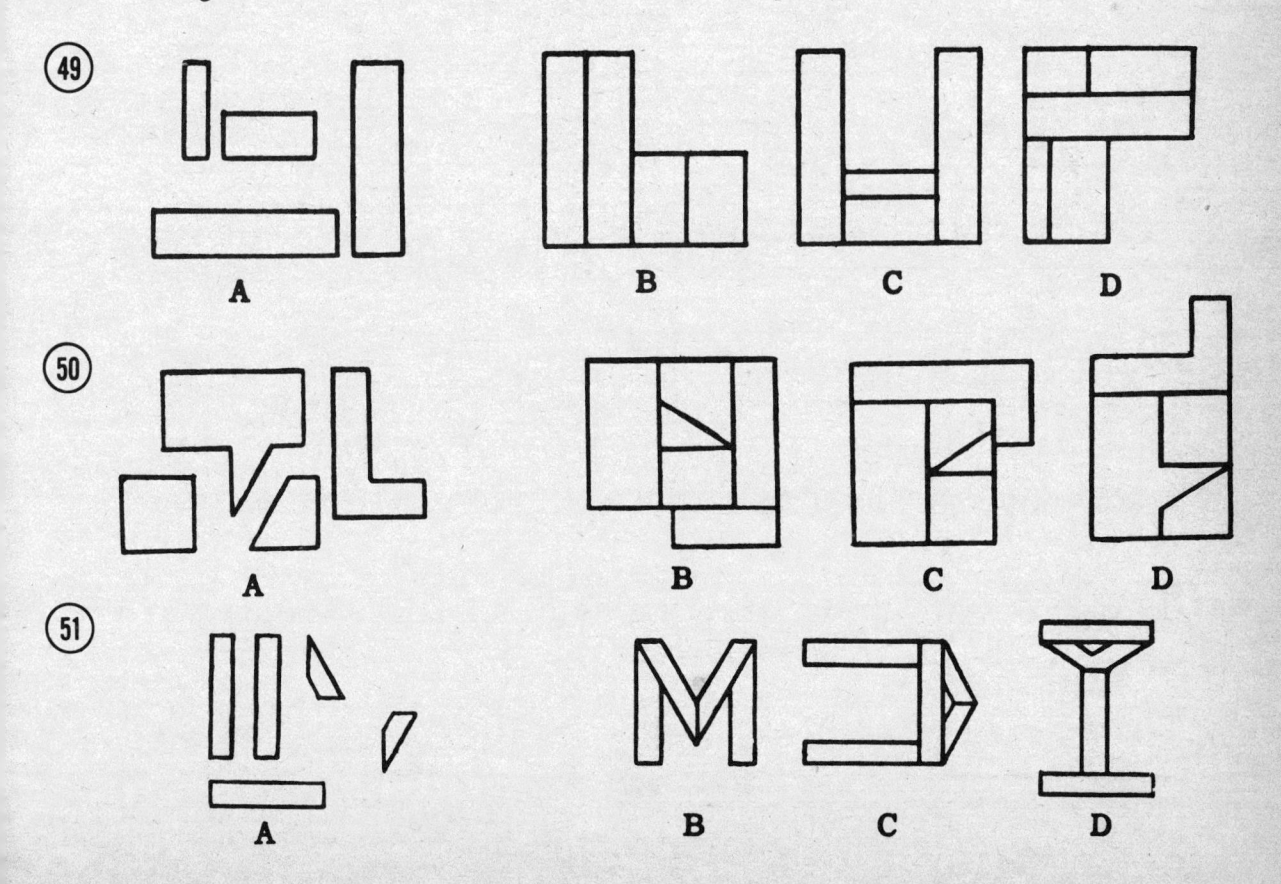

(49)
A   B   C   D

(50)
A   B   C   D

(51)
A   B   C   D

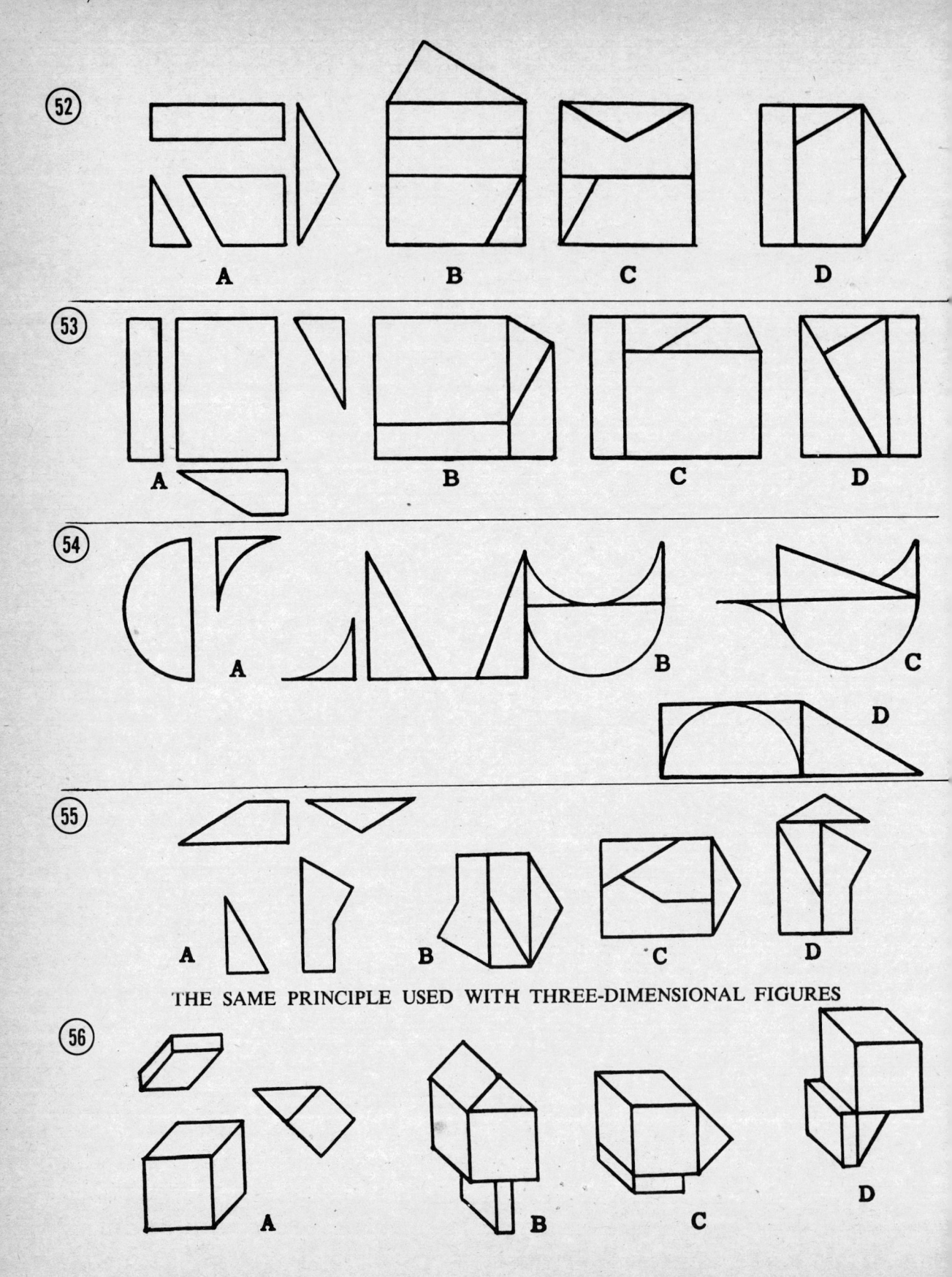

152 / *Practice For Air Force Placement Tests*

THE SAME PRINCIPLE USED WITH THREE-DIMENSIONAL FIGURES

Matching Parts and Figures / 153

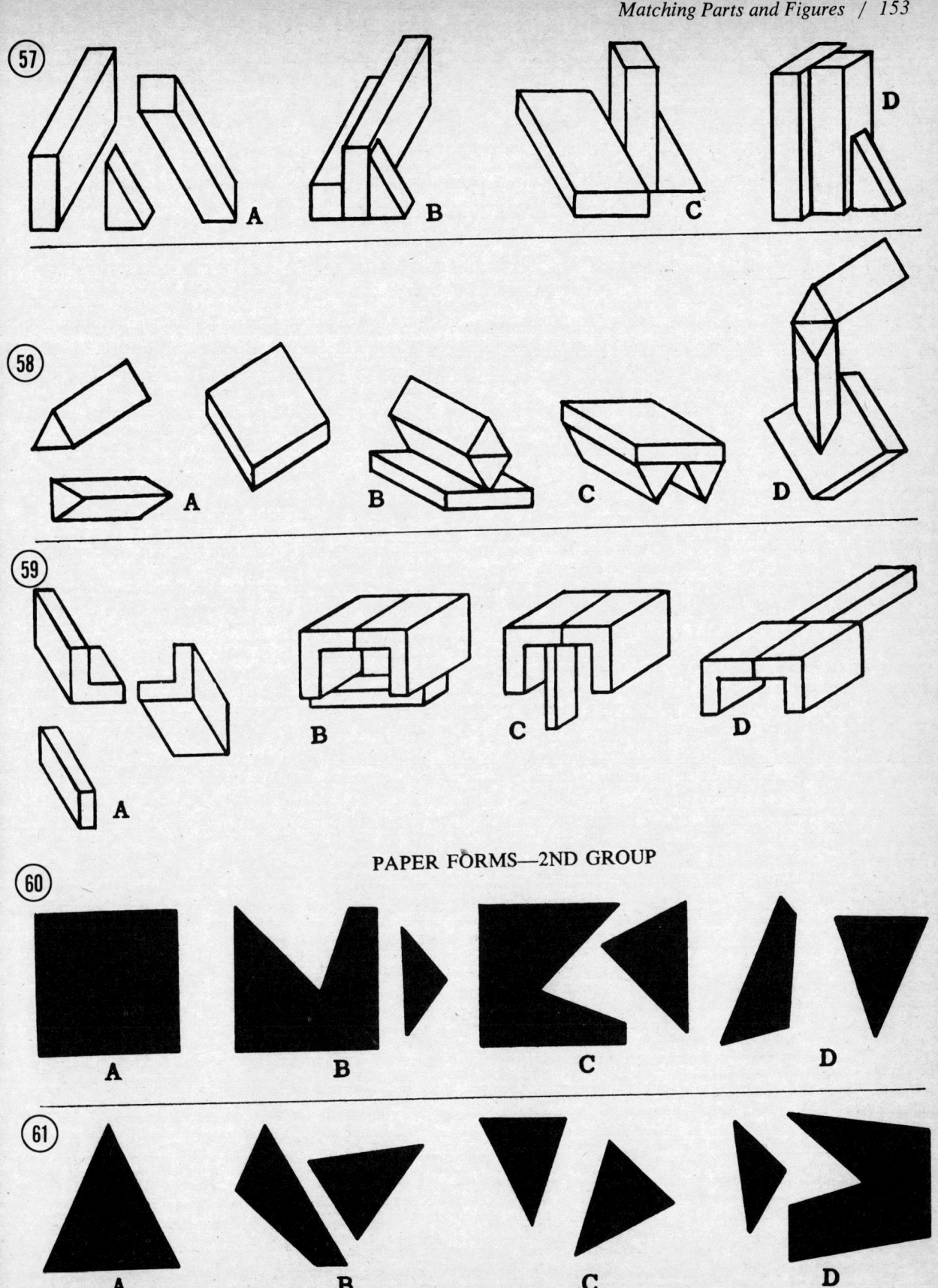

PAPER FORMS—2ND GROUP

154 / *Practice For Air Force Placement Tests*

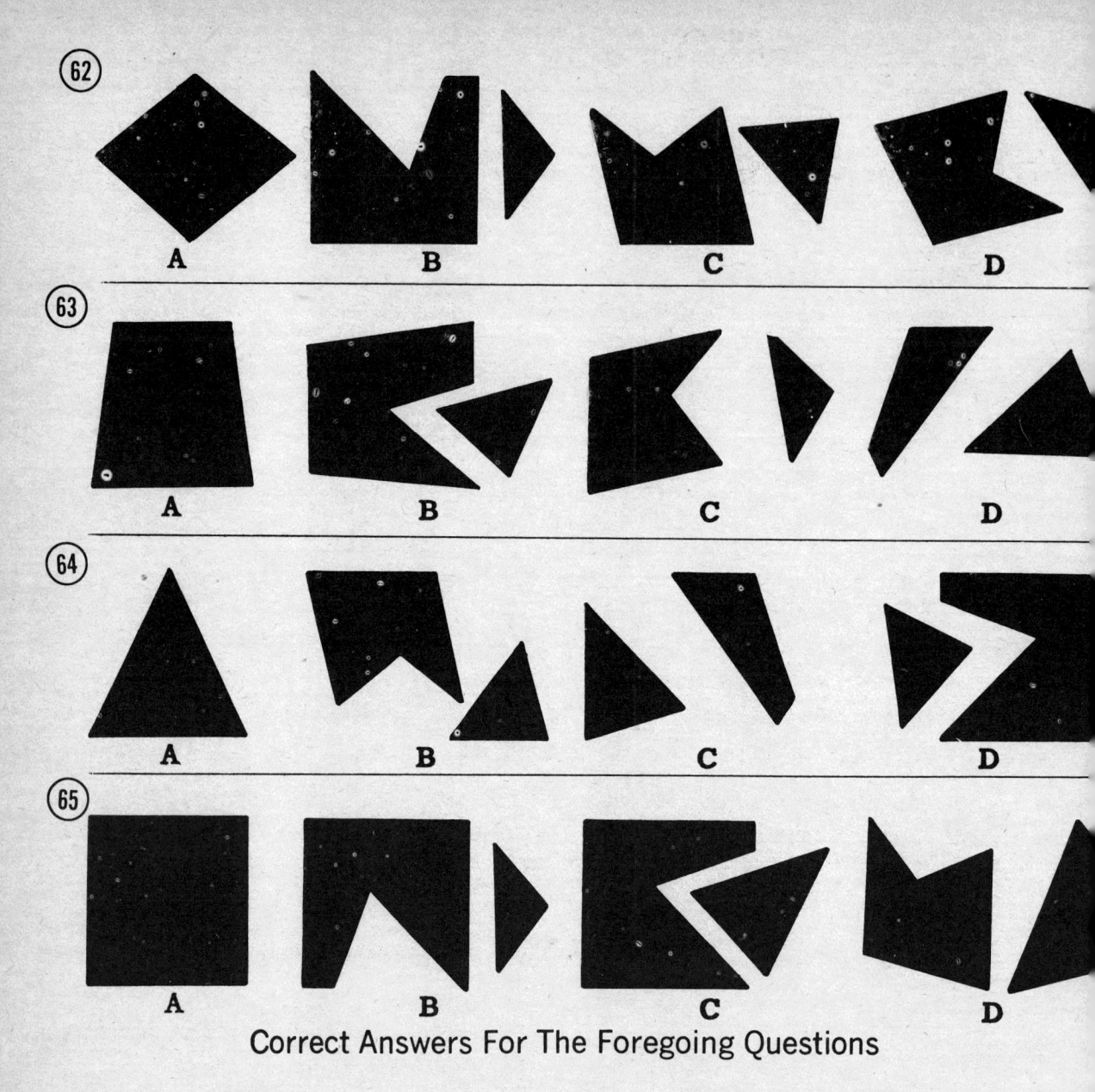

Correct Answers For The Foregoing Questions

(Please try to answer the questions on your own before looking at our answers. You'll do much better on your test if you follow this rule.)

1. BD	16. AE	31. CD	46. DE	61. B
2. BC	17. CE	32. AB	47. C	62. D
3. BE	18. CE	33. BC	48. D	63. B
4. AC	19. AC	34. BD	49. C	64. C
5. AE	20. CE	35. BC	50. D	65. C
6. AB	21. AD	36. AD	51. C	
7. AB	22. AE	37. CD	52. D	
8. BD	23. AE	38. CE	53. B	
9. BC	24. DE	39. CD	54. D	
10. AB	25. BE	40. CD	55. B	
11. AD	26. CD, DE, CE	41. CE	56. B	
12. DE	27. AE	42. CD	57. B	
13. AD	28. AC	43. AD	58. D	
14. AD	29. AE	44. AD	59. D	
15. BC	30. BD	45. CD	60. C	

AIR FORCE PLACEMENT TESTS

MECHANICAL INSIGHT TESTS

The following questions have been selected from various civil service and private industry tests. All are designed to gauge your mechanical aptitude and your inherent feeling for machinery. They all measure your mechanical ability. They will also help you determine whether or not you need to review basic arithmetic.

HUNDREDS of civil service jobs and many jobs in private industry require the ability known as "mechanical insight"; in other words, the ability to visualize the operations of a machine in motion, to see the relationships among the different parts of a machine, and the capacity to make the necessary computations which are part of the job of a man or woman whose work is around machinery.

Over many years, personnel experts and psychologists have been working together to provide a series of paper tests which will accurately predict the ability of a person to handle mechanical work. In practice it has been found that a person who does well on a pencil and paper test of this type will usually do well in the workshop.

Many questions on the following pages are designed to test the candidate's ability to think in terms of a third dimension. Others deal with hydraulics, the forces exerted by fluids in a closed system, and with the workings of valves. Some call for knowledge of the operations of pulley systems and levers. In others, it is necessary to analyze the motion of interlocking gear systems.

These questions also will enable you to discover your weak points before you take your examination. Do your best, and don't look at the answers until you have solved each problem yourself, or made your best effort to find the correct answer. You may find that the computations are difficult; that may call for brush-up in arithmetic. Or you may determine that a little review of basic physics may be what you need before you take the test.

You will find no "trick" or "catch" questions on a test of this type. The purpose of the examinations is to find the persons best qualified for work of a mechanical nature. If you have a background of mechanical experience or a natural aptitude for mechanical work, you should not find the questions too difficult.

DIRECTIONS FOR ANSWERING QUESTIONS

For each question read all the choices carefully. Then select that answer which you consider correct or most nearly correct. Write the letter preceding your best choice next to the question Should you want to answer on the kind of answer sheet used on machine-scored examinations, we have provided several such facsimiles. Tear one out if you wish, and mark your answers on it ... just as you would do on an actual exam.

In machine-scored examinations you should record all your answers on the answer sheet provided. Don't make the mistake of putting answers on the test booklet itself.

TEST I. MECHANICAL COMPREHENSION

TIME: 15 Minutes

DIRECTIONS: For each question read all the choices carefully. Then select that answer which you consider correct or most nearly correct. Blacken the answer space corresponding to your best choice, just as you would do on the actual examination.

1.

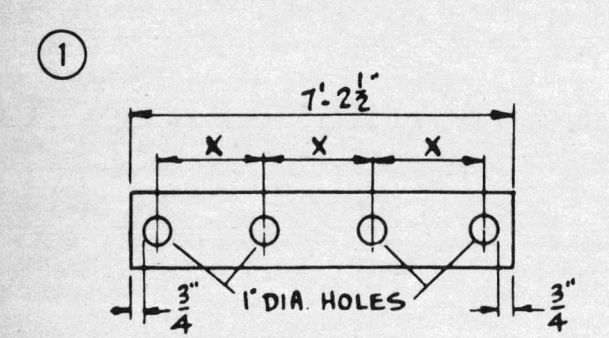

The dimension "X" on the piece shown is
(A) 2' - 3 2/3"   (B) 2' - 4"
(C) 2' - 4 1/3"   (D) 2' - 5 1/4".

2.

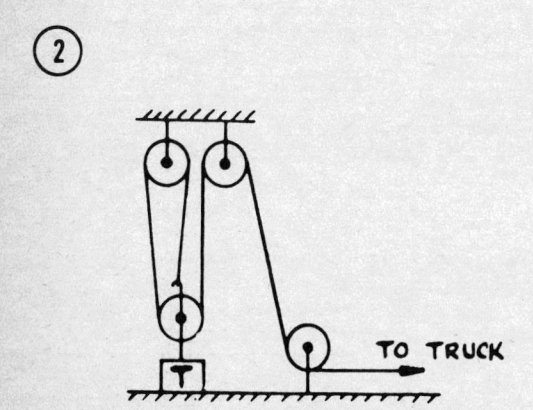

The tank "T" is to be raised as shown by attaching the pull rope to a truck. If the tank is to be raised ten feet, the truck will have to move
(A) 20 feet   (B) 30 feet
(C) 40 feet   (D) 50 feet.

3.

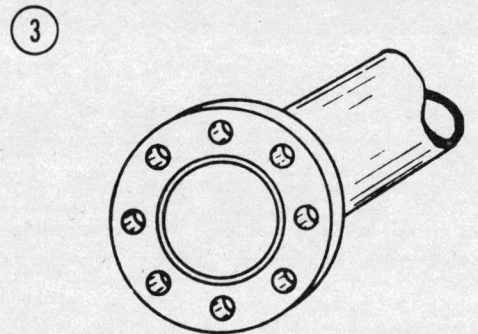

In the case of the standard flanged pipe shown, the maximum angle through which it would be necessary to rotate the pipe in order to line up the holes is
(A) 22.5 degrees   (B) 30 degrees
(C) 45 degrees   (D) 60 degrees.

4.

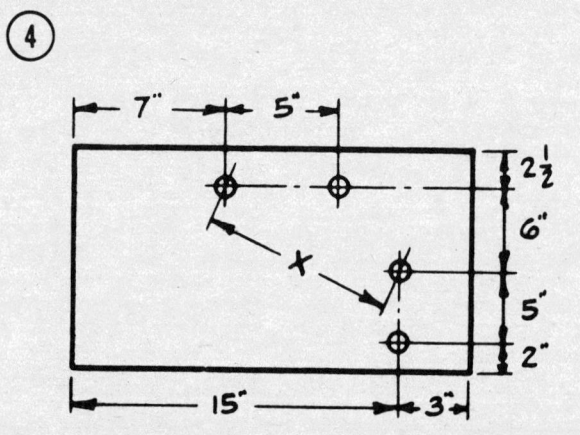

The distance "X" from center to center of the two holes is
(A) 10 inches   (B) 9 inches
(C) 8 1/2 inches   (D) 6 inches.

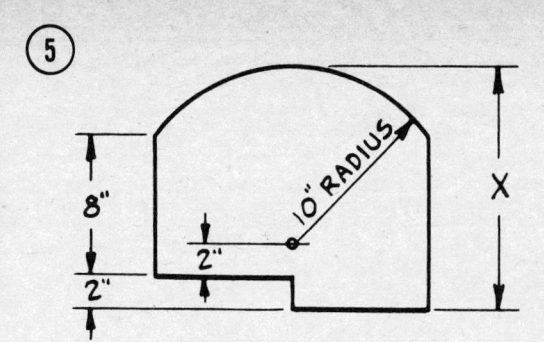

⑤ The distance "X" on the piece shown is
(A) 16 inches (B) 14 inches
(C) 12 inches (D) 10 inches.

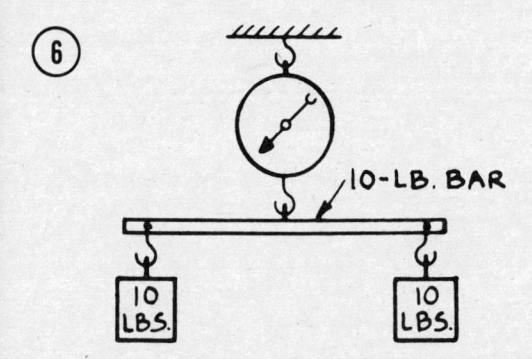

⑥ The reading on the weighing scale will be approximately
(A) zero (B) 10 lbs.
(C) 20 lbs. (D) 30 lbs.

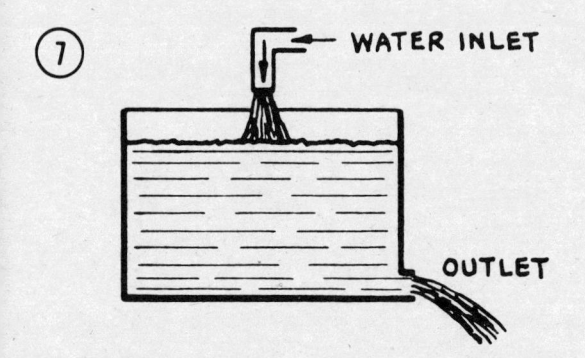

⑦ If water is flowing into the tank at the rate of 120 gallons per hour and flowing out of the tank at a constant rate of one gallon per minute, the water level in the tank will
(A) rise 1 gallon per minute
(B) rise 2 gallons per minute
(C) fall 2 gallons per minute
(D) fall 1 gallon per minute.

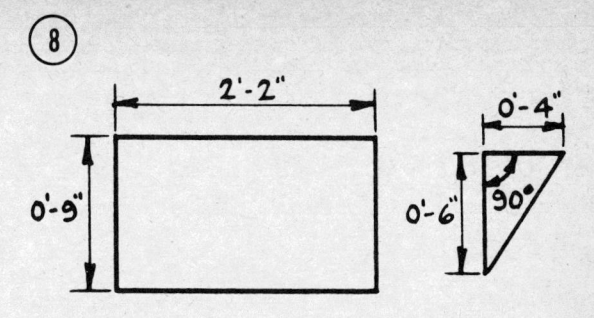

⑧ The maximum number of triangular pieces shown which can be cut from the piece of sheet metal shown is
(A) 12 (B) 16
(C) 20 (D) 25.

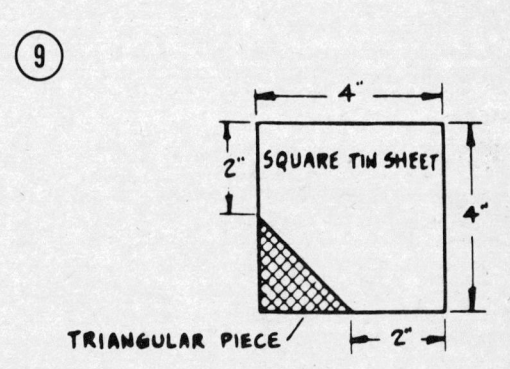

⑨ The maximum number of triangular pieces which can be cut from the tin sheet is
(A) 10 (B) 8
(C) 6 (D) 4.

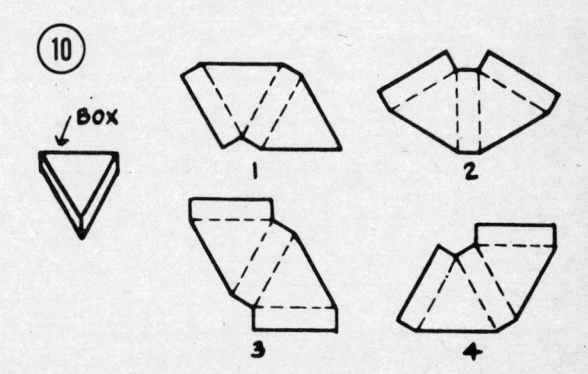

⑩ The flat sheet metal pattern which can be bent along the dotted lines to form the completely closed triangular box is
(A) 1 (B) 2
(C) 3 (D) 4.

11.

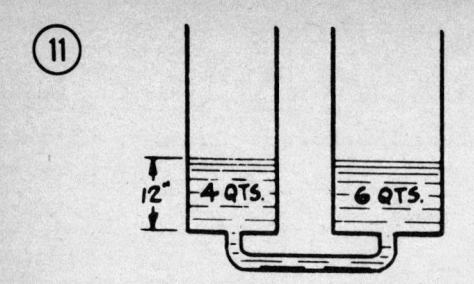

To bring the level of the water in the tanks to a height of 2 1/2 feet, the quantity of water to be added is
(A) 10 qts. (B) 15 qts.
(C) 20 qts. (D) 25 qts.

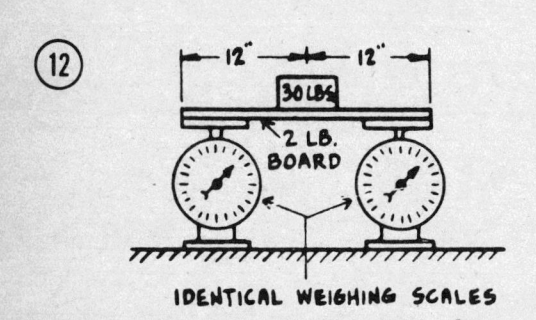

12.

The weight held by the board and placed on the two identical scales will cause *each* scale to read
(A) 8 lbs.   (B) 15 lbs.
(C) 16 lbs. (D) 32 lbs.

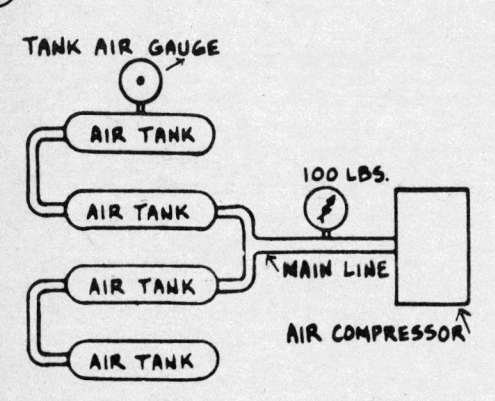

13.

Four air reservoirs have been filled with air by the air compressor. If the main line air gauge reads 100 lbs. then the tank air gauge will read
(A) 25 lbs. (B) 50 lbs.
(C) 100 lbs. (D) 200 lbs.

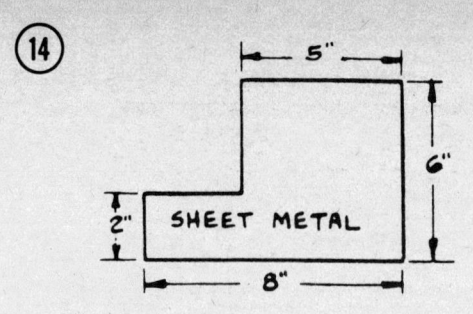

14.

The area of the piece of sheet metal in square inches is
(A) 48 (B) 36
(C) 20 (D) 16.

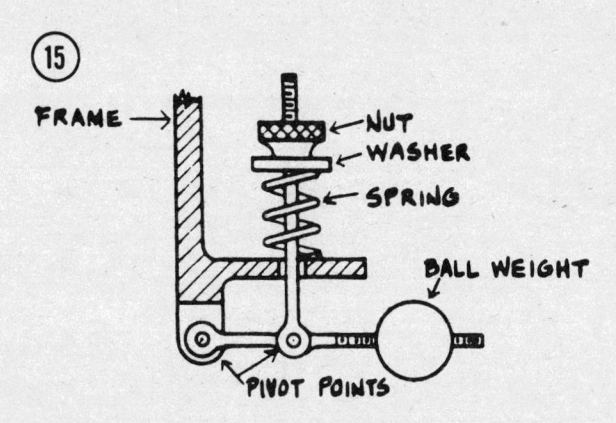

15.

If the ball and spring mechanism are balanced in the position shown, the ball will move upward if
(A) the nut is loosened
(B) ball is moved away from the frame
(C) the nut is loosened and the ball moved away from the frame
(D) the nut is tightened.

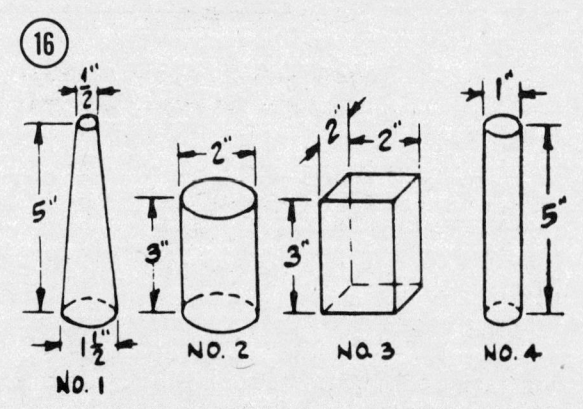

16.

The container which will hold the most water is
(A) No. 1 (B) No. 2
(C) No. 3 (D) No. 4.

17

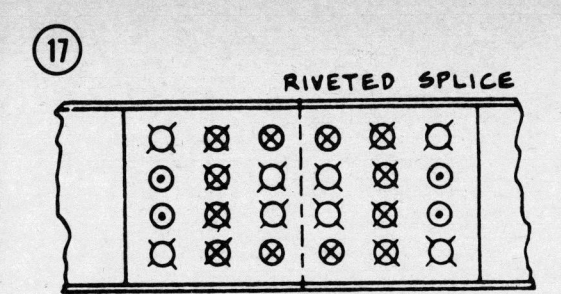

RIVETED SPLICE

In the structural steel splice the different types of rivets are shown by different symbols. The number of different types of rivets is
(A) 6 (B) 5
(C) 4 (D) 3.

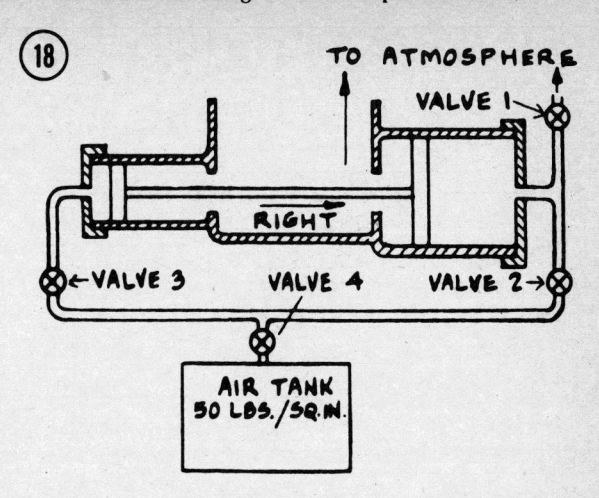

18

If all valves are closed at the start, in order to have air pressure from the tank move the pistons to the right, the valves to be opened are
(A) 2 and 4   (B) 1 and 2
(C) 2, 3, and 4   (D) 1, 3 and 4.

CONSOLIDATE YOUR KEY ANSWERS HERE

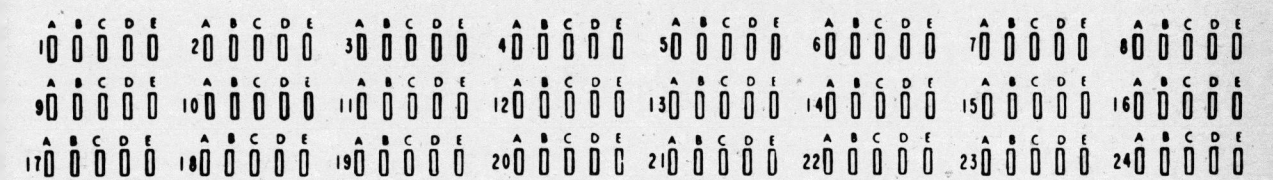

Correct Answers For The Foregoing Questions

(Please make every effort to answer the questions on your own before looking at these answers. You'll make faster progress by following this rule.)

1. B	4. A	7. A	10. C	13. C	16. C
2. B	5. B	8. B	11. B	14. B	17. C
3. A	6. D	9. B	12. C	15. D	18. D

TEST II. MECHANICAL COMPREHENSION

TIME: 10 Minutes

DIRECTIONS: For each of the following questions, select the choice which best answers the question or completes the statement.

1.

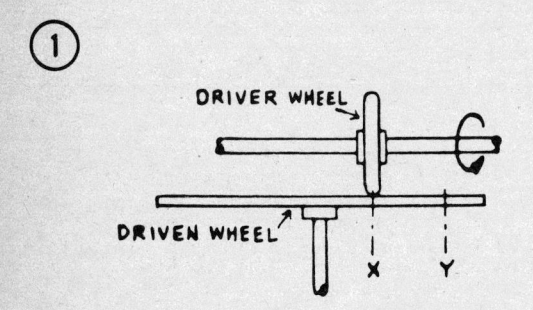

When the driver wheel is moved from location X to location Y, the driven wheel will
(A) reverse its direction of rotation
(B) turn slower
(C) not change its speed of rotation
(D) turn faster.

2.

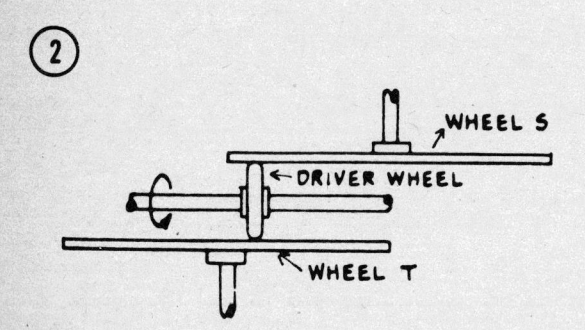

With the wheels in the position shown
(A) wheels S and T will rotate in opposite directions
(B) wheels S and T will rotate at the same speed
(C) wheels S and T will rotate in the same direction
(D) wheel S will rotate at exactly the same speed as the driver wheel.

3.

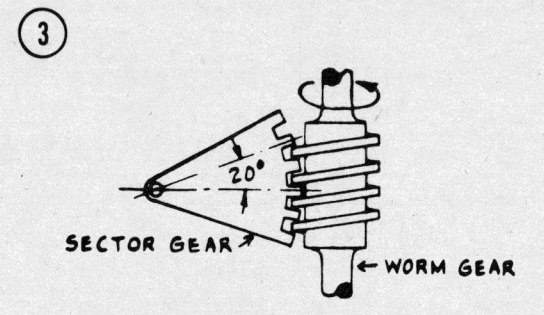

One revolution of the worm gear will turn the sector gear through the angle of
(A) 30°   (B) 20°
(C) 10°   (D) 5°.

4.

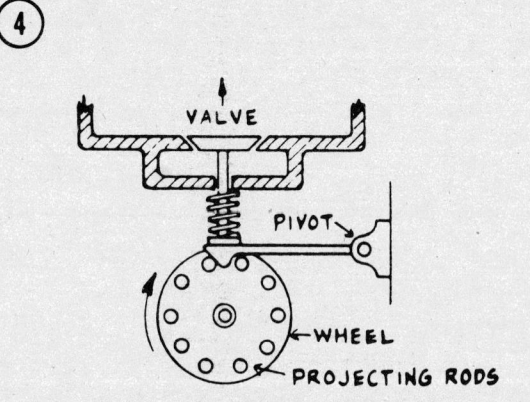

In order to open the valve once every second the wheel must rotate at
(A) 30 RPM   (B) 20 RPM
(C) 10 RPM   (D) 6 RPM

5

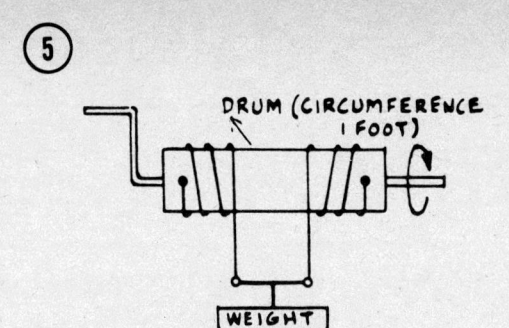

One complete revolution of the windlass drum will move the weight up
(A) 1/2 foot (B) 1 foot
(C) 1 1/2 feet (D) 2 feet.

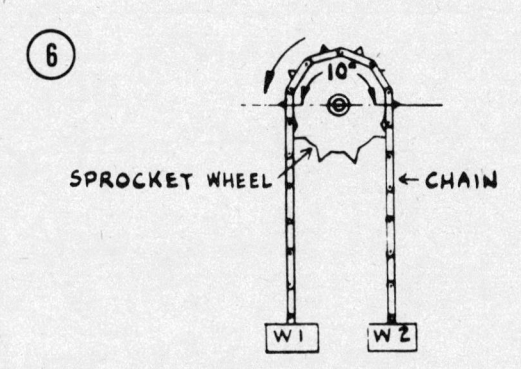

6

One complete revolution of the sprocket wheel will bring weight W2 higher than weight W1 by
(A) 20″ (B) 30″
(C) 40″ (D) 50″.

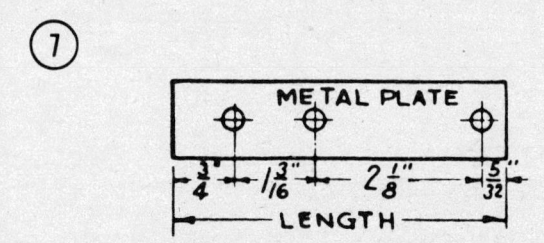

7

The total length of the metal plate shown is
(A) 3 7/32 inches (B) 3 9/32 inches
(C) 4 7/32 inches (D) 4 9/32 inches.

8

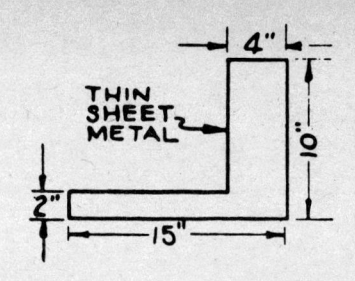

The maximum number of rectangular pieces, each two inches by eight inches which can be cut from the thin metal sheets shown is
(A) One (B) Two
(C) Three (D) Four.

9

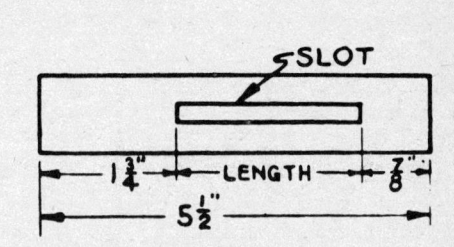

The length of the slot in the piece shown is
(A) 2 7/8 inches (B) 2 5/8 inches
(C) 2 3/8 inches (D) 2 1/8 inches.

10

The reading shown on the gage is
(A) 10.35 (B) 10.7
(C) 13.5 (D) 17.0.

11

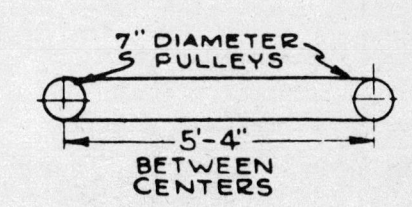

The total length of the belt connecting the two pulleys is
(A) 7 feet, 2 inches (B) 9 feet, 0 inches
(C) 12 feet, 6 inches (D) 14 feet, 4 inches.

12.

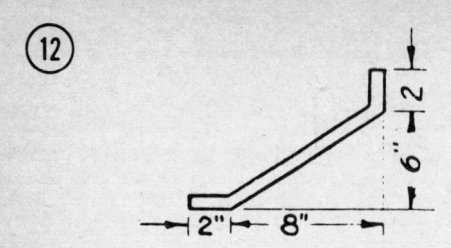

The length of the strap before bending is
(A) 18 inches (B) 14 inches
(C) 13 inches (D) 11 inches.

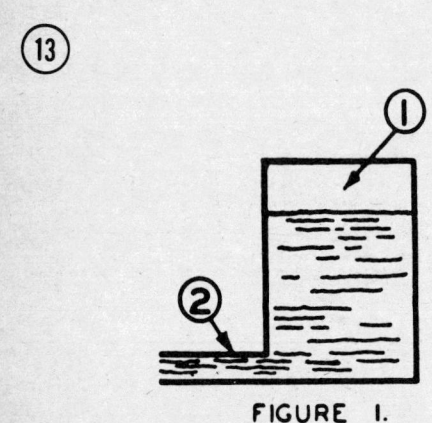

13.

FIGURE I.

Figure I represents an enclosed water chamber, partially filled with water. The number 1 indicates air in the chamber and 2 indicates a pipe by which water enters the chamber. If the water pressure in the pipe, 2, increases then the
(A) water pressure in the chamber will be decreased
(B) water level in the chamber will fall
(C) air in the chamber will be compressed
(D) air in the chamber will expand
(E) water will flow out of the chamber.

14.

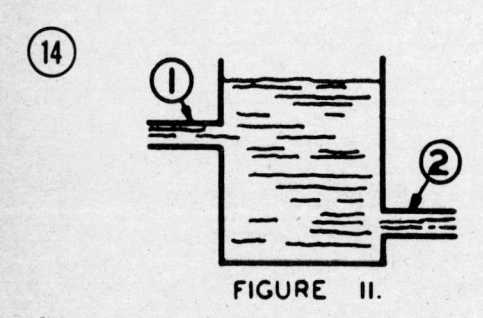

FIGURE II.

Figure II represents a water tank containing water. The number 1 indicates an intake pipe and 2 indicates a discharge pipe. Of the following, the statement which is least accurate is that the
(A) tank will eventually overflow if water flows through the intake pipe at a faster rate than it flows out through the discharge pipe
(B) tank will empty completely if the intake pipe is closed and the discharge pipe is allowed to remain open
(C) water in the tank will remain at a constant level if the rate of intake is equal to the rate of discharge
(D) water in the tank will rise if the intake pipe is operating when the discharge pipe is closed
(E) time required to fill the tank, if the discharge pipe is closed, depends upon the rate of flow of water through the intake pipe.

15.

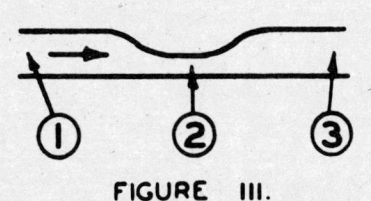

FIGURE III.

Figure III represents a pipe through which water is flowing in the direction of the arrow. There is a constriction in the pipe at the point indicated by the number 2. Water is being pumped into the pipe at a constant rate of 350 gallons per minute. Of the following, the most accurate statement is that
(A) the velocity of the water at point 2 is the same as the velocity of the water at point 3
(B) a greater volume of water is flowing past point 1 in a minute than is flowing past point 2
(C) the velocity of the water at point 1 is greater than the velocity at point 2
(D) the volume of water flowing past point 2 in a minute is the same as the volume of water flowing past point 1 in a minute
(E) a greater volume of water is flowing past point 3 in a minute than is flowing past point 2.

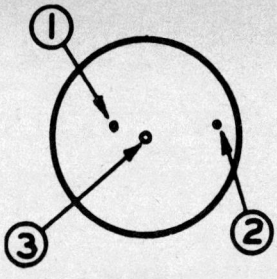

FIGURE IV.

16. Figure IV represents a revolving wheel. The numbers 1 and 2 indicate two fixed points on the wheel. The number 3 indicates the center of the wheel. Of the following, the most accurate statement is that

(A) point 1 makes less revolutions per minute than point 2
(B) point 2 makes more revolutions per minute than point 1
(C) point 2 traverses a greater linear distance than point 1
(D) point 1 will make a complete revolution in less time than point 2
(E) the product of the linear distance traversed by either point and the time required for one revolution is equal to the number of revolutions.

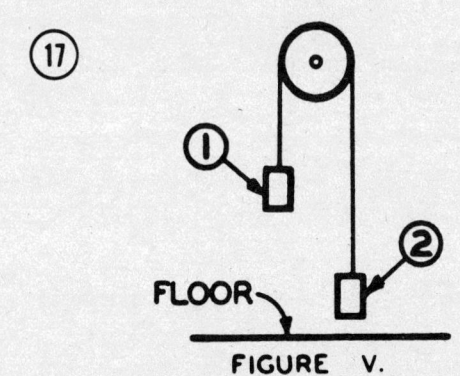

FIGURE V.

17. Figure V represents a pulley, with practically no friction, from which two tenpound weights are suspended as indicated. If a downward force is applied to weight 1, it is most likely that weight 1 will

(A) come to rest at the present level of weight 2
(B) move downward until it is level with weight 2
(C) move downward until it reaches the floor
(D) pass weight 2 in its downward motion and then return to its present position
(E) move downward a short distance before the direction of movement is reversed.

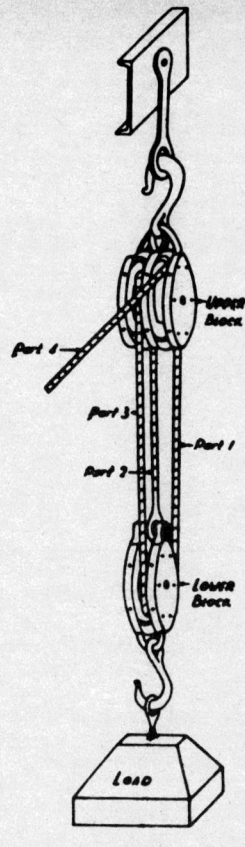

FIGURE VI.

18. Examine Figure VI and determine which part of the rope is fastened directly to the block.
(A) Part 1 (B) Part 2
(C) Part 3 (D) Part 4
(E) no part.

19. If you study Figure VI you will find that only one of the following statements is true:
(A) Each part of the rope carries about the same share of the load.
(B) A load cannot be lowered by means of the tackle shown.
(C) If the upper block were smaller but its weight unchanged, hoisting would be easier for the operator.
(D) The rope cannot possibly be connected to a winch.
(E) If the lower block were made smaller but its weight kept the same, hoisting would be easier for the operator.

20. When a load is hoisted by means of the tackle shown in Figure VI, the part that remains stationary is
(A) the load
(B) the lower block
(C) the lower hook
(D) the rope
(E) the upper block.

21. When a load is hoisted by means of the tackle shown in Figure VI, the part of the rope which is slack is
(A) Part 4
(B) Part 1
(C) no part
(D) Part 2
(E) Part 3.

CONSOLIDATE YOUR KEY ANSWERS HERE

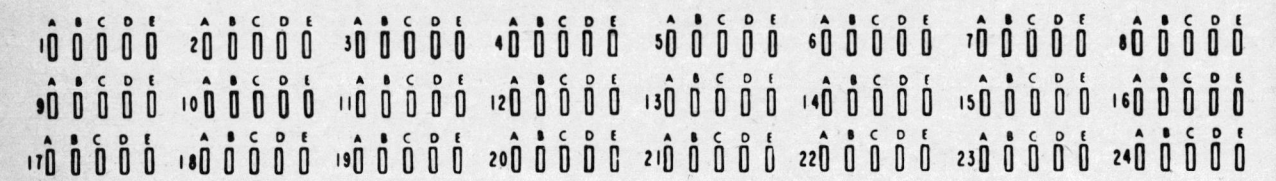

Correct Answers For The Foregoing Questions

(Please make every effort to answer the questions on your own before looking at these answers. You'll make faster progress by following this rule.)

1. B	4. D	7. C	10. D	13. C	16. C	19. A
2. C	5. B	8. C	11. C	14. B	17. C	20. E
3. C	6. C	9. A	12. B	15. D	18. B	21. C

SCORE 1
.......................%
NO. CORRECT ÷
NO. OF QUESTIONS ON THIS TEST

SCORE 2
.......................%
NO. CORRECT ÷
NO. OF QUESTIONS ON THIS TEST

AIR FORCE PLACEMENT TESTS

TOOL RECOGNITION TESTS

This is one of the kinds of question you are likely to find on your test. Given sufficient time, any intelligent person should be able to answer these fairly simple questions. But on your test you probably won't be given sufficient time. Thus you'll be tempted to rush along faster than you should, making unnecessary errors. However, by practicing with the careful selection of questions in this chapter, you will noticeably increase your speed, your skill, and your accuracy in answering this kind of question. On your test you will find that you are familiar with these questions, and that they will offer you little difficulty.

Mechanical aptitude tests are used to measure many different abilities. And the results obtained are used for many different purposes.

Sometimes they measure your ability to use your hands or to manipulate materials. Other times they measure your dexterity; and also your ability to visualize shapes and forms; and to move them around in different patterns. Some people are better at these tasks than others, even without any training. It is believed that such people have better mechanical "aptitude."

But these ideas are not absolutely clear-cut, and frequently tests that are designed to measure mechanical aptitude draw upon the knowledge a person has in mechanical matters. The theory here is that those who are likely to do well in mechanical work have interested themselves in it and have absorbed more from what they have experienced than those who are not likely to do well in such work.

As a result we find that there is in use a wide variety of questions which draw upon a person's knowledge of tools, mechanical processes, movements and information. This type of mechanical test is frequently called an *achievement* test.

Mechanical aptitude and achievement tests come in a wide variety of forms. The questions may be entirely verbal. Or they may involve the use of diagrams and pictures. They may be given orally; or they may be printed and require written answers. And sometimes the candidate may be asked to work with his hands on special testing equipment while the examiner observes and times his effort. Another form of manual test consists of actual performance on a job, or in the production of *standardized worksamples*. In such tests the work set for the candidate is very much like the work required by the job. For economy and speed, worksamples are frequently presented on simulated or miniaturized equipment.

Since every craftsman should be familiar with the tools of his trade, and since familiarity with tools is an important measure of interest and motivation, tool recognition questions have become an important feature of many mechanical ability, aptitude and comprehension tests.

In order to familiarize you with this type of question we have assembled a large variety from many different examinations. As you go through the different tool recognition tests in this chapter you will understand better how to go about answering these questions. You'll also pick up a good deal of important information about tools and tool recognition.

As you will find in the following pages, all of these questions are of a practical nature. You are given the picture of a tool in most questions, and a situation is described. You must match the tool with the necessary operation. In other questions you are shown pictures of various tools and implements and must match those which are used together.

Some of the tools which you will encounter on these pages are basic to almost every mechanical trade and you should have little difficulty in answering questions about their use. Others may be unfamiliar to you, or may have some specialized use outside your own trade. In those cases, you must apply your knowledge of mechanics to figure out which tool would seem to fit the required operation.

In answering these questions, do not try to work by elimination. When you are given a group of tools and a long list of operations, the same tool may be used for more than one operation on the list, and often one or more of the tools shown may not be used in any of the operations.

Be honest with yourself in answering these questions. Do the best you can before looking at the key answers at the end of the chapter. Usually, if you are not sure of the answer, it will be to your advantage to guess. If the test is marked in such a way that wrong guesses penalize you more than "no answer," that will be indicated on the examination paper.

A SAMPLE QUESTION EXPLAINED

DIRECTIONS: Each question in this test consists of a numbered picture followed by four lettered illustrations marked A, B, C, & D. The problem is to determine which of the four lettered pictures goes best with the numbered tool or machine part. For each question blacken the space on your answer sheet corresponding to the letter of the best answer.

EXPLANATION OF A SAMPLE QUESTION: The illustration numbered "0" shows a valve used to turn water on and off. The picture that goes best with the valve is lettered "B," the piece of water pipe. Choices "C," "A," and "D" have little or nothing to do with the valve "0." Therefore, "B" is the correct answer, and the answer strip is blackened under B.

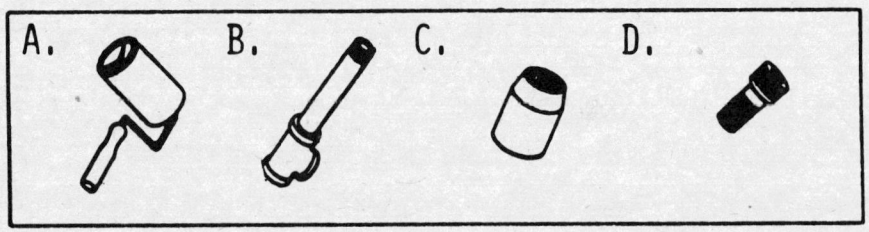

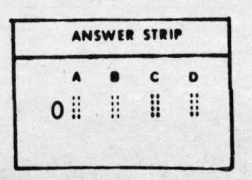

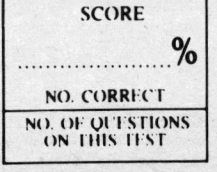

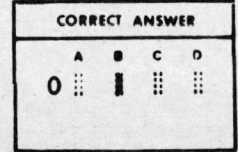

TOOL ANALOGY TEST 1
TIME: 10 Minutes

DIRECTIONS: Each question in this test consists of a numbered picture followed by four lettered illustrations marked A, B, C, & D. The problem is to determine which of the four lettered pictures goes best with the numbered tool or machine part. For each question blacken the space on your answer sheet corresponding to the letter of the best answer.

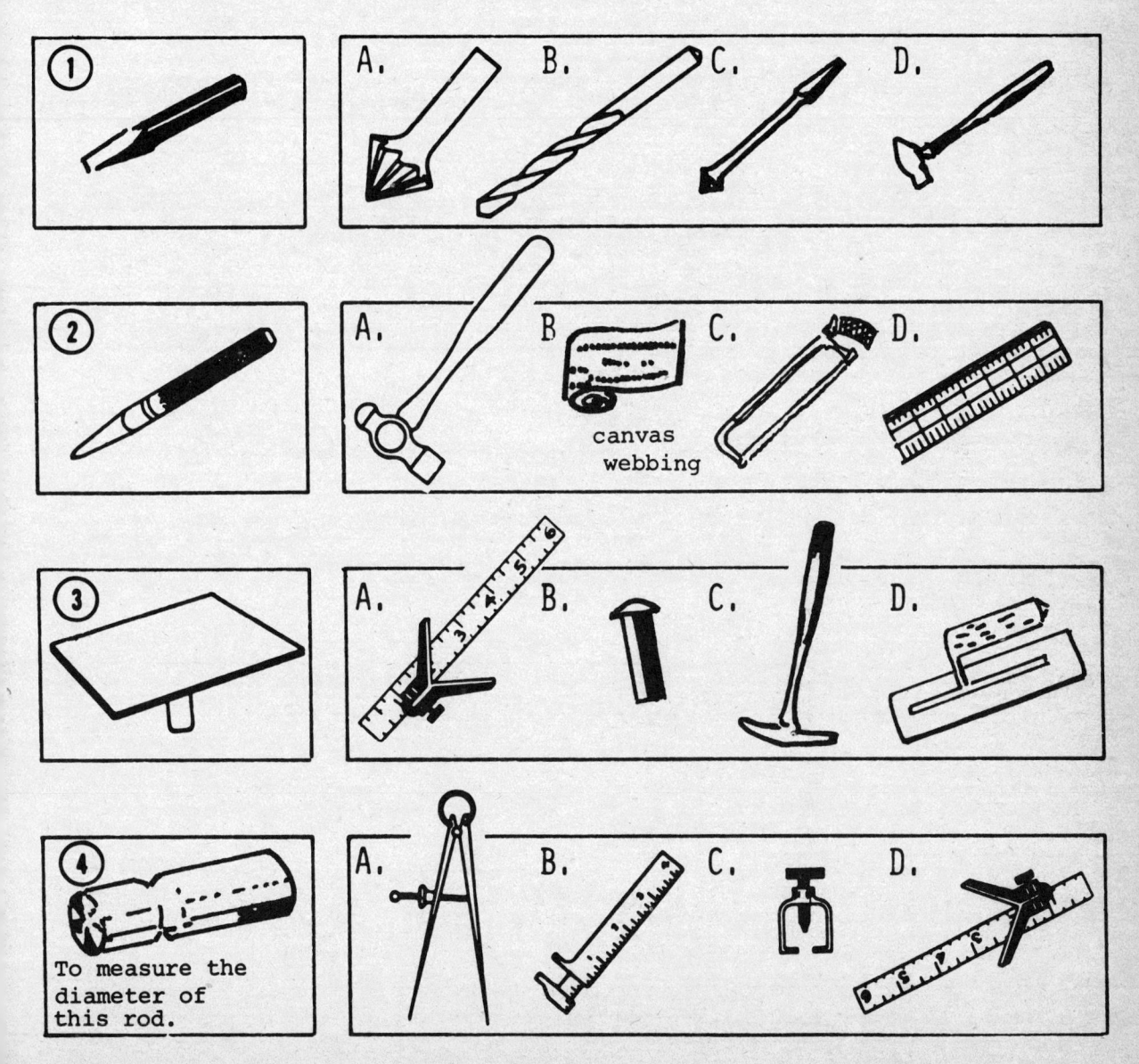

1.

2.

3.

4. To measure the diameter of this rod.

canvas webbing

168 / *Practice For Air Force Placement Tests*

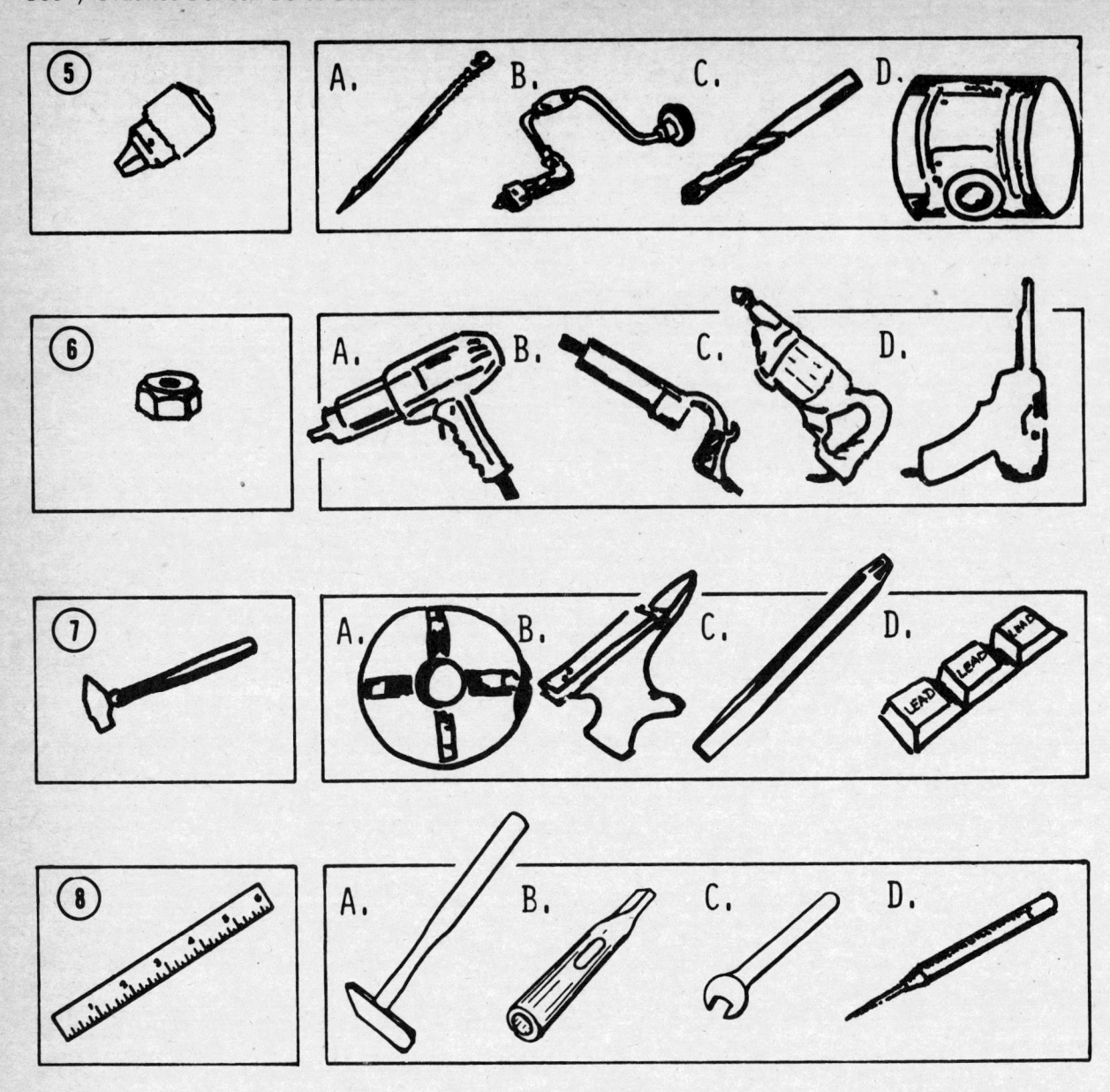

Correct Answers For The Foregoing Questions

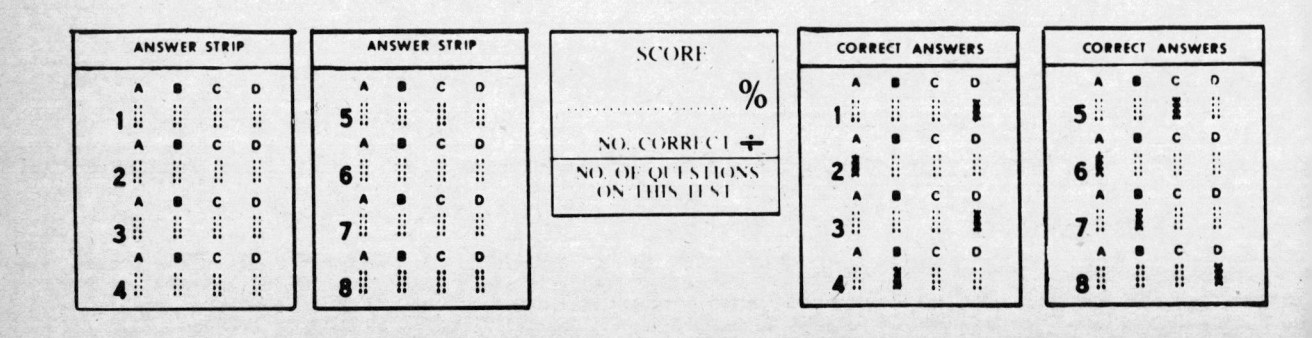

TOOL ANALOGY TEST II

TIME: 10 Minutes

DIRECTIONS: Each question in this test consists of a numbered picture followed by four lettered illustrations marked A, B, C, & D. The problem is to determine which of the four lettered pictures goes best with the numbered tool or machine part. For each question blacken the space on your answer sheet corresponding to the letter of the best answer.

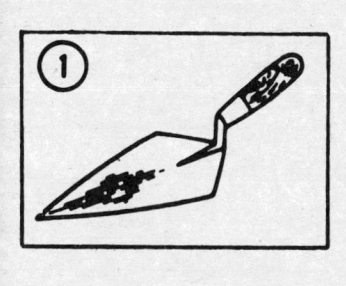

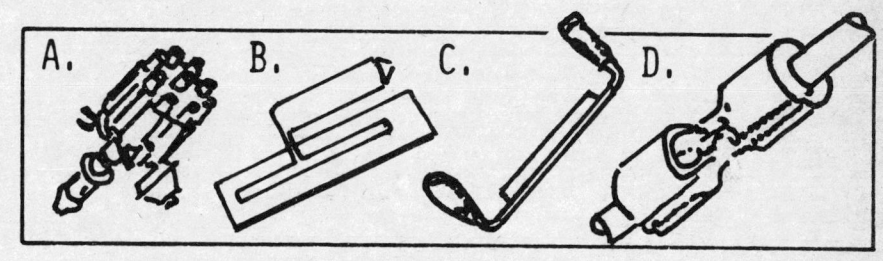

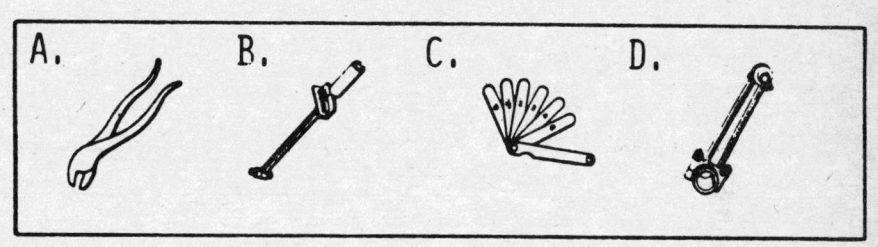

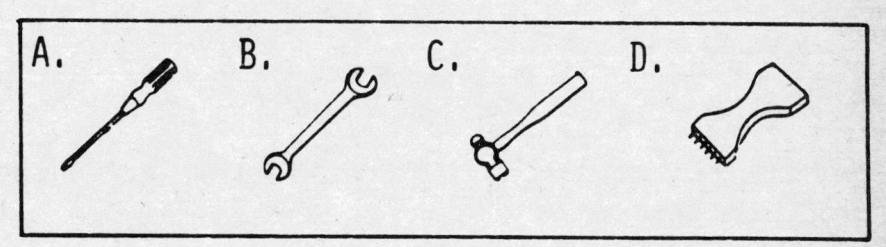

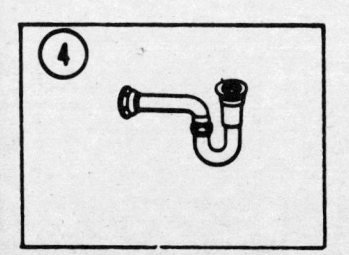

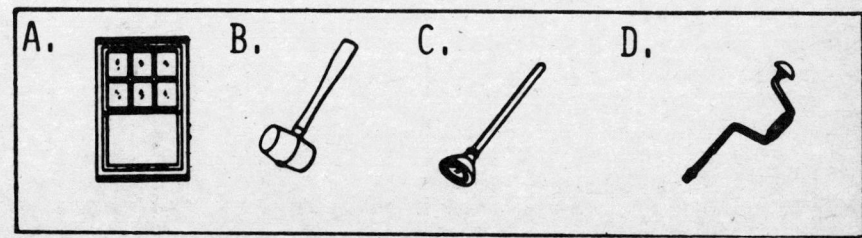

170 / *Practice For Air Force Placement Tests*

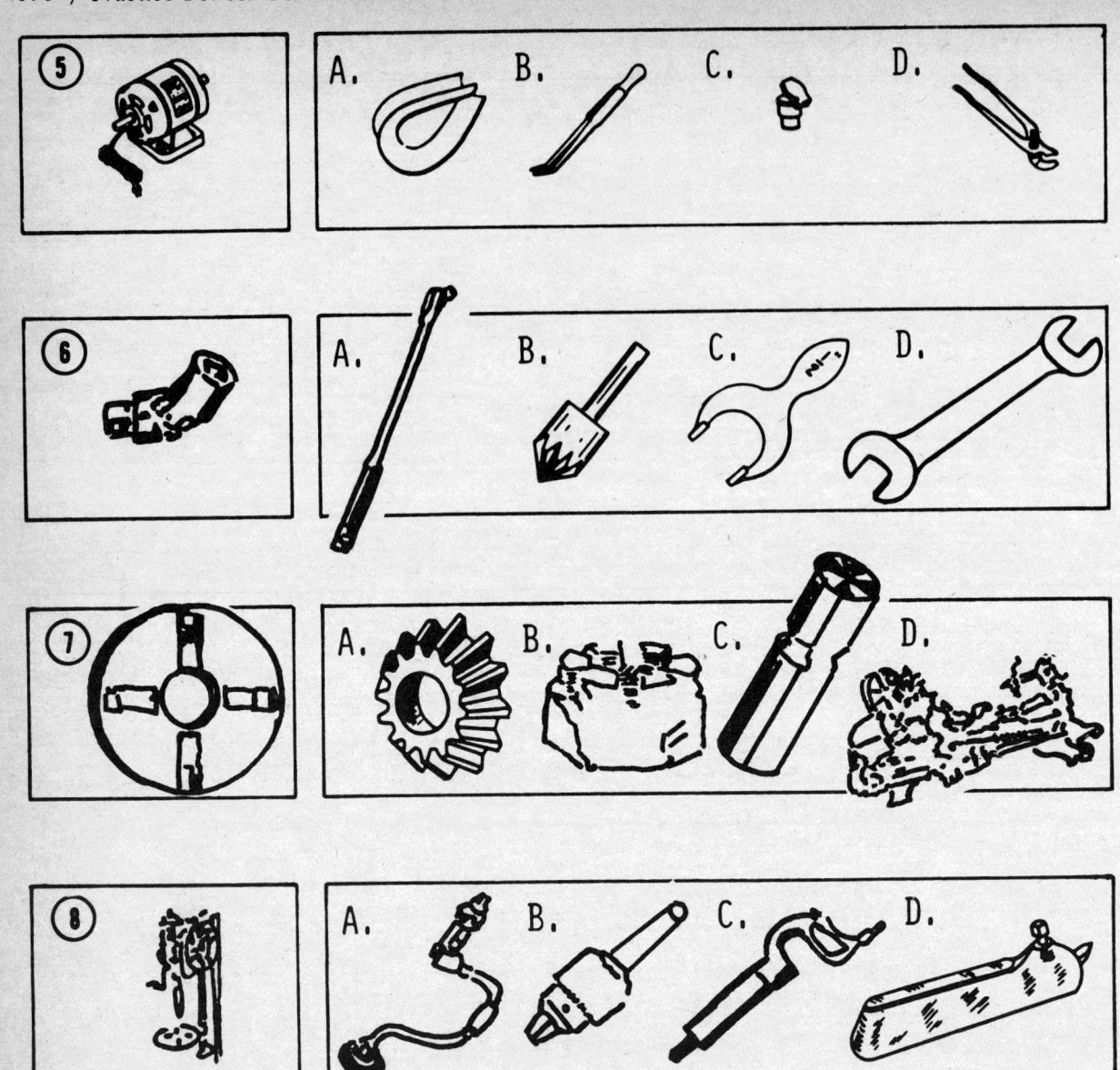

Correct Answers For The Foregoing Questions

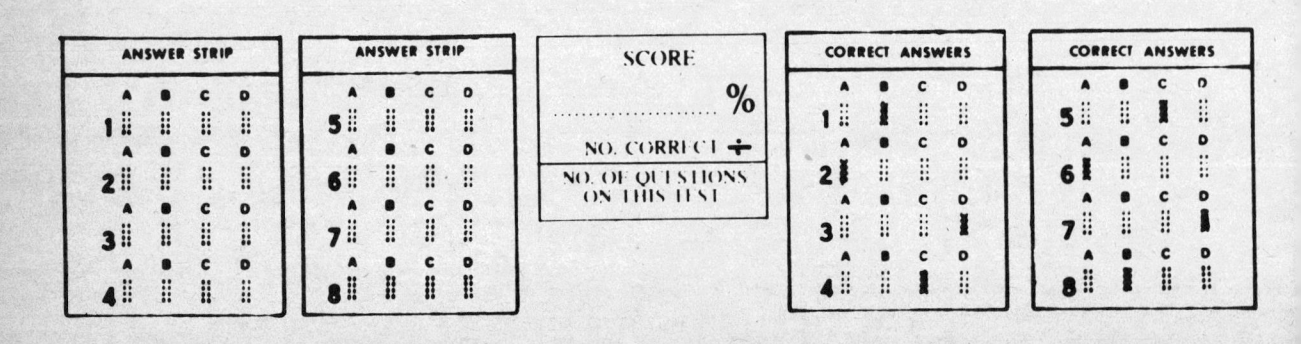

Tool Recognition Tests / 171

TOOL ANALOGY TEST III

TIME: 10 Minutes

DIRECTIONS: Each question in this test consists of a numbered picture followed by four lettered illustrations marked A, B, C, & D. The problem is to determine which of the four lettered pictures goes best with the numbered tool or machine part. For each question blacken the space on your answer sheet corresponding to the letter of the best answer.

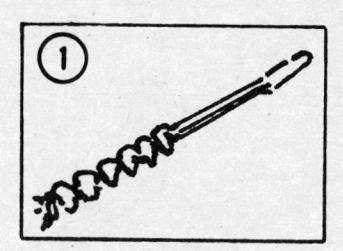

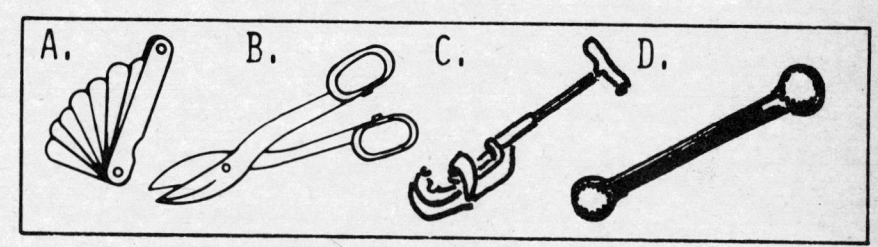

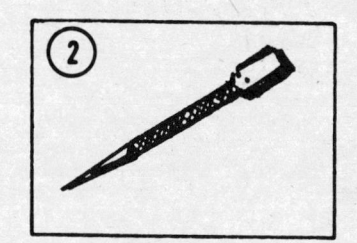

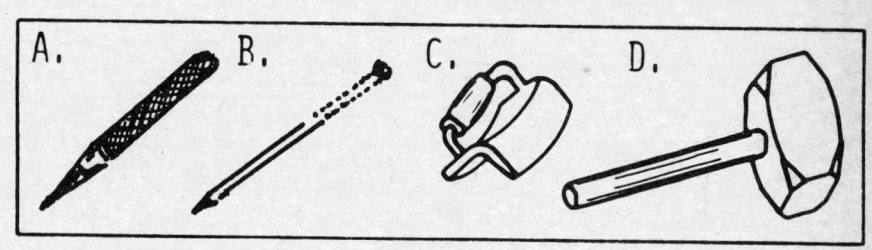

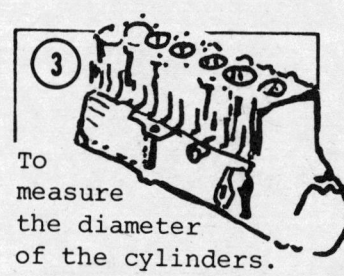

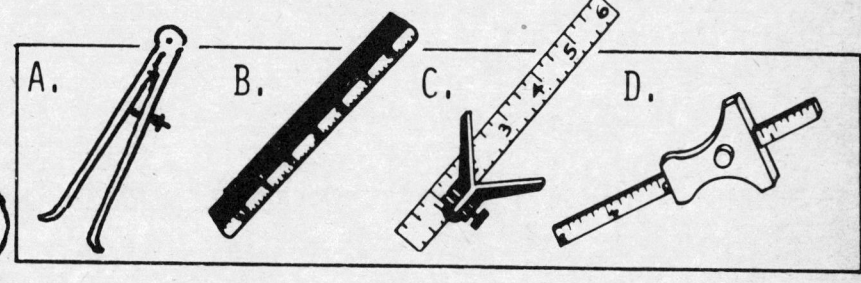

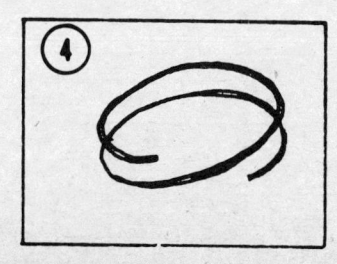

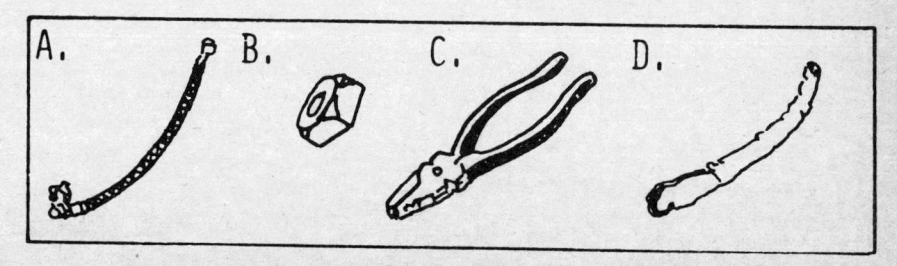

3. To measure the diameter of the cylinders.

172 / *Practice For Air Force Placement Tests*

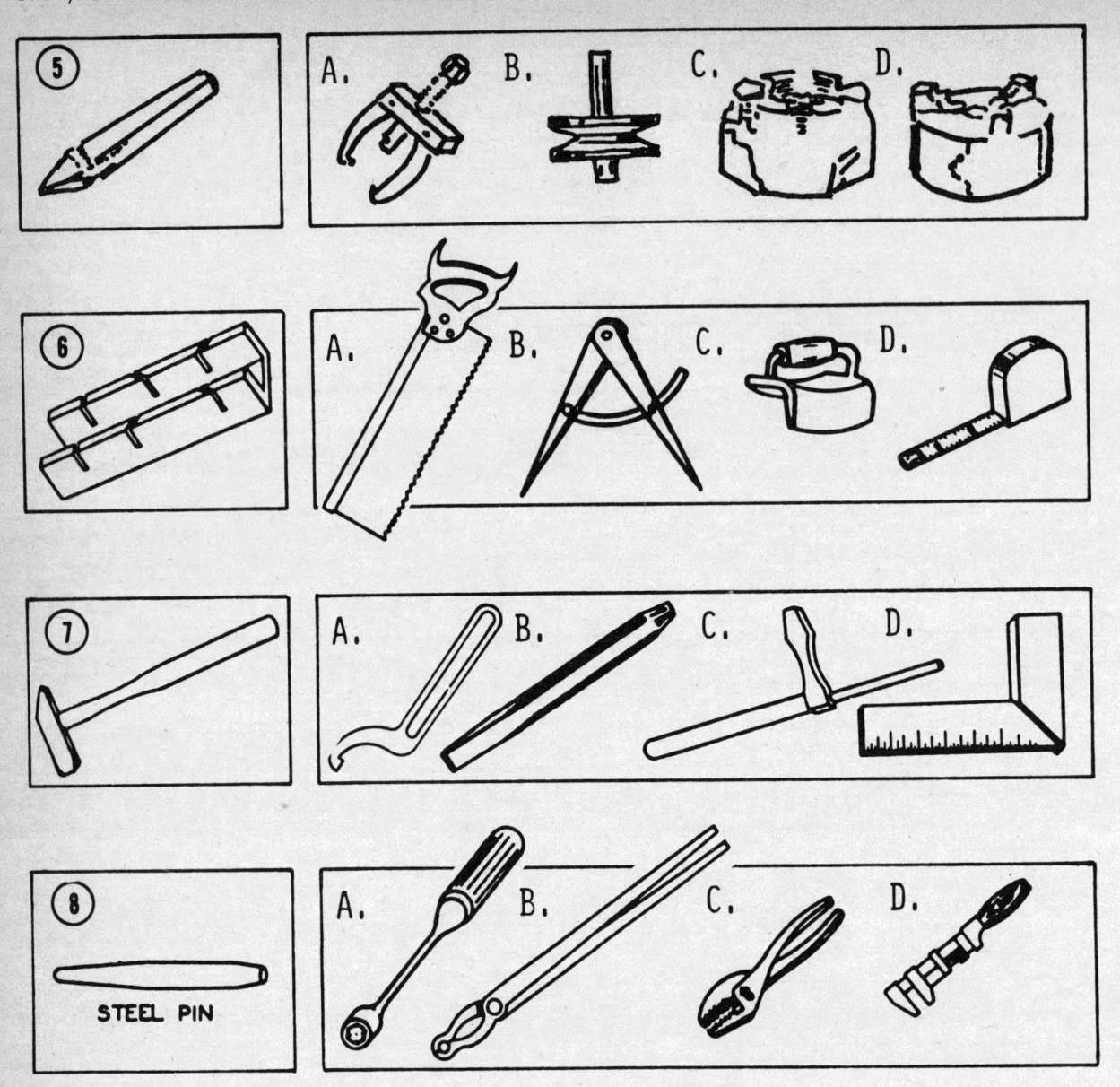

Correct Answers For The Foregoing Questions

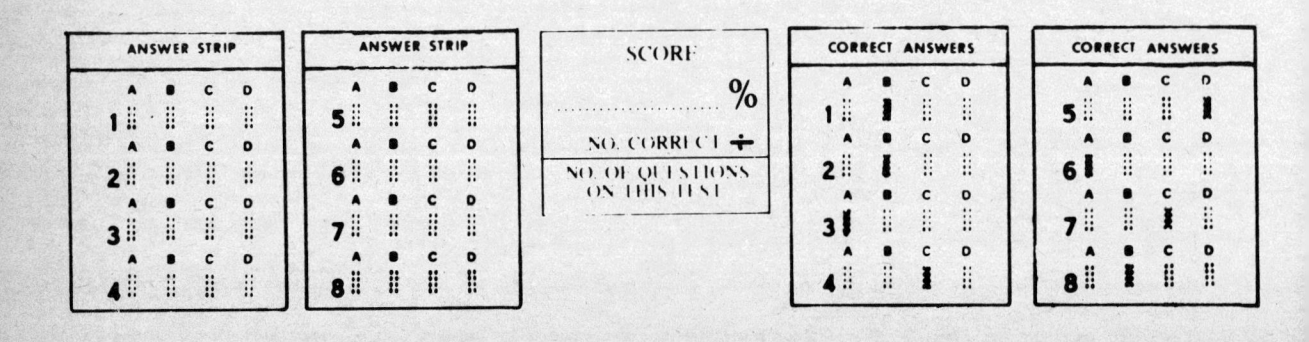

TOOL RECOGNITION TEST I

TIME: 15 Minutes

DIRECTIONS: The items listed below are jobs, each of which normally requires the use of one of the tools or pieces of equipment shown. Read the item, and for the job given, select the required tool or piece of equipment.

Correct key answers to all these test questions will be found at the end of the test.

1. Drilling a 7/8 inch hole in a brick wall.
2. Tightening a water-pipe coupling.
3. Cutting a 1/2 inch stranded steel cable.
4. Tightening a lock nut on a surface mounted outlet box.
5. Doing scroll work on wood.
6. Rounding a hole in sheet metal.
7. Chipping off the corner of a brick.
8. Removing a 1/4 inch edge from a piece of sheet metal.
9. Making a hole to tap a thread in a steel block.
10. Converting a 4-foot brass rod into 1-foot pieces.
11. Making a hole in a door for a cylinder lock.

Correct Answers

(First write your own answers. Then compare them with these answers.)

1. C	4. D	7. B	10. E
2. F	5. H	8. B	11. I
3. E	6. G	9. A	

SCORE 1 ......% NO. CORRECT ÷ NO. OF QUESTIONS ON THIS TEST

SCORE 2 ......% NO. CORRECT ÷ NO. OF QUESTIONS ON THIS TEST

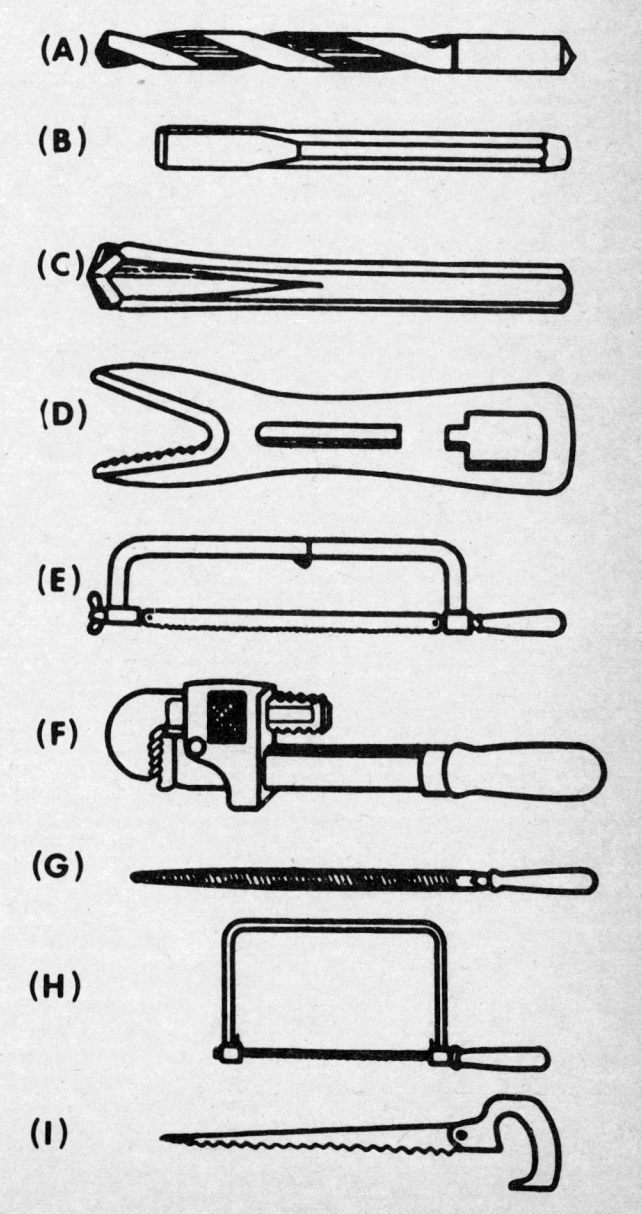

TOOL RECOGNITION TEST II

TIME: 15 Minutes

DIRECTIONS: *In this test each numbered* TOOL *in Column I is commonly associated with one of the* PIECES OF EQUIPMENT *listed and lettered in Column II. You are supposed to match up the* TOOLS *in Column I with the* PIECES *in Column II. Next to each of the* TOOLS *in Column I write the letter of the* PIECE *with which it is most commonly associated.*

Correct key answers to all these test questions will be found at the end of the test.

COLUMN I

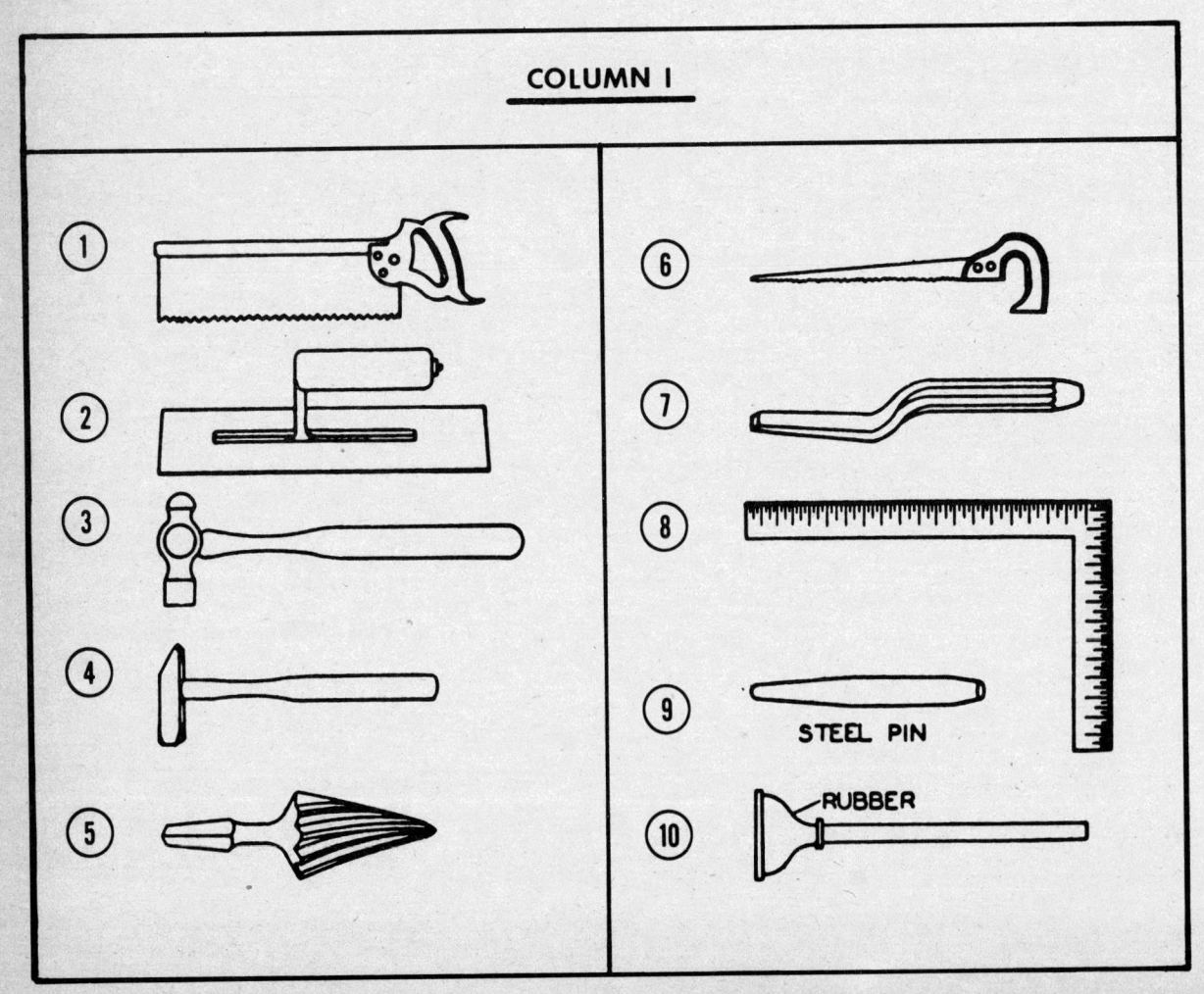

1. (hand saw)
2. (trowel)
3. (ball-peen hammer)
4. (machinist's hammer)
5. (rotary file / burr)
6. (keyhole saw)
7. (offset tool)
8. (try square / ruler)
9. STEEL PIN
10. RUBBER

S2080

Tool Recognition Tests / 175

TOOL RECOGNITION TEST II

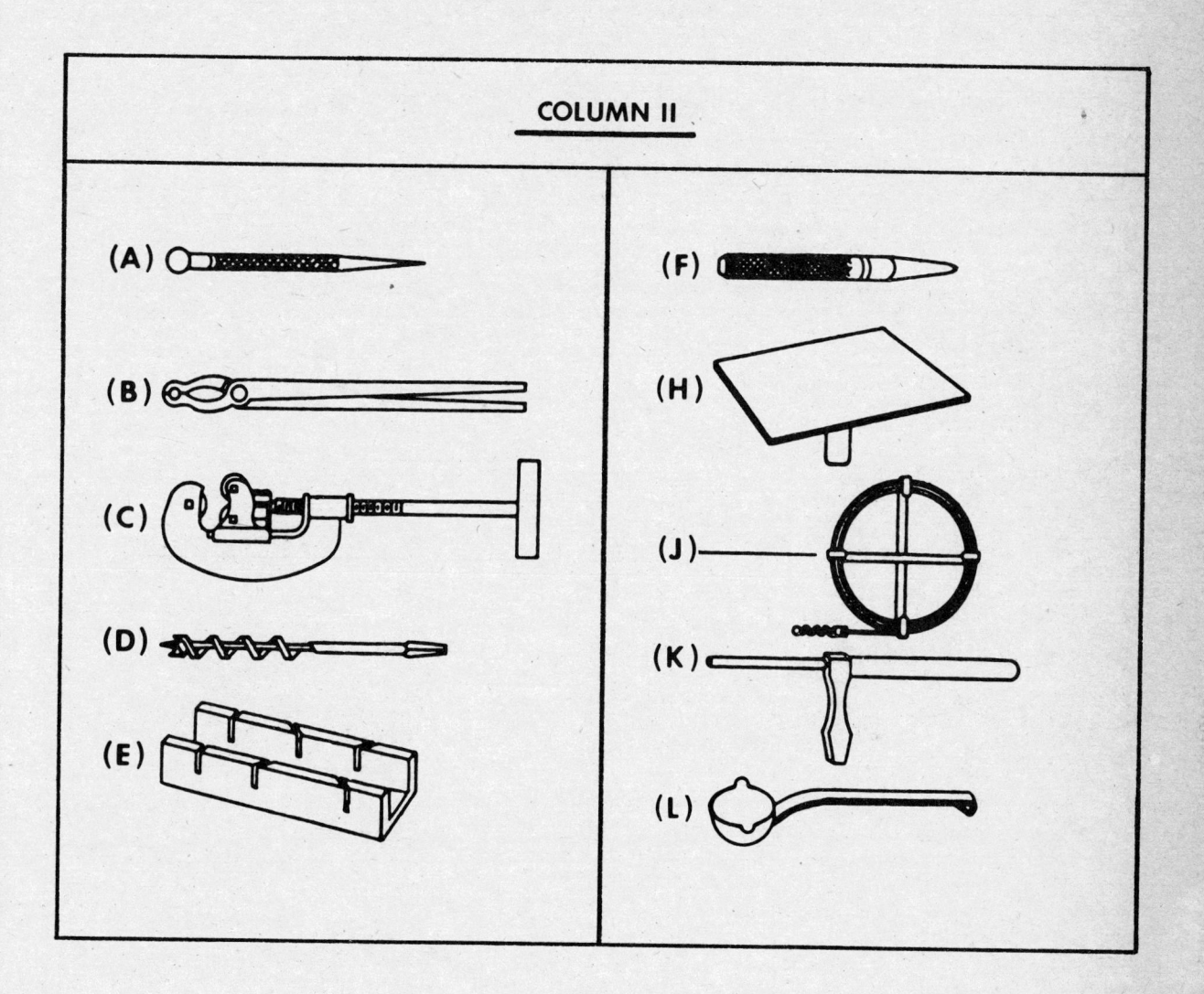

COLUMN II

(A)

(B)

(C)

(D)

(E)

(F)

(H)

(J)

(K)

(L)

Correct Answers

(You'll learn more by writing your own answers before comparing them with these.)

1. E   4. K   6. D   8. A
2. H   5. C   7. L   9. B
3. F   10. J

SCORE 1 .... %
NO. CORRECT
NO. OF QUESTIONS ON THIS TEST

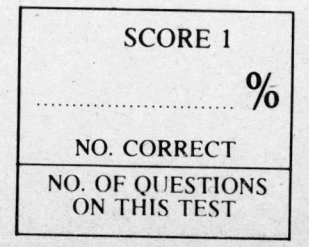

SCORE 2 .... %
NO. CORRECT
NO. OF QUESTIONS ON THIS TEST

TOOL RECOGNITION TEST III

TIME: 10 Minutes

DIRECTIONS: *The following items refer to the use of the tools labeled (A), (B), (C), etc. shown below. They are used to perform operations on the piece shown in the Figure. Read each item; refer to the Figure; and for the operation given, select the proper tool to be used.*

Correct key answers to all these test questions will be found at the end of the test.

1. Tightening a coupling on a piece of one-inch conduit.
2. Drilling a hole in a concrete wall for a lead anchor.
3. Bending a piece of 3/4-inch conduit.
4. Tightening a wire on the terminal of a standard electric light socket.
5. Cutting off a piece of 4/0 insulated copper cable.
6. Measuring the length of a proposed long conduit run.
7. Tightening a small nut on a terminal board.
8. Removing the burrs from the end of a piece of conduit after cutting.
9. Removing the flat rubber gasket stuck to the cover of a watertight pull box.
10. Knocking the head off a bolt that is rusted in place.

Correct Answers

(You'll learn more by writing your own answers before comparing them with these.)

1. D
2. C
3. A
4. N
5. K
6. T
7. P
8. M
9. N
10. H

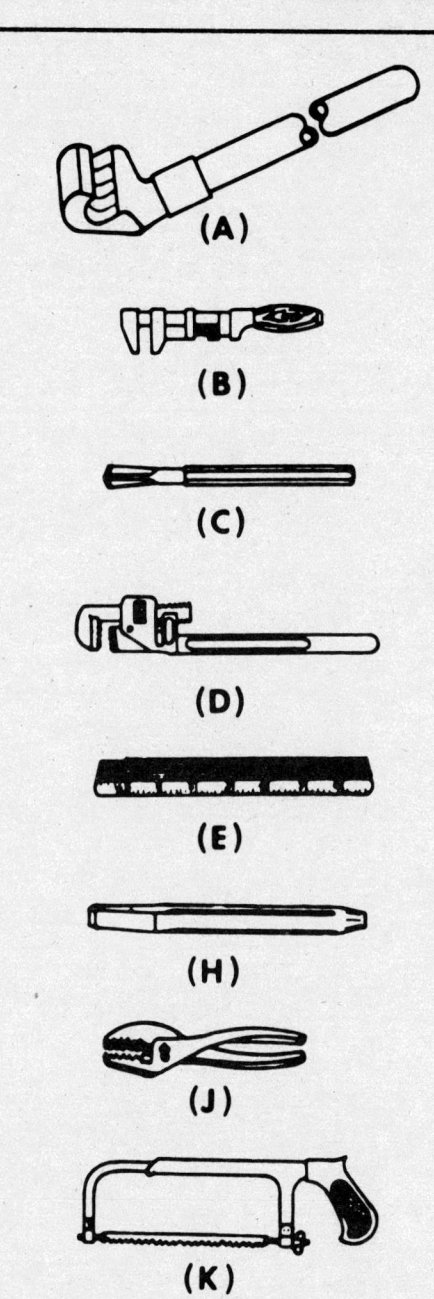

TOOL RECOGNITION TEST III

(A)
(B)
(C)
(D)
(E)
(H)
(J)
(K)

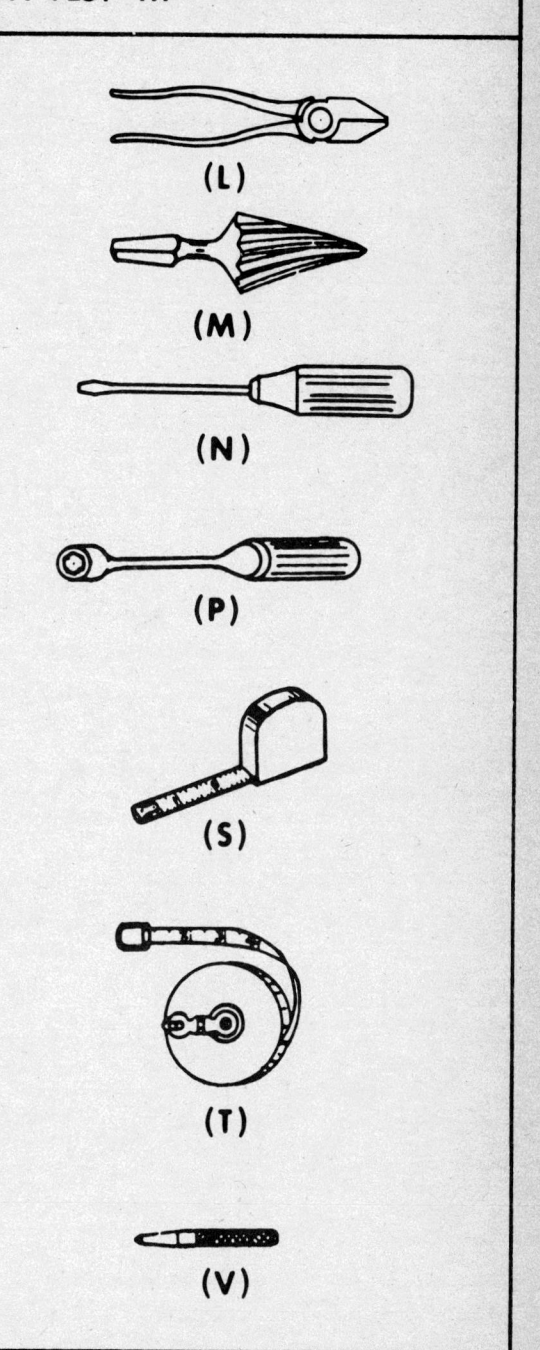

(L)
(M)
(N)
(P)
(S)
(T)
(V)

TOOL RECOGNITION TEST IV

TIME: 15 Minutes

DIRECTIONS: The following items refer to the use of the tools labeled (A), (B), (C), etc. shown below. They are used to perform operations on the piece shown in the Figure. Read each item; refer to the Figure; and for the operation given, select the proper tool to be used.

Correct key answers to all these test questions will be found at the end of the test.

1. Marking line 1 with the aid of a straight-edge.
2. Checking number of threads per inch on stud 2.
3. Making threads on stud 3, before stud 2 is inserted.
4. Removing broken stud 4 after drilling hole in center.
5. Checking depth of hole 5.
6. Removing set screw 6.
7. Removing set screw 7.
8. Measuring diameter of rod 8.
9. Removing cotter pin 9.
10. Removing nut 10.
11. Making center before drilling hole 11.
12. Removing burrs on stud 2.
13. Cutting threads in hole 5.

Correct Answers

(You'll learn more by writing your own answers before comparing them with these.)

1. C
2. L
3. H
4. M
5. W
6. N
7. K
8. S
9. P
10. T
11. B
12. J
13. A

SCORE 1	SCORE 2
.... %	.... %
NO. CORRECT ÷	NO. CORRECT ÷
NO. OF QUESTIONS ON THIS TEST	NO. OF QUESTIONS ON THIS TEST

TOOL RECOGNITION TEST IV

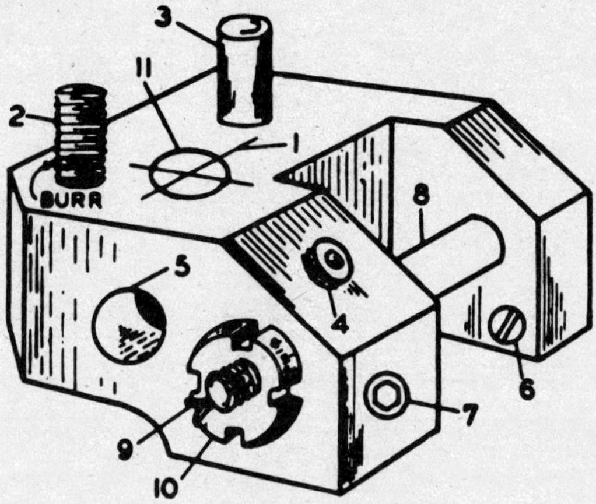

FIGURE 1

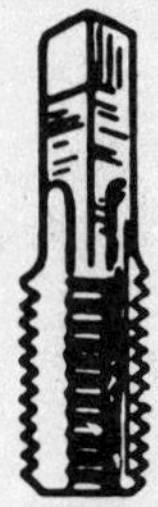
(A)

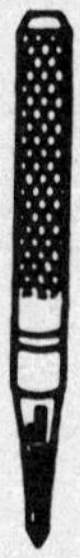
(B)

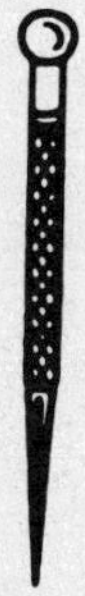
(C)

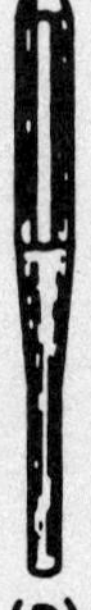
(D)

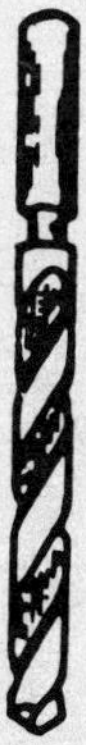
(E)

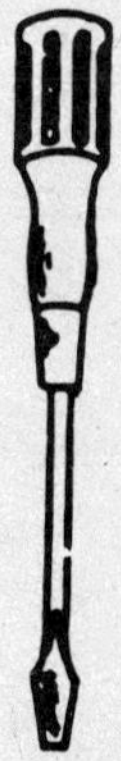
(F)

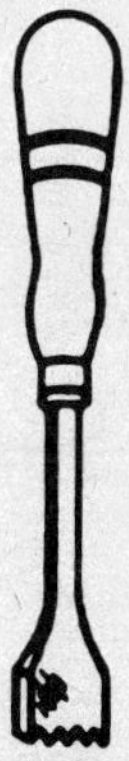
(G)

(H) 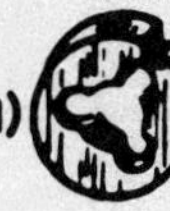

(J) 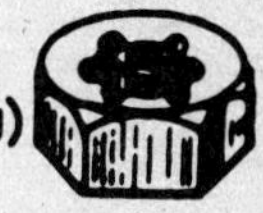

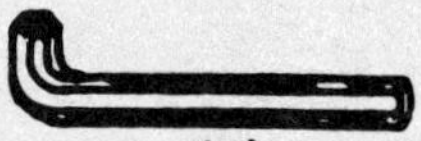
(K)

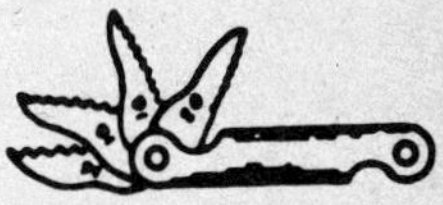
(L)

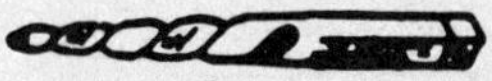
(M)

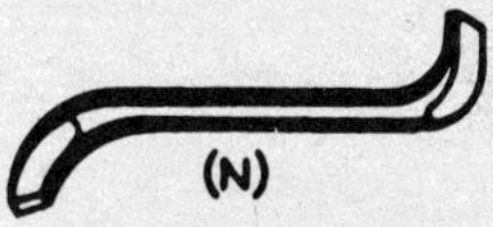
(N)

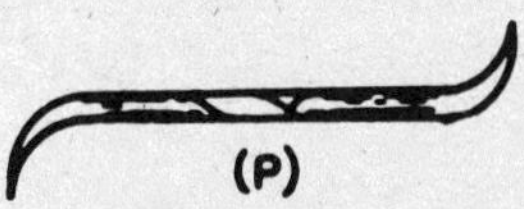
(P)

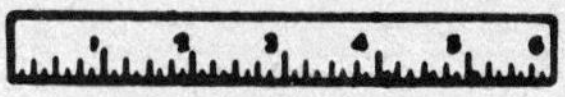
(R)

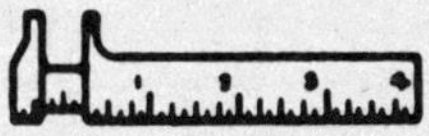
(S)

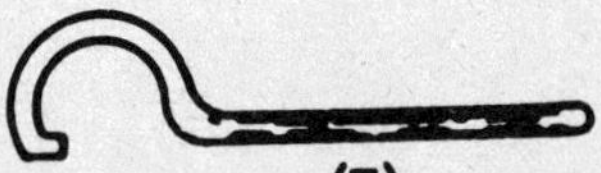
(T)

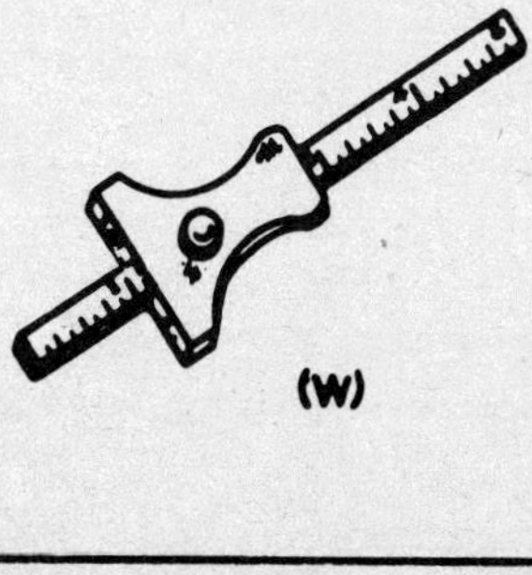
(W)

TOOL RECOGNITION TEST V.

TIME: 10 Minutes

DIRECTIONS: The items listed below are jobs, each of which normally requires the use of one of the tools or pieces of equipment shown. Read the item, and for the job given, select the required tool or piece of equipment.

Correct key answers to all these test questions will be found at the end of the test.

1. Storage battery maintenance
2. Conduit installation
3. Tool maintenance
4. Bus bar assembly
5. Winding of armatures
6. Instrument repair
7. Commutator maintenance
8. Circuit testing
9. Measurement of air gaps
10. Cable splicing

Correct Answers

(You'll learn more by writing your own answers before comparing them with these.)

1. E	4. A	6. D	8. H
2. M	5. B	or J	9. F
3. L	or J	7. K	10. C

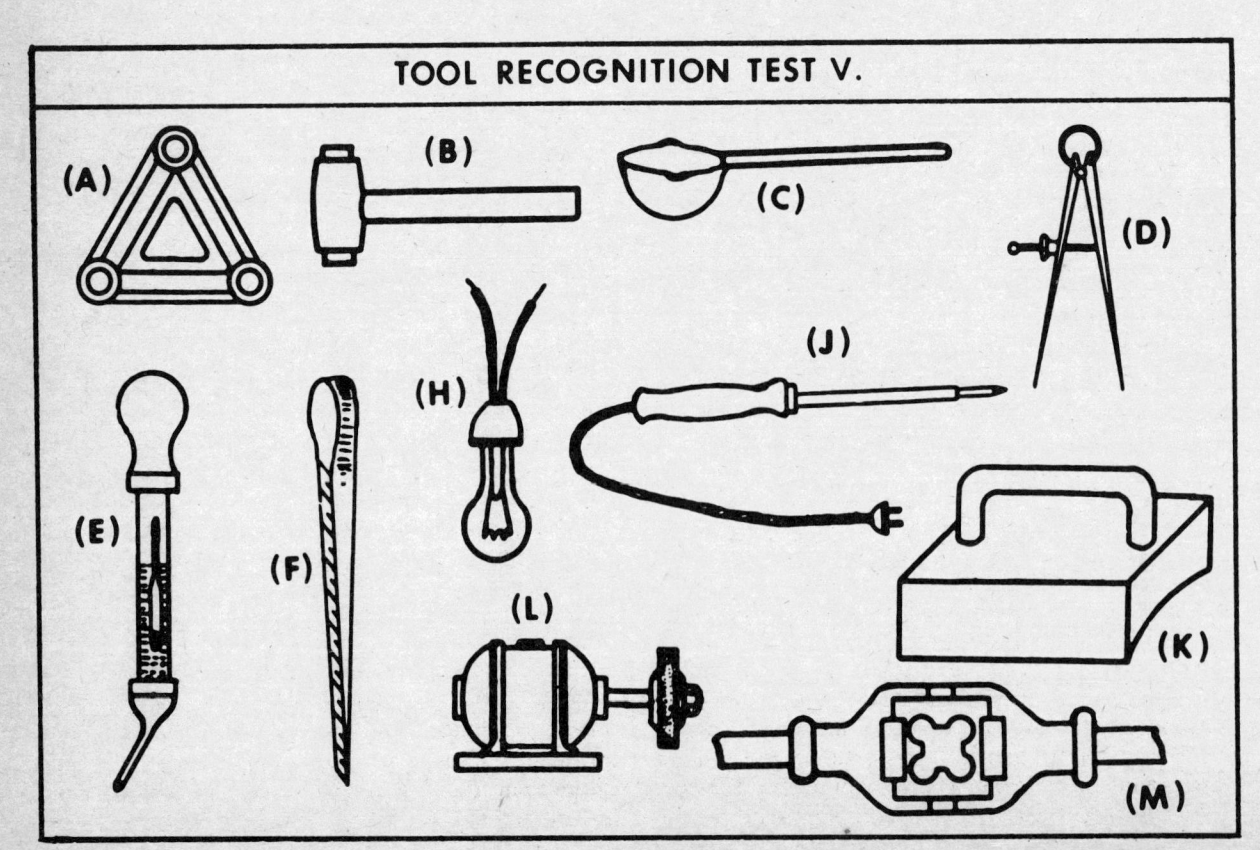

AIR FORCE PLACEMENT TESTS

TEST – TAKING MADE SIMPLE

Having gotten this far, you're almost an expert test-taker because you have now mastered the subject matter of the test. Proper preparation is the real secret. The pointers on the next few pages will take you the rest of the way by giving you the strategy employed on tests by those who are most successful in this not-so-mysterious art.

BEFORE THE TEST

T-DAY MINUS SEVEN

You're going to pass this examination because you have received the best possible preparation for it. But, unlike many others, you're going to give the best possible account of yourself by acquiring the rare skill of effectively using your knowledge to answer the examination questions.

First off, get rid of any negative attitudes toward the test. You have a negative attitude when you view the test as a device to "trip you up" rather than an opportunity to show how effectively you have learned.

APPROACH THE TEST WITH SELF-CONFIDENCE. Plugging through this book was no mean job, and now that you've done it you're probably better prepared than 90% of the others. Self-confidence is one of the biggest strategic assets you can bring to the testing room.

Nobody likes tests, but some poor souls permit themselves to get upset or angry when they see what they think is an unfair test. The expert doesn't. He keeps calm and moves right ahead, knowing that everyone is taking the same test. Anger, resentment, fear . . . they all slow you down. "Grin and bear it!"

Besides, every test you take, including this one, is a valuable experience which improves your skill. Since you will undoubtedly be taking other tests in the years to come, it may help you to regard this one as training to perfect your skill.

Keep calm; there's no point in panic. If you've done your work there's no need for it; and if you haven't, a cool head is your very first requirement.

Why be the frightened kind of student who enters the examination chamber in a mental coma? A test taken under mental stress does not provide a fair measure of your ability. At the very least, this book has removed for you some of the fear and mystery that surrounds examinations. A certain amount of concern is normal and good, but excessive worry saps your strength and keenness. In other words, be prepared EMOTIONALLY.

Pre-Test Review

If you know any others who are taking this test, you'll probably find it helpful to review the book and your notes with them. The group should be small, certainly not more than four. Team study at this stage should seek to review the material in a different way than you learned it originally; should strive for an exchange of ideas between you and the other members of the group; should be selective in sticking to important ideas; should stress the vague and the unfamiliar rather than that which you all know well; should be businesslike and devoid of any nonsense; should end as soon as you get tired.

One of the *worst* strategies in test taking is to do *all* your preparation the night before the exam. As a reader of this book, you have scheduled and spaced your study properly so as not to suffer from the fatigue and emotional disturbance that comes from cramming the night before.

Cramming is a very good way to *guarantee poor test results*.

However, you would be wise to prepare yourself factually by *reviewing your notes* in the 48 hours preceding the exam. You shouldn't have to spend more than two or three hours in this way. Stick to salient points. The others will fall into place quickly.

Don't confuse cramming with a final, calm review which helps you focus on the significant areas of this book and further strengthens your confidence in your ability to handle the test questions. In other words, prepare yourself FACTUALLY.

Keep Fit

Mind and body work together. Poor physical condition will lower your mental efficiency. In preparing for an examination, observe the commonsense rules of health. Get sufficient sleep and rest, eat proper foods, plan recreation and exercise. In relation to health and examinations, two cautions are in order. Don't miss your meals prior to an examination in order to get extra time for study. Likewise, don't miss your regular sleep by sitting up late to "cram" for the examination. Cramming is an attempt to learn in a very short period of time what should have been learned through regular and consistent study. Not only are these two habits detrimental to health, but seldom do they pay off in terms of effective learning. It is likely that you will be *more confused* than better prepared on the day of the examination if you have broken into your daily routine by missing your meals or sleep.

On the night before the examination go to bed at your regular time and try to get a good night's sleep. Don't go to the movies. Don't date. In other words, prepare yourself PHYSICALLY.

T-HOUR MINUS ONE

After a very light, leisurely meal, get to the examination room ahead of time, perhaps ten minutes early . . . but not so early that you have time to get into an argument with others about what's going to be asked on the exam, etc. The reason for coming early is to help you get accustomed to the room. It will help you to a better start.

Bring all necessary equipment . . .

. . . pen, two sharpened pencils, watch, paper, eraser, ruler, and any other things you're instructed to bring.

Get settled . . .

. . . by finding your seat and staying in it. If no special seats have been assigned, take one in the front to facilitate the seating of others coming in after you.

The test will be given by a test supervisor who reads the directions and otherwise tells you what to do. The people who walk about passing out the test papers and assisting with the examination are test proctors. If you're not able to see or hear properly notify the supervisor or a proctor. If you have any other difficulties during the examination, like a defective test booklet, scoring pencil, answer sheet; or if it's too hot or cold or dark or drafty, let them know. You're entitled to favorable test conditions, and if you don't have them you won't be able to do your best. Don't be a crank, but don't be shy either. An important function of the proctor is to see to it that you have favorable test conditions.

Relax . . .

. . . and don't bring on unnecessary tenseness by worrying about the difficulty of the examination. If necessary wait a minute before beginning to write. If you're still tense, take a couple of deep breaths, look over your test equipment, or do something which will take your mind away from the examination for a moment.

If your collar or shoes are tight, loosen them.

Put away unnecessary materials so that you have a good, clear space on your desk to write freely.

You Must Have TO GIVE YOUR **Best Test** PERFORMANCE

(1) A GOOD TEST ENVIRONMENT

(2) A COMPLETE UNDERSTANDING OF DIRECTIONS

(3) A DESIRE TO DO YOUR BEST

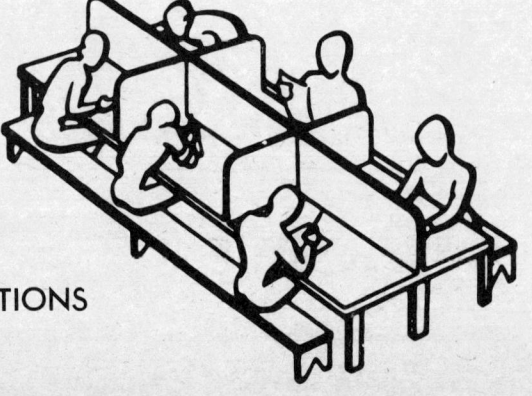

WHEN THEY SAY "GO" — TAKE YOUR TIME!

Listen very carefully to the test supervisor. If you fail to hear something important that he says, you may not be able to read it in the written directions and may suffer accordingly.

If you don't understand the directions you have heard or read, raise your hand and inform the proctor. Read carefully the directions for *each* part of the test before beginning to work on that part. If you skip over such directions too hastily, you may miss a main idea and thus lose credit for an entire section.

Get an Overview of the Examination

After reading the directions carefully, look over the entire examination to get an over-view of the nature and scope of the test. The purpose of this over-view is to give you some idea of the nature, scope, and difficulty of the examination.

It has another advantage. An item might be so phrased that it sets in motion a chain of thought that might be helpful in answering other items on the examination.

Still another benefit to be derived from reading all the items before you answer any is that the few minutes involved in reading the items gives you an opportunity to relax before beginning the examination. This will make for better concentration. As you read over these items the first time, check those whose answers immediately come to you. These will be the ones you will answer first. Read each item carefully before answering. It is a good practice to read each item at least twice to be sure that you understand it.

Plan Ahead

In other words, you should know precisely where you are going before you start. You should know:
1. whether you have to answer all the questions or whether you can choose those that are easiest for you;
2. whether all the questions are easy; (there may be a pattern of difficult, easy, etc.)
3. The length of the test; the number of questions;
4. The kind of scoring method used;
5. Which questions, if any, carry extra weight;
6. What types of questions are on the test;
7. What directions apply to each part of the test;
8. Whether you must answer the questions consecutively.

Budget Your Time Strategically!

Quickly figure out how much of the allotted time you can give to each section and still finish ahead of time. Don't forget to figure on the time you're investing in the overview. Then alter your schedule so that you can spend more time on those parts that count most. Then, if you can, plan to spend less time on the easier questions, so that you can devote the time saved to the harder questions. Figuring roughly, you should finish half the questions when half the allotted time has gone by. If there are 100 questions and you have three hours, you should have finished 50 questions after one and one half hours. So bring along a watch whether the instructions call for one or not. Jot down your "exam budget" and stick to it INTELLIGENTLY.

EXAMINATION STRATEGY

Probably the most important single strategy you can learn is to do the easy questions first. The very hard questions should be read and temporarily postponed. Identify them with a dot and return to them later.

This strategy has several advantages for you:
1. You're sure to get credit for all the questions you're sure of. If time runs out, you'll have all the sure shots, losing out only on those which you might have missed anyway.

2. By reading and laying away the tough ones you give your subconscious a chance to work on them. You may be pleasantly surprised to find the answers to the puzzlers popping up for you as you deal with related questions.

3. You won't risk getting caught by the time limit just as you reach a question you know really well.

A Tested Tactic

It's inadvisable on some examinations to answer each question in the order presented. The reason for this is that some examiners design tests so as to extract as much mental energy from you as possible. They put the most difficult questions at the beginning, the easier questions last. Or they may vary difficult with easy questions in a fairly regular pattern right through the test. Your survey of the test should reveal the pattern and your strategy for dealing with it.

If difficult questions appear at the beginning, answer them until you feel yourself slowing down or getting tired. Then switch to an easier part of the examination. You will return to the difficult portion after you have rebuilt your confidence by answering a batch of easy questions. Knowing that you have a certain number of points "under your belt" will help you when you return to the more difficult questions. You'll answer them with a much clearer mind; and you'll be refreshed by the change of pace.

Time

Use your time wisely. It's an important element in your test and you must use every minute effectively, working as rapidly as you can without sacrificing accuracy. Your exam survey and budget will guide you in dispensing your time. Wherever you can, pick up seconds on the easy ones. Devote your savings to the hard ones. If possible, pick up time on the lower value questions and devote it to those which give you the most points.

Relax Occasionally and Avoid Fatigue

If the exam is long (two or more hours) give yourself short rest periods as you feel you need them. If you're not permitted to leave the room, relax in your seat, look up from your paper, rest your eyes, stretch your legs, shift your body. Break physical and mental tension. Take several deep breaths and get back to the job, refreshed. If you don't do this you run the risk of getting nervous and tightening up. Your thinking may be hampered and you may make a few unnecessary mistakes.

Do not become worried or discouraged if the examination seems difficult to you. The questions in the various fields are purposely made difficult and searching so that the examination will discriminate effectively even among superior students. No one is expected to get a perfect or near-perfect score.

Remember that if the examination seems difficult to you, it may be even more difficult for your neighbor.

Think!

This is not a joke because you're not an IBM machine. Nobody is able to write all the time and also to read and think through each question. You must plan each answer. Don't give hurried answers in an atmosphere of panic. Even though you see a lot of questions, remember that they are objective and not very time-consuming. Don't rush headlong through questions that must be thought through.

Edit, Check, Proofread . . .

. . . after completing all the questions. Invariably, you will find some foolish errors which you needn't have made, and which you can easily correct. Don't just sit back or leave the room ahead of time. Read over your answers and make sure you wrote exactly what you meant to write. And that you wrote the answers in the right place. You might even find that you have omitted some answers inadvertently. You have budgeted time for this job of proofreading. PROOFREAD and pick up points.

One caution, though. Don't count on making major changes. And don't go in for wholesale changing of answers. To arrive at your answers in the first place you have read carefully and thought correctly. Second-guessing at this stage is more likely to result in wrong answers. So don't make changes unless you are quite certain you were wrong in the first place.

FOLLOW DIRECTIONS CAREFULLY

In answering questions on the objective or short-form examination, it is most important to follow all instructions carefully. Unless you have marked the answers properly, you will not receive credit for them. In addition, even in the same examination, the instructions will not be consistent. In one section you may be urged to guess if you are not certain; in another you may be cautioned against guessing. Some questions will call for the best choice among four or five alternatives; others may ask you to select the one incorrect or the least probable answer.

On some tests you will be provided with worked out fore-exercises, complete with correct answers. However, avoid the temptation to skip the directions and begin working just from reading the model questions and answers. Even though you may be familiar with that particular type of question, the directions may be different from those which you had followed previously. If the type of question should be new to you, work through the model until you understand it perfectly. This may save you time, and earn you a higher rating on the examination.

If the directions for the examination are written, read them carefully, at least twice. If the directions are given orally, listen attentively and then follow them precisely. For example, if you are directed to use plus (+) and minus (−) to mark true—false items, then don't use "T" and "F". If you are instructed to "blacken" a space on machine-scored tests, do not use a check (✓) or an "X". Make all symbols legible, and be sure that they have been placed in the proper answer space. It is easy, for example, to place the answer for item 5 in the space reserved for item 6. If this is done, then all of your following answers may be wrong. It is also very important that you understand the method they will use in scoring the examination. Sometimes they tell you in the directions. The method of scoring may affect the amount of time you spend on an item, especially if some items count more than others. Likewise, the directions may indicate whether or not you should guess in case you are not sure of the answer. Some methods of scoring penalize you for guessing.

Cue Words. Pay special attention to qualifying words or phrases in the directions. Such words as *one, best reason, surest, means most nearly the same as, preferable, least correct,* etc., all indicate that *one* response is called for, and that you must select the response which best fits the qualifications in the question.

Time. Sometimes a time limit is set for each section of the examination. If that is the case, follow the time instructions carefully. Your *exam budget* and your watch can help you here. Even if you haven't finished a section when the time limit is up, pass on to the next section. The examination has been planned according to the time schedule.

If the examination paper bears the instruction "Do not turn over page until signal is given," or "Do not start until signal is given," follow the instruction. Otherwise, you may be disqualified.

Pay Close Attention. Be sure you understand what you're doing at all times. Especially in dealing with true-false or multiple-choice questions it's vital that you understand the meaning of every question. It is normal to be working under stress when taking an examination, and it is easy to skip a word or jump to a false conclusion, which may cost you points on the examination. In many multiple-choice and matching questions, the examiners deliberately insert plausible-appearing false answers in order to catch the candidate who is not alert.

Answer clearly. If the examiner who marks your paper cannot understand what you mean, you will not receive credit for your correct answer. On a True-False examination you will not receive any credit for a question which is marked both true and false. If you are asked to underline, be certain that your lines are under and not through the words and that they do not extend beyond them. When using the separate answer sheet it is important *when you decide to change an answer,* you erase the first answer completely. If you leave any graphite from the pencil on the wrong space it will cause the scoring machine to cancel the right answer for that question.

Watch Your "Weights." If the examination is "weighted" it means that some parts of the examination are considered more important than others and rated more highly. For instance, you may find that the instructions will indicate "Part I, Weight 50; Part II, Weight 25, Part III, Weight 25." In such a case, you would devote half of your time to the first part, and divide the second half of your time among Parts II and III.

A Funny Thing . . .

. . . happened to you on your way to the bottom of the totem pole. You *thought* the right answer but you marked the *wrong* one.

1. You *mixed answer symbols!* You decided (rightly) that Baltimore (Choice D) was correct. Then you marked *B* (for Baltimore) instead of *D*.

2. You *misread* a simple instruction! Asked to give the *latest* word in a scrambled sentence, you correctly arranged the sentence, and then marked the letter corresponding to the *earliest* word in that miserable sentence.

3. You *inverted digits!* Instead of the correct number, 96, you wrote (or read) 69.

Funny? Tragic! Stay away from accidents.

Record your answers on the answer sheet one by one as you answer the questions. Care should be taken that these answers are recorded next to the appropriate numbers on your answer sheet. It is poor practice to write your answers first on the test booklet and then to transfer them all at one time to the answer sheet. This procedure causes many errors. And then, how would you feel if you ran out of time before you had a chance to transfer all the answers.

When and How To Guess

Read the directions carefully to determine the scoring method that will be used. In some tests, the directions will indicate that guessing is advisable if you do not know the answer to a question. In such tests, only the right answers are counted in determining your score. If such is the case, don't omit any items. If you do not know the answer, or if you are not sure of your answer, then *guess*.

On the other hand, if the directions state that a scoring formula *will* be used in determining your score or that you are *not to guess*, then *omit* the question if you do not know the answer, or if you are not sure of the answer. When the scoring formula is used, a percentage of the *wrong* answers will be subtracted from the number of *right* answers as a correction for haphazard guessing. It is improbable, therefore, that mere guessing will improve your score significantly. *It may even lower your score.* Another disadvantage in guessing under such circumstances is that it consumes valuable time that you might profitably use in answering the questions you know.

If, however, you are uncertain of the correct answer but have *some* knowledge of the question and are able to eliminate one or more of the answer choices as wrong, your chance of getting the right answer is improved, and it will be to your advantage to *answer* such a question rather than *omit* it.

BEAT THE ANSWER SHEET

Even though you've had plenty of practice with the answer sheet used on machine-scored examinations, we must give you a few more, last-minute pointers.

The present popularity of tests requires the use of electrical test scoring machines. With these machines, scoring which would require the labor of several men for hours can be handled by one man in a fraction of the time.

The scoring machine is an amazingly intricate and helpful device, but the machine is not human. The machine cannot, for example, tell the difference between an intended answer and a stray pencil mark, and will count both indiscriminately. The machine cannot count a pencil mark, if the pencil mark is not brought in contact with the electrodes. For these reasons, specially printed answer sheets with response spaces properly located and properly filled in must be employed. Since not all pencil leads contain the necessary ingredients, a special pencil must be used and a heavy solid mark must be made to indicate answers.

(a) Each pencil mark must be heavy and black. Light marks should be retraced with the special pencil.

(b) Each mark must be in the space between the pair of dotted lines and entirely fill this space.

(c) All stray pencil marks on the paper, clearly not intended as answers, must be completely erased.

(d) Each question must have only one answer indicated. If multiple answers occur, all extraneous marks should be thoroughly erased. Otherwise, the machine will give you *no* credit for your correct answer.

Be sure to use the special electrographic pencil!

HERE'S HOW TO MARK YOUR ANSWERS ON MACHINE-SCORED ANSWER SHEETS:

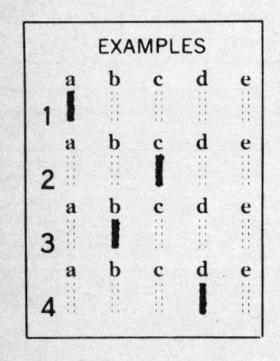

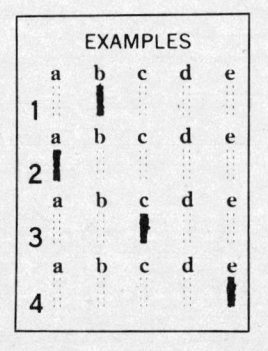

Make only ONE mark for each answer. Additional and stray marks may be counted as mistakes.
In making corrections, erase errors COMPLETELY.
Make glossy black marks.

Your answer sheet is the only one that reaches the office where papers are scored. For this reason it is important that the blanks at the top be filled in completely and correctly. The proctors will check this, but just in case they slip up, make certain yourself that your paper is complete.

Many exams caution competitors against making any marks on the test booklet itself. Obey that caution even though it goes against your grain to work neatly. If you work neatly and obediently with the test booklet you'll probably do the same with the answer sheet. And that pays off in high scores.

THE GIST OF TEST STRATEGY

APPROACH THE TEST CONFIDENTLY. TAKE IT CALMLY.

REMEMBER TO REVIEW, THE WEEK BEFORE THE TEST.

DON'T "CRAM." BE CAREFUL OF YOUR DIET AND SLEEP...ESPECIALLY
        AS THE TEST DRAWS NIGH.

ARRIVE ON TIME...AND READY.

BRING THE COMPLETE KIT OF "TOOLS" YOU'LL NEED.

CHOOSE A GOOD SEAT. GET COMFORTABLE AND RELAX.

LISTEN CAREFULLY TO ALL DIRECTIONS.

APPORTION YOUR TIME INTELLIGENTLY WITH AN "EXAM BUDGET."

READ ALL DIRECTIONS CAREFULLY. TWICE IF NECESSARY.
PAY PARTICULAR ATTENTION TO THE SCORING PLAN.

LOOK OVER THE WHOLE TEST BEFORE ANSWERING ANY QUESTIONS.

START RIGHT IN, IF POSSIBLE. STAY WITH IT. USE
  EVERY SECOND EFFECTIVELY.

DO THE EASY QUESTIONS FIRST; POSTPONE HARDER QUESTIONS
  UNTIL LATER.

DETERMINE THE PATTERN OF THE TEST QUESTIONS.
  IF IT'S HARD-EASY ETC., ANSWER ACCORDINGLY.

READ EACH QUESTION CAREFULLY. MAKE SURE YOU UNDERSTAND
  EACH ONE BEFORE YOU ANSWER. RE-READ, IF NECESSARY.

THINK! AVOID HURRIED ANSWERS. GUESS INTELLIGENTLY.

WATCH YOUR WATCH AND "EXAM BUDGET," BUT DO A
  LITTLE BALANCING OF THE TIME YOU DEVOTE TO EACH QUESTION.

GET ALL THE HELP YOU CAN FROM "CUE" WORDS.

REPHRASE DIFFICULT QUESTIONS FOR YOURSELF. WATCH OUT FOR "SPOILERS."

REFRESH YOURSELF WITH A FEW, WELL-CHOSEN REST
  PAUSES DURING THE TEST.

USE CONTROLLED ASSOCIATION TO SEE THE RELATION OF
  ONE QUESTION TO ANOTHER AND WITH AS MANY IMPORTANT
  IDEAS AS YOU CAN DEVELOP.

NOW THAT YOU'RE A "COOL" TEST-TAKER, STAY CALM
  AND CONFIDENT THROUGHOUT THE TEST. DON'T LET
  ANYTHING THROW YOU.

EDIT, CHECK, PROOFREAD YOUR ANSWERS. BE A "BITTER
  ENDER." STAY WORKING UNTIL THEY
  MAKE YOU GO.

FOR FURTHER STUDY

ARCO BOOKS FOR MORE HELP

Now what? You've read and studied the whole book, and there's still time before you take the test. You're probably better prepared than most of your competitors, but you may feel insecure about one or more of the probable test subjects. If so, you can still do something about it. Glance over this comprehensive list of books written with a view to solving your problems. One of them may be just what you need at this time ... for the extra help that will assure your success.

ARCO BOOKS FOR TESTS OF ALL TYPES

Countless attractive careers are open to test takers, as you will see from this selective listing of Arco Books. One or more of them can assure success in the test you are now taking. Perhaps you've discovered that you are weak in language, verbal ability or mathematics. You can brush up in the privacy of your own home with a specialized Arco Book. Why flounder and fail when help is so easily available? Perhaps even more important than doing your best on your present test is to consider other opportunities that are open to you. Look over the lists and make plans for your future. You might get a few ideas for other tests you can start to study for *now*. By taking job tests now you place yourself in the enviable position of picking and choosing the *ideal* job. You'll be able to select from several positions. You won't have to settle for the one (or none).

Each of the following books was created under the same expert editorial supervision that produced the excellent book you are now using.

So even though we only list titles and prices, you can be sure that each book performs a real service ... saves floundering and failure.

Every Arco Book is guaranteed. Return it for full refund in 10 days if not completely satisfied.

Whatever your goal ... CIVIL SERVICE ... TRADE LICENSE ... TEACHING ... PROFESSIONAL LICENSE ... SCHOLARSHIP ... ENTRANCE TO THE SCHOOL OF *YOUR* CHOICE ... you can achieve it through the PROVEN QUESTION AND ANSWER METHOD.

START YOUR CAREER BY MAILING THIS COUPON TODAY

ORDER NOW from your bookseller or direct from:
ARCO PUBLISHING COMPANY, INC. 219 Park Avenue South, New York, N.Y. 10003

Please Rush The Following Arco Books
(Order by Number or Title)

☐ I enclose check, cash or money order for $_____ (price of books, plus 50¢ for first book and 25¢ for each additional book, packing and mailing charge). No C.O.D.'s accepted.
RESIDENTS OF N.Y. AND CALIF. ADD APPROPRIATE SALES TAX.

☐ Please tell me if you have an ARCO COURSE for the position of _____

☐ Please send me your free COMPLETE CATALOG

NAME _____
STREET _____
CITY _____ STATE _____ ZIP # _____

S 3328

GENERAL INTEREST BOOKS

Title	Code	Price
The Psychology of Witchcraft, Ravensdale & Morgan	03501-3	10.00
Punishment—An Illustrated History, Walker	02709-6	7.95
The Riddle of Chung Ling Soo, Dexter	03826-8	3.00
The Rockhound's Handbook, Firsoff	03799-7	10.00
Roman London, Sorreell	01853-4	6.50
Secrets of the '49ers, Ballantyne	LR 03859-4	8.95
Secrets of the Sea, Mallan	03922-1	2.00
A Short History of Costume and Armour 1066-1800, Kelly & Schwabe	02906-4	12.50
Successful Public Speaking, Hull	LR 02395-3	5.95
300 Ways to Make Extra Money, Walsh	03540-A	4.95
Teach Yourself Basic Bidding, Truscott & Truscott	LR 03836-5	6.95
Trading with China, Mobius & Simmel	LR 02908-0	4.95
Treasure Hunter's Guide (How and Where to Find It), Nesmith & Potter	01806-2	5.95
Understanding Investments and Mutual Funds, Potts	02713-4	8.95
Victorian Public Houses, Spiller	02711-8	10.00
The Victorians—At Home and at Work as Illustrated by Themselves, Evans	02914-5	10.00
Warriors of the Plains, Taylor	03447-5	15.00
A Year Round Guide to Family Fun, Cleaver	03524-A	8.95
You Can Help Your Child Learn to Read, Forgan	03547-A	7.95

CHILDREN'S BOOKS

Title	Code	Price
A Child's Introduction to the Outdoors, Richey	03555-A	8.95
Carpentry is Easy—When You Know How, Marshall Cavendish Editorial Board	03480-7	4.95
Cooking is Easy—When You Know How, Marshall Cavendish Editorial Board	03481-5	4.95
Gardening is Easy—When You Know How, Marshall Cavendish Editorial Board	03482-3	4.95
Modelling is Easy—When You Know How, Marshall Cavendish Editorial Board	03483-1	4.95
Let's Explore Mathematics—Book 1, Marsh	01511-X	2.45
Let's Explore Mathematics—Book 2, Marsh	01512-8	2.45
Let's Explore Mathematics—Book 3, Marsh	01513-6	2.45
Let's Explore Mathematics—Book 4, Marsh	01824-0	2.45
Teacher's Guide: Children Explore Mathematics, Marsh	02077-6	3.00
Story of Canada, Barclay	03529-A	3.95

ARCO TAX GUIDES

Title	Code	Price
Confidential Official IRS Tax Audit Guide	03837-3	3.95
Your Federal Income Tax Annual	00865-2	1.25

AUTOMOTIVE

Title	Code	Price
Arco Motor Vehicle Dictionary: English and Spanish, Lima	LR 01927-1	5.00
Auto Repair Frauds, Engel	LR 03763-6	6.95
Auto Repairs You Can Make, Weissler	LR 02508-5	6.95
British Sports Cars Since the War, Watkins	03390-8	6.95
Car Care, Editors of Mechanix Illustrated	LR 01918-2	4.95
Car Service Data, Seale	03357-6	6.95
The Complete Book of Minibikes and Minicycles, Engel	03785-7	3.95
The Complete Book of Mobile Home Living, Engel	LR 02896-3	5.95
The Complete Book of Motor Camping (Revised), Engel	02916-1	2.95
The Complete Book of Trailering, Engel	02715-0	2.95
Famous Old Cars, Bowman	LR 00597-1	3.50
The Fastest Men in the World—On Wheels, Houlgate & Editors of Auto Racing Magazine	03305-3	5.95
The Ferrari V-12 Sports Cars, 1946-1956, Pritchard	02332-5	3.95
Fiat 1899-1972, Sedgwick	03306-1	14.95
Great Automobile Designs, McLellan	03627-3	12.00
Hot Rod Handbook, Hochman	LR 00602-1	3.95
How to Customize Cars and Rods, Barris & Thoms	LR 01151-3	3.95
The Incredible A.J. Foyt, Engel & Editors of Auto Racing Magazine	LR 02195-0	4.95
Jackie Stewart, Engel	LR 02338-4	4.95
Jim Clark Remembered, Gauld	03848-9	10.00
Karting, Smith	LR 01939-5	5.95
Learning to Drive, Stevenson	03371-1	2.95
The Lotus 49 Formula I, Hodges	02333-3	3.95
Mario Andretti—The Man Who Can Win Any Kind of Race, Engel & Editors of Auto Racing Magazine	LR 02193-4	4.95
The Mercedes-Benz Type W. 125 Grand Prix, 1937, Jenkinson	02331-7	3.95
Motorcycle Panorama, Holliday	03647-8	7.95
Motorcycle Racing Champions, Whyte	03910-8	7.95
The New Book of Motorcycles, Arctander	LR 01813-5	3.50
The New Guide to Motorcycling, Cutter	LR 02732-0	5.95
The New How To Build Hot Rods, Jaderquist	LR 00553-X	3.50
Oldtime Steam Cars, Bentley	LR 02073-3	3.50
132 of the Most Unusual Cars That Ever Ran at Indianapolis, Engel & Editors of Auto Racing Magazine	LR 02194-2	4.95
Porsche Story, Weitman & Meisl	02579-9	15.00
The Racer's and Driver's Reader, Harding & Ionicus	02689-8	6.95
Racing Car Oddities, Nye	03724-5	8.95
The Racing Driver's Manual, Gardner	03458-0	8.50
The Racing Porsches, Frere	02972-2	15.00
Racing to Win—Wood Brothers Style, Engel	02886-6	5.95
Rolls-Royce—The History of the Car, Bennett	03619-2	16.95
Vintage and Veteran Cars, Hendry	03326-6	4.95
The World's Most Powerful Road Racing Cars, Ludvigsen & Editors of Auto Racing Magazine	03304-5	5.95

ASTROLOGY, HANDWRITING, HYPNOSIS, OCCULT ARTS, AND PALMISTRY

Title	Code	Price
The Astrologer's Manual, Green	03616-8	11.95
Astrological Warnings and the Stock Market, Rieder	03539-A	7.95
Astrology, Davison	01128-9	.95
Astrology Dial-A-Scope, Wade	02393-7	3.50
An Astrology Guide to Your Sex Life, Robson	01628-0	.95
Biorhythm: A Personal Science, Gittelson	03415-7	8.95
The Book of Charms and Talismans, Sepharial	02010-5	.95
The Book of Fortune Telling, Fabia	03603-6	3.50
Cheiro's Book of Fate and Fortune, Cheiro	02507-7	5.95
Cheiro's Book of Numbers, Cheiro	01170-X	.95
Cheiro's Language of the Hand, Cheiro	01780-5	.95
Cheiro's Palmistry for All, Cheiro	01194-7	.95
Cheiro's When Were You Born, Cheiro	01168-8	.95
The Complete Guide to Palmistry, Psychos	01133-5	.95

MODELING

Bill Dean's Book of Balsa Models, Dean	02210-8	2.95
Building Flying Scale Model Aircraft, Musciano	02994-3	3.95
Collecting Model Soldiers, Garrett	03749-0	8.95
Handbook of Model Planes, Cars and Boats, Winter	LR 01308-7	3.50
How to Make Model Aircraft, Ellis	03448-3	5.95
How to Make Model Soldiers, Stearns	03446-7	5.95
International Locomotives, Durrant	02639-1	25.00
The Mallet Locomotive, Durrant	03678-8	10.00
Model Car Handbook, Plecan	LR 01465-2	3.95
Ship Modelling Hints and Tips, Craine	03348-7	6.95
World Locomotive Models, Dow	02973-0	15.00
World Steam Locomotives, Robins	03325-8	4.95

STAMP AND COIN BOOKS

American History Through Commemorative Stamps, Bloomgarden	LR 01904-2	5.95
Coin Collectors Fact Book, Zimmerman	02992-7	1.45
Coins as Living History, Schwarz	LR 03791-1	8.95
Counterfeit, Mis-Struck, and Unofficial U.S. Coins, Taxay	01000-2	5.00
How to Invest in Gold Coins, Hoppe	02999-4	2.95
An Illustrated History of U.S. Commemorative Coinage, Taxay	LR 01536-5	6.50
Money of the American Indians And Other Primitive Currencies of the Americas, Taxay	02697-9	5.95
Stamp Collector's Encyclopedia, Sutton	02647-2	1.95
Stamp Collector's Guide to Europe, Allen & Silverstone	03344-4	3.95
The Story of Paper Money, Narbeth & Beresiner	02905-6	6.95
Topical Stamp Collecting, Martin	03662-1	5.95
The U.S. Mint and Coinage, Taxay	LR 01125-4	12.50

ARMS, ARMOR, MILITARY, AND SHIPS

Allied Bayonets of World War II, Carter	01862-3	3.50
The Annapolis Story, Ilyinsky & Zink	03478-5	15.00
Antique European and American Firearms at the Hermitage Museum,	02950-1	20.00
Antique Guns, Bowman & Cary	LR 00328-6	3.50
Antique Guns From the Stagecoach Collection, Bowman	LR 01917-4	3.50
Antique Pistols, Paton & Alexander	01176-9	15.00
Antique Weapons, Akehurst	02277-9	5.95
Armoured Forces, Ogorkiewicz	02334-1	7.95
Atlas of Maritime History, Lloyd	03779-2	35.00
Best Photos of the Civil War, Milhollen & Johnson	LR 00782-6	3.95
British and American Infantry Weapons of World War II, Barker	01865-8	3.50
British and American Tanks of World War II, Chamberlain & Ellis	01867-4	12.95
British and German Tanks of World War I, Chamberlain & Ellis	01866-6	3.50
British Military Uniforms—Henry VII to the Present Day, Carman	00953-5	7.95
British Warships Of The Second World War, Ravan & Roberts	02607-3	14.95
Carbine Handbook, Wahl	01222-6	4.95
Chronology of the War at Sea, 1939-1942, Vol. one, Rower & Hummelchen	03308-8	12.50
Chronology of the War at Sea, 1942-1945, Vol. two, Rower & Hummelchen	03401-7	12.50
Collecting Militaria, Wilkinson-Latham	03879-9	15.00
Collecting Model Soldiers, Garrett	03749-0	8.95
Famous Guns from the Smithsonian Collection, Bowman	LR 01606-X	3.50
Famous Guns from the Winchester Collection, Bowman	LR 00671-4	3.50
Famous Guns that Won the West, Wycoff	03829-2	2.00
Fifty Famous Tanks, Bradford & Morgan	01583-7	1.95
Fighting Vehicles of the Red Army, Perrett	02340-6	3.95
Flags and Standards of the Third Reich, Davis	03620-6	15.00
The Gatling Gun, Wahl & Toppel	01196-3	5.95
German Army Handbook 1939-45, Davis	03376-2	7.95
German Army Uniforms and Insignia, Davis	03359-2	12.00
German Guided Missiles of the Second World War, Pocock	01647-7	4.95
German Infantry Weapons of World War II, Barker	01863-1	3.50
German Tanks and Armored Vehicles 1914-1945, White	01784-8	1.95
German Tanks 1914-1968, Nowarra	01753-8	1.95
Great Tank Battles of World War II, Bradford	02288-4	3.50
The Gun Collector's Fact Book, Steinwedel	03782-2	5.95
The Handicrafts of the Sailor, Banks	03441-6	5.95
The History of the Sailing Ship	03780-6	12.95
How to Make Model Soldiers, Stearns	03446-7	5.95
The Indian Sword, Rawson	01830-5	8.50
The Iron Ship, Corlett	03767-9	29.95
Jane's Fighting Ships, 1898, Jane	01957-3	14.95
Jane's Fighting Ships, 1905/06, Jane	LR 02269-8	19.95
Jane's Fighting Ships, 1906/07, Jane	LR 02019-9	19.95
Jane's Fighting Ships, 1914, Jane	01873-9	19.95
Jane's Fighting Ships, 1919, Jane	LR 02018-0	25.00
Jane's Fighting Ships, 1924, Jane	03379-7	22.50
Jane's Fighting Ships, 1931, Parkes	LR 02899-8	25.00
Jane's Fighting Ships, 1950/51, Blackburn	03691-5	40.00
The Metal Fighting Ship in the Royal Navy 1860-1970, Archibald; illustrated by Woodward	02509-3	19.95
Military Pistols and Revolvers, Hogg	LR 02154-3	3.50
The Modern Handgun, Hertzberg	LR 01464-4	3.50
The Naval Annual, 1913, Hythe	LR 02267-1	12.50
Naval Wargames, Carter	03748-2	10.00
North Atlantic Seaway, Vol. I, Bensor	03679-6	19.95
Pacific Liners 1927-1972, Emmons	03380-0	8.95
Russian Infantry Weapons of World War II, Barker	02336-8	3.50
The Sherman, Chamberlain & Ellis	LR 01860-7	1.95
Ship Modelling Hints and Tips, Craine	03348-7	6.95
The Ships of the German Fleets, 1848-1945, Hansen	03648-6	25.00
Sword, Lance and Bayonet, ffoulkes & Hopkinson	01645-0	7.50
U-Boats Under the Swastika, Showell	03457-2	10.00
Warships 1860-1970, Thornton	03319-3	6.95
The Wooden Fighting Ship In the Royal Navy, AD 897-1860,	02369-4	19.95

KEY UNIFORM GUIDES

British Eighth Army, Adair	03363-0	1.95
British Parachute Forces, 1940-45, Davies	03362-2	1.95
German Parachute Forces, 1935-45, Davis	03365-7	1.95
Luftwaffe Air Crews, Davis	03364-9	1.95
U.S. Army Airborne Forces, Davis	03366-5	1.95
U.S. Infantry, Europe 1942-45, Davies	03361-4	1.95

WORLD WAR II FACT FILES

American Gunboats and Minesweepers, Lenton	03610-9	3.95
Anti-Aircraft Guns, Chamberlain & Gander	03818-7	3.95

ARMS, ARMOR, MILITARY, AND SHIPS

Title	Code	Price
Anti-tank Weapons, Chamberlain & Gander	03607-9	3.95
British Escort Ships, Lenton	03609-5	3.95
Heavy Artillery, Chamberlain & Gander	03898-5	3.95
Infantry, Mountain, and Airborne Guns, Chamberlain & Gander	03819-5	3.95
Light and Medium Artillery, Chamberlain & Gander	03820-9	3.95
Machine Guns, Chamberlain & Gander	03608-7	3.95
Mortars and Rockets, Chamberlain & Gander	03817-9	3.95
Self-Propelled Anti-Tank and Anti-Aircraft Guns, Chamberlain & Gander	03897-7	3.95

AVIATION

Title	Code	Price
Air War in Viet Nam, Drendel	01817-8	2.95
Aircraft of The Vietnam War—A Pictorial Review, Drendel	02513-1	3.95
Airliners of the World, Morgan	01541-1	2.95
Allied Aces of World War II, Hess	01555-1	2.95
The American Aces of World War II, Hess	01757-0	2.95
Aviation and Space Museums of America, Allen	03631-1	6.95
Bill Dean's Book of Balsa Models, Dean	02210-8	2.95
Bomber Aircraft of the United States, Morgan	01597-7	1.95
Building Flying Scale Model Aircraft, Musciano	02994-3	3.95
Civil Aircraft of Yesteryear, Munson	01713-9	5.95
Crack Up!, Morgan	01759-7	2.95
Fasten Seat Belts: The Confessions of a Reluctant Airline Passenger, Morgan	LR 01821-6	5.00
Fifty Famous Fighter Aircraft, Groh	01751-1	2.95
Fighter Aircraft of the United States, Morgan	01554-3	1.95
Fighters Over the Desert, Shores & Ring	02070-9	8.50
Forgotten Fighters and Experimental Aircraft of the U.S. Army: 1918-1941, Bowers	02403-8	3.95
Forgotten Fighters and Experimental Aircraft of the U.S. Navy: 1918-1941, Bowers	02404-6	3.95
How to Make Model Aircraft, Ellis	03448-3	5.95
Illustrated History of World War I in the Air, Ulanoff	LR 01768-6	8.95
Jane's All the World's Airships, 1909, Jane	01956-5	17.50
Jane's All the World's Aircraft, 1913, Jane	01880-1	14.95
Jane's All the World's Aircraft, 1919, Jane	01955-7	25.00
Jane's All the World's Aircraft, 1938, Jane	LR 02646-4	35.00
Jane's All the World's Aircraft, 1945-46, Jane	LR 02390-2	29.95
The Lockheed Constellation—Aircraft Classic No. 1, Hardy	02885-8	10.00
Luftwaffe Colors, Volume I, 1935-45, Merrick	03652-4	16.95
Mustang—The Story of the P-51 Fighter, Gruenhagen	03912-4	15.95
1972 Aircraft Annual, Taylor	02581-6	4.95
Pictorial History of the Luftwaffe, Price	02144-6	5.95
Pictorial History of the RAF, Volume I: 1918-1939, Taylor	01857-7	7.95
Pictorial History of the RAF W.W. II—Volume II: 1939-1945, Taylor & Moyes	02137-3	5.95
Pictorial History of the RAF, Volume III: 1945-1969, Taylor & Moyes	02421-6	5.95
Pictorial History of the USAF, Mondey	02479-8	6.95
Pilot's Handbook of Aeronautical Knowledge, FAA	03479-3	5.00
The Private Pilot's Dictionary and Handbook, Polking	02932-3	3.95
Stuka at War, Smith	02503-4	6.95
Warplanes of the World, Taylor	01502-0	4.95
Warplanes of Yesteryear, Munson	01468-7	5.95
World Military Aviation, Krivinyi	03360-6	10.00
World War II Aircraft in Combat, Bavousett	LR 03823-3	8.95

AIRCRAFT ALBUMS

Title	Code	Price
Heinkel—Aircraft Album No. 1, Turner	02414-3	3.95
Messerschmitt—Aircraft Album No. 2, J. Richard Smith	02505-5	3.95
Junkers—Aircraft Album No. 3, Turner & Nowarra	02506-9	3.95
Boeing—Aircraft Album No. 4, Munson & Swanborough	02582-4	4.95
Hawker—Aircraft Album No. 5, James	02699-5	4.95
North American—Aircraft Album No. 6, Swanborough	03318-5	4.95
Focke-Wulf—Aircraft Album No. 7, Smith	03349-5	4.95

ARCO-AIRCAM AVIATION SERIES

Title	Code	Price
No. 1—North American P-51D Mustang, Ward	02093-8	2.95
No. 2—Republic P-47 Thunderbolt, McDowell & Ward	02095-4	2.95
No. 3—North American Mustang MK. I, Shores & Ward	02097-0	2.95
No. 4—Supermarine Spitfire MK. I-XVI, Merline Engine, Hooton & Ward	02099-7	2.95
No. 5—North Amer. P-51 B/C Mustang, Ward & McDowell	02101-2	2.95
No. 6—Curtiss Kittyhawk MK. I-IV, Ward & Shores	02103-9	2.95
No. 7—Curtiss P-40D-N Warhawk	02105-5	2.95
No. 8—Supermarine Spitfire Mk. XII-24, Supermarine Seafire Mk. 1-47	02107-1	2.95
No. 9—Spad Scouts SVII-SXIII	02110-1	2.95
No. 10—Lockheed P-38 Lightning	02113-6	2.95
No. 11—Consolidated B-24D-M Liberator	02115-2	2.95
No. 12—Avro Lancaster	02117-9	2.95
No. 13—Battle of Britain Hawker Hurricane, Supermarine Spitfire, Messerschmitt Bf. 109	02119-5	2.95
No. 14—Finnish Air Force 1918-1968	02121-7	2.95
No. 15—Nakajima Ki. 43, Hayabusha I-III	02292-2	2.95
No. 16—Republic F/RF-84FThunderflash/Thunderstreak	02294-9	2.95
No. 17—Boeing B-17 Flying Fortress	02296-5	2.95
No. 18—Mitsubishi Abm-Zero-Sen	02298-1	2.95
No. 19—North American F-86A-H Sabre, Volume I	02301-5	2.95
No. 20—Nakajima Ki. 27	02303-1	2.95
No. 21—Sharkmouth, Volume I	02225-6	2.95
No. 22—Sharkmouth, Volume II	02328-7	2.95
No. 24—Canadair Sabre Nk I-VI/Commonwealth Sabre Mk. 30-32	02305-8	3.25
No. 25—Luftwaffe, Volume I	02307-4	3.25
No. 26—Luftwaffe, Volume II	02308-2	3.25
No. 27—Kawasaki Ki. 61-I/III Hien/Ki. 100	02310-4	3.25
No. 28—Vought F4U-1/7 Corsair	02314-7	3.25
No. 30—Czechoslovakian Air Force	02322-8	3.25
No. 31—Hawker Hunter	02311-2	3.25
No. 32—North American B-25C-H. Mitchell	02312-0	3.25
No. 33—Hawker Hurricane Mk I-IV	02316-3	3.25
No. 34—Douglas A-4 Skyhawk	02313-9	3.25

MORGANS FAMOUS AIRCRAFT SERIES

Title	Code	Price
The A-1 Skyraider, Birdsall	02188-8	2.95
The AT-6 Harvard, Morgan	01413-X	2.95
B-17 Flying Fortress, Birdsall	01292-7	2.95
The B-24 Liberator, Birdsall	01695-7	2.95
The B-58 Hustler, Robinson	01662-0	2.95
The Boeing 707, Schiff	01664-7	2.95
The Douglas DC-3, Morgan	01294-3	2.95
The F-4 Phantom, O'Rourke	02221-3	2.95
The F-86 Sabre, Childerhose	01414-8	2.95
The Lockheed Constellation, Morgan	01659-0	2.95
LZ 129 "Hindenburg", Robinson	01295-1	2.95
The Messerschmitt Bf. 109, Craig	01666-3	2.95
The P-38 Lightning, Gurney	02015-6	2.95
The P-40 Kittyhawk, McDowell	01755-4	2.95
The P-47 Thunderbolt, Morgan	01297-8	2.95
The P-51 Mustang, Morgan	01298-6	2.95
The Planes the Aces Flew, Morgan & Shannon	01296-X	2.95
The Seaplanes, Palmer	01293-5	2.95